Dr Eastman has written a persuasive and po  the inevitability and the necessity of the family. Twenty years ago, perhaps, her theory would have been considered conventional wisdom. Now, it represents radical dissent.

ANDREW GREELEY

I especially appreciated her analysis of how government, education, and other institutions continue to ignore their role in supporting healthy families.

DOLORES CURRAN, national columnist and author of *Traits of a Healthy Family* and *Stress and the Healthy Family*

Dr Eastman's chapter on family strengths is the best I've found anywhere. At the Working with Families Institute we use it not only for training family physicians but also in all family assessments.

EDWARD BADER, Co-ordinator Working with Families Institute, Associate Professor, Faculty of Medicine, University of Toronto

Moira Eastman has performed an invaluable service for those who have been arguing for a family policy which is concerned with family relationships as well as with family poverty, and for a policy of preventing family breakdown.

JIM CRAWLEY, former Executive Director, Marriage Guidance Council of Western Australia

Without question, this book should be read by all of us. It could make a tremendous contribution to the current issues being raised about what we should do to improve the quality of family life in the United States.

Dr DANIEL ANDERSON, President Emeritus, Hazelden Foundation, U.S.A.

Dr Eastman's book is a 'must' reading for anyone really interested in the well-being of families today . . . Her insights on public policy and family life are useful worldwide.

Dr STEVEN PREISTER, Deputy Executive Director, American Association for Marriage and Family Therapy

Eastman is a sensible and sensitive critic who goes much beyond the usual platitudes and panaceas to offer a humane and plausible philosophic and political analysis of what families do and what families need in order to do what they do right.

JEAN BETHKE ELSHTAIN, Centennial Professor of Political Science, Vanderbilt University, author of *Public Man, Private Woman* and *Women and War*

FAMILY

The Vital Factor

Moira Eastman

CollinsDove
A Division of HarperCollins*Publishers*

For my parents
Doreen and Pat

my brothers and sisters
Peter, Margaret, Frank and Hilary

my husband Garry
and my children
Margaret, Stephen and Nicholas.

Thank you for teaching me
what is worth living for.

Published by CollinsDove*Publishers*
A Division of HarperCollins*Publishers* (Australia) Pty Ltd
22-24 Joseph Street,
North Blackburn, Victoria 3130

First published 1989
Reprinted 1991

Typeset in 11/12 Sabon by Bookset
Printed and bound by Griffin Press Limited, South Australia

The National Library of Australia
Cataloguing-in-Publication Data:

Eastman, Moira, 1940–
   Family: The Vital Factor

   ISBN 0 85924 735 X

1. Family — Australia. 2. Family policy — Australia, I.
Title.

306.8'5'0994

Acknowledgements

A number of people have contributed to this book. Colleagues who read an earlier version of the manuscript include John Hunt, John Bushell, Monica Marietti, Jim Crawley, Olga Spooner and Cyril Halley. Their criticisms, suggestions, encouragement and additional information forced me to reconsider a number of issues and to clarify some statements. Rosemary Sutherland's detailed discussion of the manuscript and her research assistance on several issues was particularly helpful. The book is much better for their help.

I am grateful to John Bushell, Director of Catholic Family Welfare Bureau, for making an arrangement whereby I was able to have time to write this book. Rosalie Cotter, librarian at the Bureau, gave invaluable assistance in tracking down books and articles and included in the service stimulating discussion of ideas.

Madeleine Wright of Collins Dove has steered the manuscript through the publishing process with the right blend of patience, encouragement, severity and ingenious solution of difficulties. Her choice of Dr Elizabeth Wood Ellem as editor allowed me to benefit from Elizabeth's learning, skill and meticulous care in the reviewing of the manuscript.

My family supported me through the protracted period of Ph.D. study on which the book is based. My husband, Garry Eastman, drew attention to articles, books, conferences and visiting speakers. Thanks are due also for the many ways in which he relieved me of other responsibilities to enable me to finish the book. In his other role as my publisher, I thank him for the efficient and friendly working environment in which each stage of the process took place.

Our children, now grown, also offered a variety of support and encouragement. I appreciated particularly the often expressed opinion from Margaret, Stephen and Nicholas that 'this book really is important'.

Moira Eastman

Contents

Introduction

There is something about the intimacy, flexibility, loyalty, belonging, support and love of family life that is the essence of being human. We reserve the word 'inhuman' for those who seem not to feel the attachments, the responses, the caring and the responsibility that family life demands. Yet, the family is not in favour. One of the themes of this book is to explore the reasons for this poor image.

One reason may be that the very idea of family is emotive and controversial. All of us who have participated in family life perceive family issues through the filter of our own experiences, which, by their very nature, are deeply felt. And while family can give immense satisfaction, it is also the area where we experience the most pain. To find rejection, criticism or lack of interest where we most seek acceptance and unconditional belonging is singularly upsetting. It is inevitable, then, that we feel ambivalent about the idea of family.

A second reason for the poor image of family in recent years is its link to the area of values. Modern science arbitrarily distinguishes between the world of facts and the world of values. Increasingly, the view is accepted that we cannot talk meaningfully about values, as they lie outside the world of facts and of meaningful propositions about facts. But to avoid a topic as fundamental to human life and to a human future as family on the basis that to address it is somehow to be involved in values questions is to co-operate in a widespread process of handing our future over to irrational forces outside of human control and will.

Not only is family linked to values, it is closely linked to controversial and often conservative values. Those who argue for family support are at times seen to be trying to return to a mythical past. Although the retreat of dogmatism and superstition due to enlightened thinking has been accompanied by 'fragmentation, discontinuity and loss of meaning',[1] we have options other than to abandon the project of enlightenment. Some say we need a second enlightenment: an enlightenment of values and social concern to accompany our cognitive enlightenment. In other words, we can choose to redirect, not abandon, the project of the enlightenment.

Some want to retain capitalist economic and social modernisation, yet seek refuge from its fragmenting effects through demanding forcible imposition of traditional family forms and values.[2] In the area of family, those critics who most vehemently attack the evident deterioration in the stability and integrity of family life often seem to be unaware of the links of this disintegration to the wider structures of society that they just as frequently defend. Evidence of fragmentation of families (like evidence of the destruction of the environment) poses tough questions about the whole direction of modern societies.

Families and family values are sometimes seen as the antithesis of feminist values, yet there is no inherent conflict between feminism and family values. Family, far from being the major enemy of women, has in fact suffered with them similar denigration and demeaning. The source of that belittling is the same in both cases. Women and families have been identified with the undervalued private realm, and both have been ignored and silenced by the powerful, technocratic, competitive, public world. While significant advances have been made in women's roles in the public sphere, there has been little improvement in the power and status of women's private roles. It may be that the roles of home-maker and child-nurturer are even less valued than they were fifty years ago.

A consistent theme of the women's movement has been both the need to change the public world and to revalue the despised, private, personal world. Sex-role stereotyping combined with the exclusion of women from the public world effectively denuded the public world of the 'feminine' nurturing and compassionate values. Both women and these feminine virtues must be returned to the public. Hence family issues and women's issues are intimately linked.

Some see the essence of family life as consisting of traditional notions of male dominance within families. There is absolutely no evidence to support this notion in studies of families that create well-being in their members. Dominance (and its frequent companion, manipulation) is destructive of family life and individual competence. Hence it is not proposed that we could or should re-impose this dominance.

Family values have also been seen as opposed to liberal social values. It is paradoxical that families have come to be seen as representing the ultimate in conservatism. Those on the political left have too readily accepted the notion that families are a symbol of, and tend to embody, the most extreme reactionary values. This over-simplification is understandable to the extent that family imagery has been captured and used by fundamentalist groups to disguise individualism and competitiveness. But to concede family imagery and family values to the ultra-right is a failure of critical thinking. The fact that families are not inherently conservative is demonstrated by the use of the family imagery of sisterhood and brotherhood in two of the most influential and radical movements of the century.

In fact, families are one of the few groupings in society that embody values alternative to the technocratic and profit-centred motives that are endemic in contemporary society. Families and family values are the major alternative to a selfish, individualistic mentality. In this view, families should be supported not only because they create the stuff of society, human beings, but because the sharing, flexibility and communality of family life at their best provide a different model of what society can be.

Family functioning is based on co-operation rather than competition, sharing of resources rather than individual aggrandisement, unconditional acceptance rather than acceptance only on the condition of performance. It could be argued that the only group in Western societies that has operated on the principle of 'from each according to ability, and to each according to need' has been the family. And, for all the faults and weaknesses of family groups, which have received so much criticism recently, most families do operate on this principle.

There has been considerable concern over those families where resources are not shared, especially where the mother is unable to gain access to the husband's income to enable her to meet her own and their children's needs. This reality should not be ignored, denied or diminished, but it does not nullity the fact that it is difficult to find another area in society where co-operation and sharing of resources takes place more routinely than it does in most families.

Perhaps the greatest danger facing society in the family issues area is that there are signs that families are beginning to be invaded by the maximising values of the commercial world and the market-place. One sign of this is the number of parents who, following family breakdown, abandon their children to poverty, even when they themselves enjoy an enhanced standard of living. (Of course, not only some separating or divorcing parents betray their children in this way. There are parents who stay married and who fail to support or care for their children.) The rising costs of the Supporting Parent Benefit have brought this problem to public attention, whereas before it remained a private problem for the parent who alone accepted responsibility for the children's support. If this individualistic, competitive attitude to family life was to occur on an even larger scale, it is inconceivable that a truly human society could survive. Already it is causing serious problems, with long-term consequences.

Disillusion with families and awareness of serious problems and dysfunction within many families has led to a readiness in some circles to assume that the family has had its day and that it is time to seek alternative arrangements for child-rearing. While not denying the seriousness of the stresses on families or evidence of dysfunction within families, that perspective is excessively pessimistic. As Mount and the Bergers have argued, to do away with families will not lead to an increase in freedom. Rather it leads to the terror of totalitarism, with the individual exposed to the naked power of the state and all intermediaries removed.[3]

Another theme is that the topic of families has been silenced in public debate. Families are readily blamed, but their capacity to make positive contributions to the public realm is rarely acknowledged. One outcome of this silencing is that while families are the strongest influence on the development of human competence, they are not given the status and support from the public realm that would allow them to fulfil their unique, irreplaceable roles.

Two institutions (the economy and education) had clear evidence in the 1960s of the vital roles played by familes. The Coleman Report into Equality of Educational Opportunity and the Moynihan Report into indicators that family factors had the potential to undermine the gains made in the 'war on poverty' in the USA showed that the public institutions and policies in these areas were reliant on family factors for their effectiveness. In neither case was the evidence responded to. I have sought to discover the reasons for this and it seems that the blind-spots that prevented a response to these influential reports in the 1960s still exist. It is not too extreme to claim that there has been a constraint on debate of family issues.

An important aspect of the women's movement has been a battle over language, with women raising consciousness of the ways sexist biases within language have contributed to and maintained the ignoring, silencing and denial of women. At the same time, language has been involved in restricting debate over family issues. The thorny question of the definition of family is one area where language battles rage. No matter what definition is proposed, it is not accepted on the grounds that it excludes some variant of family or living arrangement. Another is the insistence that the word 'family' be abandoned on the grounds that no such entity can be meaningfully discussed, the differences in family types being so extreme as to preclude any common name.

Definitions of family vary from the abstract and technical formulae adopted for legal, sociological and statistical purposes to the more personal 'the place where you are loved and nurtured'. In my study of families, I allowed families to use their own definition of family — and in fact it was an issue that never arose. Even children as young as two know who is in the family and who is not.

The difficulty of achieving an acceptable definition of family, such a basic aspect of human life, indicates a battle over the very concept of family. Fundamental disagreements over exactly what is education, or health, or politics do not have the same power to force the participants to retire from the field as they do in this area of family. Nor is every discussion of politics, education or health preceded by the demand that the protagonists define 'health' or 'politics' or 'education' to the satisfaction of all possible participants before any other statements be made. If such a demand were made, it would be clear to all that the demand was unreasonable and that it could be fulfilled only when consensus had been reached. That such a demand is made suggests that ideology is involved. One indication of the presence of ideology is that certain topics are debarred from discussion. It is suggested in chapter 10 that technocratic consciousness and the ideology of the public institution have been damaging to family interests. The interests of the new class of bureaucrats and information workers are closely tied to the power of the public institution, and their attitudes to family a critical factor in the current situation of families.

I have assumed that readers are aware of the changes in family demographics and status in recent years. There has been such widespread coverage of the facts of higher rates of divorce, fewer choosing to marry, marriage being delayed and smaller families that I have not attempted to review this ground. The effects of longer life-expectancy, of marriages in which child-rearing dominates only a small percentage of the life-span, of relationships extending over three and four generations have likewise been thoroughly aired.

These dramatic demographic changes, combined with changes in the status of marriage (it is no longer seen as 'odd' not to marry or to choose not to have children, and little stigma attaches to divorce or to living together without formal marriage), mean that there is little legal or social coercion on couples to remain married if this is disagreeable. These changes are neither insignificant, nor do they portend *only* gloom and doom.

These changes cannot be lightly dismissed as 'families changing their function', because both European and American research shows that the pattern of smaller families, high divorce rates and high rates of single-parenthood are linked to established indicators of social pathology, including higher suicide rates.[4] A classic sociologist (such as Durkheim) would consider the rising rates of youth suicide as statistics of the greatest social significance. The fact that statistically these correlate with changing family patterns indicates that family is not just a 'private' concern but of central social significance. The failure of social scientists to analyse these links and their tendency to bless or legitimate them by reframing them as merely 'changes of family function' is a failure of the intellectual role.[5]

On the other hand, the stable family-patterns of the past hid a great deal of anguish and pain, and it may be that our current patterns hold the potential for a more free, more fully human concept of marriage and family life. However, this is a possibility to be struggled and fought for. It is unlikely to emerge spontaneously without our addressing the challenging issues raised by current family statistics.

Another theme that recurs throughout this book is that of the public and the private. While the private realm's value and integrity is affirmed, this is not to say that a retreat into privatism is supported. Erosion of the cultural values that make sense of contemporary social, economic, and political conditions results in inaction and indecision in individuals. Loss of cultural values manifests in a fascination with family concerns, leisure time, consumption and the growth of 'civil privatism'. It leads to de-politicisation, the process of failing to participate in the process of reasoned debate through which a consensus of mutual interests can be arrived at and values established. The only solution to the difficulties families face is through a revival of the public realm. Public and private cannot be done away with. Both realms are essential. What is at issue here is the relationship between the two realms, especially evidence that the public realm is actually removing resources from the private realm, and this is damaging to families.

The argument of the book can be simply summarised.

Families are the strongest factor in the development and maintenance of human competence. There is an accumulating body of evidence on the characteristics of families that create competence and well-being in their members. The vital factor is the family's own internal dynamics, the way family members relate to each other and the outside world. The way family members communicate, value the unique qualities of each member and recognise and affirm each other is a strong predictor of the competence of the individuals. Clear leadership, the wise use of power, the ability to make decisions, shared family-time, humour and a supportive network of friends and relations are other aspects of well-functioning families. Yet, though families are the strongest factor in human competence, there is evidence that in the late twentieth century they lack the infrastructure of support that they need to fulfil their uniquely valuable roles. Current family statistics point to fragmentation and stress in families. The social and personal costs of family breakdown are staggering, yet there is a failure by public bodies to respond with preventive measures. In Australia it is estimated that the cost of marriage breakdown amounts to $175 per head per year, while only 44 cents per head are allocated to prevent this cost. The major response has been to make divorce easier and more dignified, but there has been little attempt to lower the incidence of divorce, despite evidence that it is by no means a solution to family conflict that is free of side-effects.

In the area of education there has been a slowness to respond to evidence of the impact of families on children's learning in schools. The finding that the solution to the problem of children who did not benefit from schooling did not lie in devoting more resources to schools, but in doing something about the way the parents treat the child at home, has been virtually ignored. While family breakdown is a major cause of poverty, anti-poverty campaigns rarely address the issue of family breakdown.

In searching for the 'reason' that supports this failure to provide the infrastructure of support that families need, two culprits are found. One is the excessively narrow definition of knowledge or reason that gives the status of knowledge only to those matters that can be ascertained by observations based on sense data. This definition precludes learning to communicate, learning to nurture children, developing the attitudes and commitments that sustain family life as true learning. At best the latter are mickey mouse subjects for the not-too-bright. A second barrier to an adequate response to family needs is an antipathy between the public and the private. There is a tendency to forget that the formal public institutions with responsibility for health, education, the economy and so on rely on an informal world of families and communities. There is a tendency to assume that the effective actors are the institutional ones rather than the family and community ones. There is a tendency to overlook the private realm, to assume its input will always be there and does not need resourcing or status. In fact, at times it seems that both status and resources are being progressively withdrawn from this informal world with disastrous results for families.

Another reason for the failure to respond to the evidence of the lack of an adequate infrastructure of support for families is that no one knows what to do. Hence the last chapter reports some of the ways different institutions are adapting their practice in order to become more supportive of families. None of these programs is a radical, earth-shattering intervention that would overcome all the problems and issues that confront families. They are mostly small and local and have a limited impact. But they demonstrate that it is possible to support families, and they indicate that a variety of approaches by a variety of agencies and institutions are needed. There will be no single answer or solution to the stresses faced by today's families. A multitude of responses are needed, and these require that we recognise the value of families and the uniqueness of the contribution they make to social life, that we devote resources to support and enrich and understand families and the issues they face, and that we consult with families and work in partnership with them.

Bettelheim advances the notion that human beings evolve by evolving their social structures. Families, at their best, are the most creative, flexible, loving, growth-promoting group we know. We can learn a lot from them for the future evolution of our other social structures.

Part 1

The Impact of the Family

1

Families and Intellectual Development

It is the family that constitutes our 'common humanity', for our use of language, the basis of that humanness, has its origin in family forms. This makes the family 'the universal basis of human culture ... As language constitutes the essence of man as a species, and not reason, so the family and not the social order, is the setting that humanizes him'.
Jean Bethke Elshtain, quoting Stuart Hampshire.[1]

The story of the wild boy of Aveyron who was discovered in 1800 in a district in the south-west of France, having been lost or abandoned and having survived in the wild without human companionship, throws into stark relief a fact we take for granted. Human beings are essentially social creatures: to grow up in isolation, without human society, precludes the development of full humanity.

Despite the devoted and inspired teaching and care of his protector, Dr Jean-Marc-Gaspard Itard, an outstanding scientist and doctor, it was impossible for the wild boy to develop the ordinary capabilities essential for even the simplest role in human society. It seemed that Victor (as he came to be called) had been deprived of human company from about the age of three, and was probably about twelve when he was found.

Although he aroused initial enthusiasm and interest, those first responsible for him soon gave up in disgust. Far from being the noble savage, he was

> a disgustingly dirty child affected with spasmodic movements and often convulsions who swayed back and forth ceaselessly like certain animals in a menagerie, who bit and scratched those who opposed him, who showed no sort of affection for those

1

who attended him; and who was, in short, indifferent to everything and attentive to nothing.[2]

The most striking lack was his total failure to develop language — despite evidence of acute hearing, sight and intelligence. It seemed a vital stage had been missed, a door had been closed, and the opportunity to develop language had been irretrievably missed. The modern case of Genie, an abused and neglected child who was isolated in a small room and not spoken to from the age of twenty months to thirteen-and-a-half years, shows similar outcomes, although Genie did learn a few words, and the notion of language was not entirely foreign to her.[3]

The Abbé Sicard, who early gave up the care of Victor, declared that he was abandoned because he was an idiot. Itard believed that he was an idiot because he was abandoned. With the onset of adolescence his developing sexuality, unfocused and unbound, dominated his actions. He reverted to being 'wild', unsocial and unreachable. Eventually he had to be placed under even greater restraint than formerly.

Of course, the wild boy grew up without *any* society, but his story draws our attention to an aspect of life that is so pervasive as to be hidden. We take for granted the complex socialisation procedures that make human beings human. Because they are so pervasive and because they normally operate reasonably successfully, it is possible for us to overlook their existence or their importance. It is normally in a family that the wild boy would have learned language, social skills and restraint on his instinctive behaviour so as to enable him to fit into society.

In recent years, the family has had a chequered career though forecasts of its imminent death seem to have been a little premature. At the same time, alternatives to the family have, in turn, lost a little of their lustre.[4] Studies of kibbutz children find that, while the children are usually secure and stable, they are group-oriented, and lack the strong individual identity and autonomy assumed to be a sign of healthy psychological functioning (and, incidentally, assumed essential to the maintenance of democratic societies). It was hoped

2

that the attenuation of family bonds would result in greater personal freedom and autonomy. In fact, the reverse seems to have happened. The most striking example of this is the tendency of kibbutz children to choose group-oriented, highly structured environments. For example, while only 6 per cent of Israel's population were members of a kibbutz, kibbutz members made up 40 per cent of Israel's officer corps during the Six Day War of 1967.

Studies of commune children have found them to be neglected, even to the extent of being under-nourished.[5] On the other hand, successful communes (success was defined only in terms of survival) were characterised by strong, charismatic leadership, clear roles and rules, strong boundaries (which severely restricted or totally prevented members from having contact with the world outside the commune) and ritualised celebrations of the community's life and values.[6] In other words, they had institutionalised the supposedly oppressive aspects of family life in a far more rigid and inflexible form than is normally found in traditional family life.

A book whose title foretold *The Death of the Family*[7] was published in 1971. Meanwhile a great deal of evidence was mounting to indicate that while there is no doubt that certain families and certain styles of family can destroy their members' emotional stability and stamina, other family styles have the reverse effect. The latter create robust mental health, provide an ability to withstand stress, and have an equally strong impact on other areas of human functioning, such as intellectual development and success in school. Later job and social status, physical health, social concern and action, parenting and family styles, and the ability to create and sustain networks of support for family life are all influenced by experience within the family of origin.

Families have a greater impact on at least some areas of the moral development of adolescents than peers or school, and they are a major influence on the style of religious attitudes, practices and beliefs developed. A child's experience in the family of origin provides the pattern for later parenting styles. Through learning and experience, individuals may choose to alter that pattern in various ways. Social concern and action are also nurtured by certain family backgrounds.[8]

Families are one of the most valued aspects of life, and membership of a family is associated with personal happiness.[9] Australians derive more satisfaction from family than from work, play, religion or possessions, and for them, family is a prime value, something for which everything else, even life itself, could be sacrificed.[10] Despite the high rate of marriage breakdown in the USA, research there finds that most people report family life to be one of their greatest satisfactions in life.[11]

Of adult Americans, 92 percent rate the family as their most important personal value (followed, in descending order, by friendship, work, patriotism and religion): 83 percent would welcome more emphasis on *traditional family ties*; 33 percent said they place more emphasis on family togetherness than their parents did; 55 the same and only 12 percent less; 78 percent said they consider the family to be the most meaningful part of their life (as against only 9 percent making this claim for work).[12]

Dr Don Edgar, the Director of the Australian Institute of Family Studies, uses the phrase 'the crucible of competence' to refer to families. In fact, no other group or aspect of life outweighs the family's contribution to well-being and happiness. Some of the research on which the above claim is based needs to be examined more closely. The institution with the formal responsibility for intellectual development (and, to a large degree, social development) is the school. Yet there is evidence to suggest that families rather than schools are the prime influence in both of these areas. This is a suitable place, then, to begin an exploration of the positive impact of, families.

The influence of the family on intelligence

Parenting style has emerged as the key to the social and intellectual development of young children. Even studies of infants show this relationship.

The infant phase
Some strong evidence showing links between parenting styles

and intelligence emerges from the work of Klaus, Kennell and their colleagues at Case Western Reserve School of Medicine in the USA.[13] Klaus and Kennell based their work on the observation that animal mothers, immediately after giving birth, have quite specific and complex patterns of relating to their infants. The patterns differ from species to species, but were consistent to each species. They decided to explore human mothers and infants in order to discover whether there were human patterns of mother-response to newborn infants.

At the time they conducted their research, hospitals were run in a way that allowed virtually no contact between mothers and newborn infants. The researchers were able to alter the hospital conditions to allow the mothers to have their naked infants with them for about an hour immediately after delivery and for several hours each day of their hospital stay. Heat panels were provided over the mothers' beds to prevent chilling, and mothers were randomly assigned to either the experimental situation of extended contact with their newborn infant or to the standard hospital procedure of a glance at the baby shortly after birth, a short visit six to twelve hours later to identify the baby, and twenty to thirty minutes for feeding every four hours during the day. Each mother of a full-term baby in the extended-exposure group proceeded to relate to her baby in a similar way, showing an ordered progression of behaviour.

> The mothers started with fingertip touch on the infants' extremities and proceeded in 4 to 8 minutes to massaging, encompassing palm contact on the trunk . . . Mothers of normal premature infants permitted to touch them in the first 3 to 5 days of life followed a similar sequence, but at a much slower rate.[14]

The mothers of full-term babies who were given this opportunity for extended contact with their infants showed a remarkable increase in the time spent in face-to-face contact with their infants. A second study replicated the findings with a new sample, and follow-up a month later found that the extended-contact mothers had a different pattern of behaving towards their infants than did the mothers who experienced the normal hospital procedure of limited contact with new-borns.[15] The extended-contact mothers stood beside the babies during a hospital examination and soothed them when they cried. They fondled the babies more during feeding, had more eye-to-eye contact, and were more willing to pick up the babies when they fussed. They expressed more reluctance and anxiety about leaving the baby in someone else's care. Amazingly, these differences were still evident between the two groups of mothers when the infants were re-examined at twelve months of age.[16] After two years, the two groups of mothers were still measurably different in their responses to their babies. The mother's conversation with the child was observed and recorded during a free-play period in a setting containing toys and books.

Speech patterns of the mothers revealed that those who had been given extra contact with their infants during the neonatal period used significantly more questions, adjectives, words per proposition, and fewer commands and content words than did the control mothers.[17]

A more recent study replicated the findings with a larger sample of sixty mothers in a different cultural setting.[18] The use of two extended-contact groups enabled researchers to test whether the 'special attachment period' occurred in the few hours after birth or whether it extended over several days. One group received an early contact time of forty-five minutes immediately after birth and the other had the same contact time beginning twelve hours after the birth. Only the mothers in the immediate-contact time were affected.

Mothers who had contact with their neonates immediately after birth showed significantly more affectionate behaviour ('en face' looking at the baby, talking to the baby, fondling, kissing, smiling at the infant) when compared to the mothers in the delayed and control groups ... No significant differences were noted between the delayed and control groups. This study indicates that the maternal sensitive period is less than twelve hours in length, suggests the importance of skin to skin contact and compels reconsideration of hospital practices that even briefly separate mother and infant.[19]

Follow-up studies of the infants when they were five years of age found statistically significant differences between the two groups. In comparison with the controls

> The five-year-olds of the early contact mothers had significantly higher IQ's, understood language as measured by a receptive language test significantly better and comprehended significantly more phrases with two critical elements.[20]

The extended-contact children were seven IQ points ahead of the control group. There were significant correlations between the complexity of the mother's speech patterns to her infant at two years of age and the child's understanding of language and intellectual performance at age five. A significant correlation was found between the amount of time women spent looking at their babies during the filmed feeding at one month of age and the child's IQ at five years of age.[21]

Klaus and Kennel call these mutually satisfying patterns of relationship 'mother-child bonding' and their research prompted much of the current concern about bonding of infants to mothers. It also led to the changed hospital practice of mothers 'rooming-in' with infants, which was designed to facilitate such early bonding or, more accurately, to reverse hospital practices that were thought likely to interfere with a bonding process.

In view of how difficult it is to devise any program that can raise a group of normal children's IQ seven points once school age has been reached, it is hard to exaggerate the importance of Klaus and Kennell's research and its focus on mother-infant interaction as a key area for the development of human competence, including intellectual development. Other studies of mother-infant interaction support these findings of Klaus and Kennell.[22]

In fact research on the whole phase from birth to three years indicates that this brief period may be more important for educational success than the whole period of formal schooling.

The toddler phase
A study of the development of human competence carried out

under the auspices of Harvard University during the 1960s and 1970s demonstrated particularly clearly the relationship between parenting patterns and the development of children's competence.[23] This study was led by Burton White, and began with the Harvard Preschool Project in 1965.

The Head Start Programs had already been introduced in the USA in an attempt to respond to the knowledge that children who performed poorly in first grade rarely improved over their school career, and could be expected to fall farther and farther behind their age-mates the longer they stayed at school. Early evaluation of Head Start indicated that very few of the programs had long-term, or even short-term, success. In 1974 the eminent child-development researcher Urie Bronfenbrenner reported that the only early intervention programs to have any success were ones that *altered family interaction in a positive way*.[24] Some programs had concentrated on formal group processes, which had the effect of giving parents the message that *their* contribution was less vital than that of the educational experts; and falling measures of their children's achievements indicated the negative effect that conviction had on their children's development. (Presumably, the parents withdrew some of their involvement and activity with the child, deciding to leave these to the experts.)

Burton White had noticed that by three years of age a small number of children had spurted ahead of their age-mates. These are the ones who later do well in school and develop superior competence in a range of areas. Because these superior-competence children are easily identifiable at three, but indistinguishable from their peers at fifteen months of age, White assumed that the period from one year to three years must be the one of particularly interesting developments in the growth of human competence. Benjamin Bloom's *Stability and Change in Human Characteristics* had recently been completed, showing that 50 per cent of all intelligence is acquired by age four.

For all these reasons, the period of early childhood was chosen as likely to yield the best results. In the first phase of the research, a wide range of pre-school children were studied. Children who were (according to a broad group of researchers and child-development specialists) of a particularly high level of competence for their age and were 'most likely to succeed in pre-school and school' were identified. The children selected came from a wide range of socio-economic and cultural backgrounds, but shared a variety of linguistic, intellectual and social skills that set them apart from their average and below-average contemporaries. The researchers also selected, as a comparison, children whom they deemed were not likely to succeed. In all, four groups were studied: children from advantaged and disadvantaged families who were doing well, and children from advantaged and disadvantaged families who were not doing well.

In the next phase, researchers studied the home environments of the highly competent children and their less competent age-mates. They inquired which families were expecting another child. When the new infants were between one and three years old, the researchers began visiting their homes every other week and recording everything they could about the child-rearing practices of their parents. This involved many hours of visiting homes, interviewing parents, and just being around and observing. The observations continued for two years, with the observers spending long enough in the homes for family members to forget their 'just for the outsiders' manners and to revert to their usual patterns. In these target families researchers noticed a variety of at-home practices that seemed to be related to the exceptional competence of the children in the highly competent groups. The researchers were particularly interested in those disadvantaged families where children were developing high competence, as they assumed that to develop high competence from a position of disadvantage indicated that the families were having a particularly positive impact.

To test these findings, the researchers decided to teach these at-home practices to a variety of other parents. After this parental coaching the researchers studied the children to see if there were discernible effects on their competence. The researchers used three control groups to help them distinguish the effects of their experiment from irrelevant factors. One control group was given a different treatment by an expert child-development team in order to control for the placebo effect by comparing the treatment given with some of the best standard knowledge available. Another group was a measurement-only control group, for it is known that measuring procedures are a significant intervention. The measurement-only group went through all the tests of the other controls, but were not given the treatment of the experimental group.

The researchers were able to teach the at-home practices to parents with relatively little difficulty, and the follow-up study of the children's development showed a very high level of competence in the children reared in this way. These patterns of parenting related to high human competence were not restricted to any social group. Parents of different racial and ethnic and religious groups were found either to have these patterns naturally or to be able to learn them and apply them at home. As Burton White said of a later parent-education program based on these findings, 'We had success with families in which both parents had doctoral degrees and with families in which both had failed to finish high school.'[25] However, in *The Origins of Human Competence* study, parents who already had one or more children, though able to learn the skills in a group situation, tended not to put them into practice at home. Instead, they fell back into the patterns they had already established with their older children.

This was a significant and influential study. It showed a strong link between parenting practices in the home and the development of a broad range of human competencies. It showed that these important parental practices could be taught to parents and that many parents were ready and even eager to learn and benefit from knowledge in the area of effective family-patterns. It showed that the timing of educational interventions in the area of family life is critical: programs directed to first-time parents are much more likely to be successful than programs for parents of later-born children.

White's estimates of the number of families in which parents naturally employ the competent parenting style varies from one in ten to one in thirty. He thinks only one in thirty 'does a great job without really knowing what is happening'.[26] For this reason he concludes that 90 per cent of children are under-achievers. The two major reasons he gives for less than successful child-rearing are ignorance and stress. Parents are not given the information they need to perform the parenting role as well as they could. White acknowledges that his own chidren were well past the critical early years before his own enlightenment took place under the tutoring of the families who naturally possessed this highly effective parenting style.

White also speaks with feeling of the stress of caring for children, especially if they are closely spaced. He considers that only those who have cared for children, by which he means the mothers (this research was undertaken in the 1970s), and of course the researchers who observed it, have any idea what it is like. He offers three simple rules to enable the child-rearing process to go well: design the world of the child sensibly and safely; act as the child's personal consultant; set limits effectively. His primer for parents (see pp. 188–9) expands these essentials.

The Origins of Human Competence study is only one of many that have indicated the importance of family settings for the development of human competence. Other researchers measured a number of parental behaviours, including 'maternal involvement with child', 'provision of appropriate play materials' and 'emotional and verbal responsivity of the mother' when children were two years old. The latter behaviours correlated highly with the children's development when the children were four-and-a-half years old.[27] Yet another study found that children who have a high level of resistance to stress and an ability to cope with highly stressful situations are characterised by a particular style of family background, which seems to account for their robust nature. However, evidence of the importance of family settings is not restricted to the pre-school period. Studies of those children who do well in schools even more strongly indicate the importance of family settings.

Success in schooling and family factors

Families not only have a strong impact on the intellectual,

emotional and social development of infants and young children, they also powerfully affect the ongoing development of older children, adolescents and even adults. The impact of families on school achievement was shown very clearly by the series of large-scale research projects undertaken in the 1960s into equality of educational opportunity.

The Equality of Educational Opportunity Report

The USA led the way in research into whether schools provided equality of educational opportunity for children. The findings were sobering. It had previously been a cherished belief in the USA that all children had the opportunity to succeed in life. It was known that there were great inequalities of wealth, but it was thought that the lack of formal class barriers and the provision of universal schooling provided the opportunity for anyone who was prepared to work to reach the level of achievement of which each was capable. The research into whether schools actually provided this access to achievement for all children was a very large and expensive project, involving massive collection and analysis of data. Data were collected from approximately 570,000 students and 60,000 teachers, and on the facilities available in 4000 schools.

The findings were published in the *Equality of Educational Opportunity Report*, often referred to as the Coleman Report, after James Coleman, who led the research team. The major finding was that schools do not overcome educational disadvantage and that 'differences between schools account for only a small fraction of the differences in pupil achievement.'[28] While there are obviously differences between the most advantaged schools and the least advantaged, the Coleman Report findings were that it is the family backgrounds, rather than the school inputs, that most strongly account for this difference.

This was a significant finding, one that called into question one of the most cherished American beliefs: that theirs was a society that provided equality of opportunity to all. The research sparked world-wide interest, and similar studies were conducted in other countries, with similar thought-provoking results.

Family versus school

Another striking finding of the research concerned the impact of families on success in school. Of the seven major conclusions of the Coleman Report, the first three related to the strength of this family factor and several others were indirectly related to family factors. The seven major findings were:

1. Family background has great importance for school achievement;
2. The relation of family background to achievement does not diminish over the years of school;
3. Family background accounts for a substantial amount of the school-to-school variation in achievement and, therefore, variations in school facilities, curriculum and staff can only have a small, independent effect;
4. There is a small amount of variance explicitly accounted for by variations in facilities and curriculum;
5. Although no school factor accounts for much variation in achievement, teacher characteristics account for more than any other;
6. The social composition of the school body is more highly related to achievement, independently of the student's social background, than is any other factor;
7. Attitudes, such as sense of control of the environment, or a belief in the responsiveness of the environment, are strongly associated with achievement, and appear to be little influenced by variations in school characteristics.

In 1972 the findings of the Coleman Report were subjected to critical review by a number of leading researchers. Marshall Smith, for example, stated that in the five years since the publication of the Coleman Report there had been general agreement on points 1 and 7, so he would concentrate on the other five which had proved controversial. After reassessing the evidence he wrote:

> in general, the results of the reexamination affirm and strengthen the overall conclusions of the Report:
> That schools bring little influence to bear on a child's achievement that is independent of his background and general social context; and that this very lack of an independent effect means that the inequalities imposed on children by their

home, neighbourhood, and peer environment are carried along to become the inequalities with which they confront adult life at the end of school. [p.325][29]

Coleman himself wrote in the same report:

schools do not constitute an important enough modification of the child's environment to interrupt the family process that in the absence of school would be expected to show the same constant correlation with achievement that they now show. [Three modes of analysis provide] a rather strong base of evidence for the inference that school factors constitute a relatively minor modification of the child's learning environment — a firm foundation for the argument that much more radical modifications of the environment are necessary in order to greatly increase achievement of presently low-achieving groups.[30]

David Armor, who re-analysed the findings on school and family factors, affirmed the strength of family background over school factors on achievement: 'This complete and independent reassessment shows that community inputs are clearly stronger predictors of student achievement.'[31] In searching for factors that might have the potential to reduce the differences in achievement between white and black students, Armor wrote:

School factors may be important for a certain basic level of achievement, but this does not necessarily mean that *improving* those factors will help bring black achievement closer to white achievement. If one wants to reduce this differential, Coleman's and our analysis point to *family background factors as the more promising area for improvement*.[32] [Emphasis added]

Christopher Jencks summed up the findings in a particularly pithy statement: 'variations in what children learn in school depend largely on variations in what they bring to school, not in variations in what schools offer them.'[33]

In the United Kingdom, the Plowden Report, *Children and their Primary Schools*, supported by massive statistical data and extensive interviews with parents, identified parental interest in a child's education as the most important single

14

influence on his or her progress (more important, for example, than size of family, or parents' income or social class). The report stressed the interdependence of school and home: 'It has been recognised that education is concerned with the whole man; henceforth it must be concerned with the whole family.'[34]

Education Priority Areas (EPA) were declared as a result of the realisation of the influence of both home and neighbourhood environments. Through the EPA policy, play-groups and home-visiting schemes brought young pupils, parents and teachers together in informal educational environments and situations. The emphasis chosen was that of increased collaboration between home and school rather than the development of specific programs to increase parenting skills. No national program was developed to address the situation of those children whose parents did not exhibit the satisfactory level of interest or ability to encourage and stimulate their children's learning. It seems this failure was due to financial reasons.[35]

The Bullock Report, which was issued several years later, in 1975, also stressed family factors in children developing *A Language for Life*.[36] It recommended that secondary school students should be involved in the care of young children, particularly in play-groups, both to assist in early language development of the children and for the older students to observe early learning in progress. Parents were to be helped in the selection and use of books at home for early reading experiences. Again funds were not made available to implement most of the Bullock Report proposals, although the report was widely accepted and warmly received.

Parental interest

The Plowden Report's finding on the impact of the parents' interest in the child's education was significant. The strength of the 'subjective' family factors of parental interest in children's schooling and expectations of success had puzzled the North American Equality of Educational Opportunity researchers. Smith was inclined to put the strength of the subjective factors down to faulty data:

15

The variable *Parent Interest*, on the other hand, is intended to assess the behaviour of the parent before the child entered school (whether the child was read to or not) and how often the parent asks the child about his schoolwork. It seems unlikely that either of these behaviours is a direct cause of a child's success in school after 1st grade.[37]

Smith was expressing the common-sense view of the time. It seemed ridiculous that merely talking to a child about school should affect the child's achievement in school. But this common-sense view fails to understand how significant the parents are to the child.

When the parent asks about school, she or he conveys to the child that school matters and it matters to the parent how the child is performing in school. Further, presumably the parent does not just ask about school. Presumably the parent listens to the child and then has an opportunity to guide and advise the child or to take appropriate action if action is required. The close-up studies of families that are described later are important in this context as they show how this factor of 'interest in education' is translated into an effective spur to children's development, not just in educational endeavours, but in the whole realm of human competence. These studies give reason to believe that 'asking the child about school' is a pointer to a whole realm of family activities and interaction *known* to powerfully affect human competence.[38]

An international study

An international study, which included investigation of seven subject-areas in eighteen countries, was conducted under the sponsorship of the International Association for the Evaluation of Educational Achievement (IEA).[39] This study, too, found the importance of home background even in subjects such as science, modern languages and civic education, which appear on the surface to the much more school-dependent than others, such as mother-tongue fluency. Re-analysis of this data at Aston (UK) attempted to quantify the effects of family and school factors and came to the conclusion that if a school had to choose between using a certain financial resource to lower class-sizes and using it to improve the family environment for education, 'there is much evidence which would prompt the latter'.[40]

Australian research

Australian researchers come to conclusions similar to those already cited. H. H. Penny's investigations of barriers to Aboriginal children's educational achievement focused on the need for changes at the level of home and community. For example, Penny stated the need for Aboriginal parents to be better informed of the links between school achievement and access to jobs and status, and also of the home practices that can enable their children to benefit from the school experience. While obviously impressed with the warmth and conviviality of Aboriginal community life, Penny considered that parents needed to understand that children who were up late at night joining the adults in talking and singing could not be alert and attentive the next day in school.[41]

Professor Kevin Marjoribanks has made use of Australia's diverse population to research the links between social class, ethnic groups and children's learning environments. He concludes that there can be no major breakthrough in school effectiveness without intervention at the family and neighbourhood level. He envisions a new relationship between children, schools, families and neighbourhoods to enable equality of educational opportunity to become more of a reality.[42]

Professor Bob Connell's innovative research into schooling for middle-class and working-class students broke away from the individualistic model. Interviewing of students was done in 'clusters'. Students and their parents, teachers and headteachers were interviewed, so as to gather an integrated picture of the students in their social matrix. This technique vividly demonstrated how families mediate expectations, attitudes and skills, and these powerfully affect young people's ability to negotiate the educational structure and institutions. For some working-class youngsters, doing well at school means to accept the behaviour and style of teachers rather than those of parents as models. Such acceptance can be seen by the youngster as a denial or betrayal of family values and style. Sometimes youngsters receive verbal messages about doing well at school, but to do well at school may mean breaking many patterns that are part of the whole fabric of family life and values. This study is particularly enlightening on the family's role in mediating to children the expectations and patterns of behaviour that are vital to schooling succcess.[43]

One-parent families and school success

One aspect of family life that has undergone considerable change in recent years is the marked increase in the numbers of one-parent families. Hence it is of interest to know whether this change in family structure affects children's educational chances.

Many studies have shown that one-parent or two-parent status does not affect the school achievement of children. As long as the children have the interest and support of one parent (and preferably of both) and are not caught up in conflicts between their parents, they can do well in school. Paul Amato, in *Children in Australian Families: The Growth of Competence*, reports on a study of 402 families. One-half of the children were attending primary schools and the other half secondary schools. Half of the families in each group were intact, and the others were separated, divorced, other one-parent status or step-families. Children and parents were interviewed separately. Amato found that

of the 13 high-competence primary school children, five lived in intact families, seven lived in one-parent households, and one lived with neither parent. Of the 11 low-competence children, five lived in intact families, two lived in stepfamilies, and four lived in one-parent households. These distributions indicate that living in a one-parent household was no barrier to achieving a high level of general competence. Indeed, whereas only 31 per cent of the children in the sample came from one-parent households, they made up 54 per cent of high-compentence children.[44]

Yet one American study found schooling deficits to be associated with one-parent status. In 1980 a study called *The*

Most Significant Minority: One-Parent Children claimed to be the first longitudinal study of the needs of children of one-parent families. The report found that

> one-parent children, on the whole, show lower achievement in school than their two-parent peers . . . Among two-parent children, 30 per cent were ranked as high achievers, compared to only 17 per cent of one-parent children. At the other end of the scale, the situation is reversed. Only 24 per cent of two-parent children were lower achievers — while 40 per cent of the one-parent children fell into that category.
>
> There are more clinic visits among the one-parent (secondary) students, and their absence rate runs far higher than for students with two parents.
>
> One-parent students are consistently more likely to be late, truant, and subject to disciplinary action by every criterion we examined, and at both the elementary and secondary levels . . . one-parent children are more than twice as likely as two-parent children to give up on school altogether.[45]

Both UK and USA figures report that children who have experienced the divorce or separation of their parents have, on the whole, lower educational achievement, lower job status and lower income, which indicates that while much evidence points to family processes as the key to family and individual competence, family structure too may be relevant and should not be dismissed too readily. However, many children of one-parent families are performing very well in school.

Evidence of the impact of families on intellectual development and success in schooling comes from studies of parental behaviour with newborns and young children, from a wide range of studies of families and human competence that will be reviewed throughout this book and from studies of schooling achievement, particularly the body of work that emerged from the equality of educational opportunity debates. In all, this latter body of work represents a major segment of the educational research effort of the last quarter-century. The conclusions are clear and have never been seriously disputed. Who succeeds and who fails at school is being decided outside the school, primarily by family factors. Family factors outweigh school factors in determining educational success. Yet the implications of this research have been poorly comprehended.

Educational research and practice has continued as if the findings were the reverse of what they actually are: as if children's learning in school were primarily related to school policies and programs — curriculum, books, buildings, teacher-training programs and so on — and only very marginally affected by family factors.

However, it is not just in the area of education that family factors have a powerful impact. Emotional or psychological strength and flexibility are essential for human competence, and this dimension, too, is primarily formed by family experiences.

2

Families and Health

Emotional and mental health

Therapists and counsellors find that experiences in the family
of origin and in the current family are the most significant
factors creating the depression, anxiety, confusion or stress
that lead people to seek counselling. Their experience is
borne out by research. Many studies have found strong links
between an individual's mental and emotional health and
early experiences in the family of origin. Experiences in the
current family can exacerbate or heal earlier wounds. Forms
of psychopathology (such as certain schizophrenias) are
linked to family patterns. Both alcoholism and drug addiction are often found to have a family component. Robust
psychological well-being is almost always associated with
optimal or at least competent family functioning. A study of
college students and their family backgrounds is typical of
many that have found this link between family context and
mental and emotional health.

Emotional health of college students
In 1969 a report was published of an investigation of the
relationship between college students' emotional health and

the organisation of their families.[1] One hundred first-year university students were screened to assess their psychological health. The study focused on the ten students at the top and the bottom of the ranking and on their families. Family-patterns clearly distinguished those students with high-level psychological functioning from those at the bottom of the ranking. Many family-patterns were seen to be relevant, such as the ability to communicate and solve problems, warmth, the expression of feelings, the balance between autonomy and dependence, and the balance of parental dominance. This study found that when both parents are disturbed, the children are usually disturbed also. When both parents are healthy, so are the children. If one parent is disturbed and the other healthy, the children will be healthy if the parental relationship is warm and supportive, a finding that places as much significance on the parental relationship as on the parental mental health.

Many studies before and since this time have supported Westley and Epstein's findings on the relationship between family patterns and children's emotional health and none has seriously questioned it.

Drug and alcohol abuse
One of the most common forms, symptoms or causes (depending on your viewpoint) of emotional disturbance is addiction, and one of the most disturbing trends of our time is the increase in drug and alcohol abuse and addiction. Again, family-patterns seemed to be relevant and even crucial. Blum and his colleagues concluded after a number of studies of drug patterns that 'drug risk is best predicted by family factors'.[2] He noted differences between the low drug-risk and high drug-risk families he studied. Communication patterns, father's authority and participation, the use of power and humour in the family and the degree of mutual respect differentiated the two groups. He concluded that 'the peer group has little influence as long as the family remains strong'.

Blum concurs with earlier researchers who found that youthful illicit drug-use begins as a group activity, and peers supply one another with drugs, provide justifications for and interpretations of drug experiences, and teach the use of drugs. They also agree that, over a generation, peer influence may have increased in patterns of use of tobacco (and hence, presumably, of illicit drug-use). It seems that US teenagers compared with some other nationalities are more attuned to group-norms than to a conscience that meets cultural standards. It can be expected, then, that teenagers' drug-use would be strongly related to the drug-use in their environment. Blum found evidence that, in general, as far as *drug experimentation* went, this was true. Despite this pattern, when it came to assessing middle-class, *high-risk drug-use*, he asserts that 'knowing the characteristics of the family allows us to make almost completely accurate predictions'.[3] Blum found that even in superior family environments, teenagers or young adults will experiment with drugs. However, they seem to be protected from destructive drug involvement. Teenagers from families that offered sufficient emotional support offered explanations for either giving up drug involvement or forgoing drug experimentation. Reasons such as 'I am satisfied with my real-world orientated self' or 'You can't really respond to others' sadness when you are on pot' underlay their decisions.

Protection of the addictive behaviour has been identified as a pattern within alcoholic families. Contradictory messages to the developing addict are common. As well as intense opposition to drug involvement, there can be hidden messages approving or allowing the behaviour. The parents may be expressing their own unhealed pain through the behaviour of their child. Sometimes their protective behaviour is associated with a great fear of a member leaving the family. The seemingly perverse behaviour of such parents is not easily altered and rarely responds to the urgings and warnings of friends, teachers, doctors and others who may express the misgivings they feel. It seems that in such cases the parents' own instinctive parenting responses have been disturbed or distorted.

A study that demonstrated this pattern particularly clearly was undertaken by Dr Sandra Coleman.[4] She found intergenerational family-patterns of unresolved mourning and a lack of spiritual beliefs to be associated with heroin addiction. Coleman found that the parents of heroin addicts had experienced traumatic and unresolved grief far more frequently than had the parents of control families (normal subjects and psychiatric outpatients).

Of special interest is the fact that a far greater number of the addict parents lost relatives from accidents, murders, suicide, war and crib deaths. Only rarely did the parents of the psychiatric outpatients have a family member die of unusual circumstances, and parents of normal subjects had no such experiences. With regard to separation, none of the parents of the normals were ever separated from a natural or foster mother during either childhood or adolescence. In contrast both heroin addict parents and psychiatric outpatient parents had such experiences. Unlike the other groups, the parents of normals were never separated from their entire families or sent to live with relatives during their childhood.

This pattern of unexpected and untimely death (or separation) was often repeated in the addict's own life-experience. It is not bereavement, loss or separation *alone* that causes the problem. In families where the loss is 'creatively grieved' the youngsters may develop outstanding competence.[5] Again it is the *family* that offers or thwarts the possibility of 'creative mourning' for the child or teenager. It seems that addict families minimise the impact of death and tend to avoid death-related issues. This pattern is almost certainly related to their failure to provide a context in which 'creative mourning' enables a resolution of the loss.

Other researchers agree with Coleman's findings.[6] They find parental fear and unwillingness to allow the adolescent or young adult to separate and establish successful marital relationships. Excessive dependency of the addict on his parents (masked by the apparent independence of unacceptable behaviour) is common. And the addictive behaviour as part of a continuum of self-destruction in the family has also been noted.

The studies by Coleman of heroin addicts are an example of how severe disturbances in family-patterns are often found to involve more than one generation. The equally significant finding by Eisenstadt that loss may be associated with genius or high competence is supported by Wallerstein and Kelly's finding that the crisis of parental divorce sometimes acts as a spur to children's development and results in superior competence in some children. It seems that some families have the ability to protect their members from the effects of bereavement and loss by enabling their members to 'creatively mourn'[7] and hence eventually achieve a resolution of the loss. Wolfenstein finds that children do not mourn as adults mourn. Those children who achieve a positive outcome after parental bereavement are the ones who have an ability to make new attachments, a 'relatively low level of ambivalence toward the parent who has died', and for whom there is a readily available, probably already loved and trusted, substitute.[8] Again, it is the family's previous patterns and ability to provide these needs of the child that determines the outcome of loss of parent in childhood.

Family dynamics and mental illness
In 1976 Lewis and his co-researchers at Timberlawn in Texas reported their experience that mental illness in adolescents could usually be traced to either developmental difficulties or to ongoing, interaction patterns within families. Earlier, a spate of publishing by psychiatrists and researchers reported finding links between family-patterns and the development of forms of mental illness, such as schizophrenia.

The pioneering work of writers such as Cooper, Laing and Esterson remains of influence.[9] They played a significant part in the development of the 'Family Systems' approach to therapy in which certain forms of neurosis, psychosis and behaviour difficulties are seen to be triggered or induced by family-patterns and are best alleviated by addressing the family-patterns rather than pressuring the 'identified patient' alone to change.

One clue that indicated to these psychiatrists the negative power of some patients' families was that patients frequently got better in hospital but relapsed immediately they returned home, or even after being visited by family members. When psychiatrists studied the families involved, they felt that one reason the patient had become sick in the first place, and the reason why relapses occurred after the return home, was to be found in the dynamics of the sick person's family. It was early believed that schizophrenia was due to the suffocating attentions of mothers who live through their children and prevent them from developing separate identities of their own. Although attention never shifted from the mother, it gradually came to be believed that the wrong kind of fathers (weak, submissive, indifferent, negligent or passive) and severe conflict could lead to equally unsatisfactory results. The psychiatrist Lidz[10] coined the terms 'marital skew' and 'marital schism' to describe the family styles often associated with the development of schizophrenia in the young. 'Skewed' families are characterised by a dominant mother who also displays 'rather serious psychopathology' and is able to impose her pathology on her family because her spouse tends to passivity. Lidz uses the term 'marital schism' to describe the relationship between spouses in families where chronic hostility, withdrawal, threats of separation and undercutting of each other's worth to the children prevail. The lack of a firm parental coalition leads to parents competing for their children's loyalty and affection. Both these styles of family were often found when psychiatrists investigated the background of schizophrenic patients.

Wynne[11] stressed the negative effects of 'pseudomutuality' or lack of warmth and of stereotyped and rigid roles in the families of schizophrenics. The families Wynne describes show a desperate preoccupation with harmony, which they try to preserve by preventing anyone from departing from her/his accustomed role. Families such as these have been studied more recently by Rolv Mikkel Blakar, in Oslo, who found that parents of schizophrenic offspring could perform a problem-solving task involving giving each other directions from maps and finding a particular route *when there was no conflict*.[12] But in induced conflict situations (where members are following different maps, which they believe to be the same) their desperate need to agree with each other prevents them from making the discovery that 'the map must be wrong'. Their refusal or inability to even admit that there is a difference between them prevents them from solving the communication difficulty.

The double-bind

Gregory Bateson, whose earlier work was in anthropology, developed his famous double-bind theory: the parents of schizophrenics send double messages to their children. The messages contradict one another, but the child is prevented from commenting on the contradiction. Often one message is verbal and the other non-verbal, which is further mystifying for the child. The following example, 'Sons should love their mothers but keep their distance', illustrates what Bateson meant by the double-bind.

A young man who had fairly well recovered from an acute schizophrenic episode was visited in the hospital by his mother. He was glad to see her and impulsively put his arm around her shoulders, whereupon she stiffened. He withdrew his arm, and then she asked, 'Don't you love me anymore?' He then blushed, and she said, 'Dear, you must not be so easily embarrassed and afraid of your feelings'.[13]

If the son accepts the mother's simulated warmth as genuine and approaches her with affection, the mother draws away. If the son then withdraws, she accuses him of being unloving. No matter how he responds, he is in the wrong.

It would not be surprising if a child who is attempting to learn language, understand society and find his own identity in such a family should develop schizophrenia. This at least was the opinion of the 'anti-psychiatrists'. Laing, Cooper and Esterson presented their findings as a radical criticism of both family and psychiatry and won the label of 'anti-psychiatrists' or 'radical psychiatrists'. Later research has supported them in finding that there are marked communication differences between families containing schizophrenic members (and families where members later develop schizophrenia) and normal control families, though other of their findings have been challenged, especially the double-bind theory. The objection that the differences are due to the stress placed on a family by a schizophrenic member has been answered by studies that also include families with adolescents with serious heart disease, and families including anorexic members and also by prospective studies.[14]

The work of Bjorn Rishovd Rund in Oslo indicates that although there are marked deviances in communication patterns found in the parents of schizophrenic patients, these differences are found only in the parents of non-paranoid schizophrenics.[15] Lewis's study was based on a small sample (only twelve patient families and forty-four non-patient families), but twelve independent raters, unaware of whether the families contained a patient, reliably classified the families containing patients at the lower end of the well-functioning family spectrum. Bowen speaks of the 'undifferentiated egomass' in his descriptions of the family style that is often found to produce schizophrenic offspring.

A protracted debate on the cause of the schizophrenic illnesses continues. The main conflict is between bio-medical and psycho-social theories. There is ample evidence of genetic factors in chronic schizophrenia. However, it is now thought that genetic factors contribute to vulnerability rather than directly *cause* schizophrenia.[16] Chemical, viral and enzyme theories are all supported by research evidence, as are childhood characteristics, social class factors and stressful life events. In other words, schizophrenia is a complex, multifaceted illness. No one factor alone explains its etiology. But of the known contributing factors, family communication is at least as important as any other.

Attachment and emotional strength
The psychiatrist John Bowlby, best-known for his work in developing the theory of attachment and its central role in the growth of human competence, supports these observations on the role of families in the development of some very serious disorders. Bowlby uses different terminology. He proposes that the infant or young child gradually builds 'working models' of his attachment figures and of himself in relation to them. The information for these models comes from a variety of sources, such as his own day-to-day experience, statements made by his parents, and information coming from others. Usually these different sources are reasonably compatible, and the child constructs a working model of her or his world that is internally consistent and which enables her or him to make firm and accurate predictions of

what is likely to happen. She or he can then act effectively. But for some children, the information reaching them from their parents is incompatible with their own day-to-day experience:

> To take a real, though by no means extreme, example: a child may experience his mother as unresponsive to him and unloving and he may infer, correctly, that she had never wanted him and never loved him. Yet this mother may insist, in season and out, that she does love him. Furthermore, if there is friction between them, as there inevitably is, she may claim that it results from his having been born with a contrary temperament. When he seeks her attention, she dubs him insufferably demanding; when he interrupts her, he is intolerably selfish; when he becomes angry at her neglect, he is held possessed of a bad temper or even an evil spirit. In some way, she claims, he was born bad. Nevertheless, thanks to a good fortune he does not deserve, he has been blessed with a loving mother who, despite all, cares devotedly for him.[17]

It is clear from the above that Bowlby is describing a situation with many similarities to Bateson's 'double-bind'. Bowlby lists the unacceptable options open to a child in such a position. The child may persist in accepting the evidence of experience, in which case the parent often enforces her own viewpoint with threats to abandon the child or to become ill or to commit suicide.[18] Under such pressure, the child may give up the evidence of her or his experience and accept the definition of herself or himself as inherently 'disturbed', a person whose behaviour is quite incomprehensible and in no way accounted for by the family context. A third option is an uneasy compromise: the child attempts to accept both viewpoints and oscillates uneasily between the two. Yet another option is a desperate attempt to integrate the two viewpoints. Because they are incompatible, this attempt is doomed to failure and may lead to cognitive breakdown.

Bowlby differs slightly from others who have found such patterns in the family background. He noted (in the early 1970s) a bias in psychiatry and psychoanalysis to accept the parent's definition of the situation and to discredit the child's. He also noted the growing tendency from those who espoused an anti-psychiatry stance to judge the patient right and sane and the parents in the wrong. Bowlby never perceived the evidence that families *can* make their members mad as evidence that families inevitably do make people mad. Nor did he condone the blaming of parents for their offspring's dysfunction. Quite the reverse:

> . . . while parents are held to play a major role in causing a child to develop a heightened susceptibility to fear, their behaviour is seen not in terms of moral condemnation but as having been determined by the experiences they themselves had as children. Once that perspective is attained and rigorously adhered to, parental behaviour that has the gravest consequences for children can be understood and treated without moral censure. That way lies hope of breaking the generational succession.

Families as mediators of socially induced stress

As well as having a primary role in creating robust psychological health, families play a powerful role in mediating stresses emanating from broad social conditions to family members. However, their ability to buffer stress, while considerable, can be overwhelmed.

A historical and social study of families during and since the Depression of the 1930s shows both that families have an ability to protect members from stress and the vulnerability of families to socially induced stress. It also indicates that socially induced stress can have *beneficial* effects on families and individuals, *provided the family is able to cope with the stress and is not prevented from nurturing the most vulnerable members, the little children.* Elder studied teenagers from middle-class and working-class families in Oakland who lost a significant amount of their income and resources due to the Depression. He followed these teenagers through their life development and found that this 'deprived' group experienced an enhancement of almost every area of life, and the enhancement continued throughout their lives. Their educational and job success, income, marital satisfaction and physical health were all better than their counterparts from middle-class families who suffered little or no loss of income in the Depression. The experience of stress and learning to cope with it were, in fact, beneficial, and the way the families coped with the stress was critical.

The families were strengthened in their response in that everyone else was suffering the same thing, so there was less reason for self-blame for the loss of income. Boys from middle-class families who were hardest-hit by the Depression benefited most from the Depression experience, but girls and boys from working-class backgrounds also benefited. Youngsters from families who escaped economic ruin were less successful both educationally and vocationally. A greater proportion of them had later psychological problems. Elder concludes that a childhood that shelters the young from the hardships of life fails to develop or test adaptive capacities that are called on in life-crises: 'To engage and manage real-life (though not excessive) problems in childhood and adolescence is to participate in a sort of apprenticeship for adult life.'[19]

Elder also studied a group from Berkeley who were young children at the onset of the Depression. Their life stories are the reverse of the teenagers' experience. Because they were so young when the Depression hit, they were exposed to its impact as children for a longer time, which may account for the very different outcomes in their case. Also it disrupted the family when they were at a much more vulnerable age. One reason that the teenagers benefited from the Depression experience was that they were able to do something about it (work, help the family, help mind the little children), and hence the experience introduced them early into the world of adults and strengthened their sense of their own efficacy.

Those who were small children at the onset of the Depression suffered the failure of their families to meet their needs for nurture and support in those formative years. In this second sample, sons from both middle-class and working-class families who lost significant income during the Depression ranked lower on high school grades, expressed lower aspirations and were less likely to complete college. The girls showed less evidence of trauma. This is referred to later. Boys who entered college showed deficits, such as lack of self-esteem, a tendency to withdraw from adversity and to avoid commitments. They displayed a sense of victimisation and vulnerability to the judgements of others.[20] For those who did not enter college, the negative consequences were more severe, resulting in longer periods in manual jobs and greater instability of working life. In the final follow-up at around age forty, a higher proportion of the deprived than of the non-deprived of this latter, Berkeley, sample exhibited some health problems, chronic fatigue or energy decline and heavy or problem-drinking. These symptoms are more often present among the high-achievers than among the low-achievers.[21]

The effects of this Depression deprivation were *not* strongest when the boys entered first grade, when the Depression stress was still current, but became evident *only* during the boys' adolescent years. It seems that developmental limitations surface when children encounter 'demanding situations that call upon their adaptive resources, as in the transition from the protective environment of an elementary school to the achievement pressures of adolescence'.[22]

One of the most surprising findings of Elder's research was that the effects of the Depression on this second sample of families (those where the children were quite young at the outset of the Depression) were linked to the family-patterns *prior to* the Depression. Using data from interviews conducted prior to 1929, Elder created an index of the marital relationship, which turned out to be a predictor of the effect of the Depression on the children. Usually, the father's loss of his bread-winner role resulted in loss of status within the family, a weakened tie between father and son, and a strengthened tie between mother and daughter. This in turn was related to reduced competence in the boys but not in the girls.

But in families where, previous to the Depression, a very positive tie existed between the spouses, the experience of deprivation 'actually enhanced the relationship of father with son *and* daughter'.[23] This enhanced relationship of father with son and daughter protected both from the otherwise expected side-effects of Depression deprivation. In fact, for boys the loss of a close tie to the father and the consequent attractiveness of the peer group was linked to the most damaging consequences of Depression deprivation.[24]

These findings show that families have a great power to mediate social events and experiences to their members; but if families are stressed beyond their ability to protect and nurture the most vulnerable members, the little children, then the destructive impact affects the future life-course of those children and probably sets in train dysfunctional inter-generational patterns.

There are very serious questions raised by Elder's research in view of the number of children in poverty. Both Australia and the USA have many children living in poverty, and the high rates of marriage breakup add to the numbers of children who also are separated from one parent. Elder's research indicates that economic stress does not always result in negative outcomes for children, though there are obvious limitations to this (once a certain limit of poverty is exceeded, the damaging results are well documented). But he finds poverty plus attenuated ties to parents puts children at risk of the painful and depressing life-pattern that the Berkeley Depression cohort (the group who were quite young when the Depression entered their lives) experienced.

Both the USA and Australia have more poor children than poor old people. In fact, the slogan 'the feminisation of poverty' could well be altered to 'the transfer of poverty to the children' as one aspect of the number of women caring for children who are poor is that it is *children more than any other group who are bearing the brunt of poverty*. In Australia in 1986, one in five children were in families receiving family-income support.[25] The Social Security Minister, Brian Howe, commented on this when he launched the Australian Government's Child Support Scheme, which will enforce the collection and payment of maintenance from non-custodial parents.

We have as a society neglected what we have constantly projected as being our greatest concern. There are very few communities in the world that pretend to be so committed to family as we are in Australian society, yet we have allowed the spectre of 800,000 children in poverty.[26]

The number of children who are suffering severe disturbances to their attachment to parents due either to dysfunctional families or to family break-up is also cause for concern.

Families are the primary moulders of mental and emotional well-being and they also have a marked ability to mediate externally induced stressors to family members. Most people readily agree that families have a powerful effect on mental and emotional health. Not so many are aware that families are also either a protector of physical health or, when dysfunctional, destroyers of health.

Physical health

There are strong correlations between family styles and family dynamics and the degree of physical health of family members: those families who nurture intellectual, social and emotional competence also build strong physical health.[27] A satisfying family life (or other intimate support group) is a powerful protector of physical health, while severe distress or disruption in family life is a considerable threat to health.

In the *No Single Thread* study (see chapter 4), family members were asked to keep notes of all illnesses, accidents, medication and hospital visits. Analysis of these records showed an unexpected correlation. Those families that were able to discuss loss and death and to consider the implications of loss of family members in a concrete way had lower rates of all illnesses, including the day-to-day colds, flu, headaches and accidents. The ability to face and deal with loss was mentioned earlier in relation to drug risk.

Other research shows that rates of illness increase when stress in families rises. It is known that during the crisis of marriage separation and divorce, or in the aftermath of bereavement, family members suffer a markedly higher rate of illness and even death.[28] For example, widows die at rates three to thirteen times higher than married women for every category of cause of death.[29] Widowers, divorced men and single men exhibit similar statistics compared with married men.

These statistics are not repeated to induce a cloud of gloom on those who may already be feeling the pain of loss. For those who are able to go through a mourning process, the health risks described are almost cancelled out. The key factor is having someone to talk to, especially about the grief and the loss. And those who are not in a traditional family structure but enjoy intimate companionship are likewise protected. However, the statistics also illustrate that for most people that health-protecting intimacy is provided by marriage and family, and that intimacy is not easily replaced by other groupings.

Yet another researcher found evidence of family factors related to health in the longitudinal, prospective study of medical students entering the Johns Hopkins University in the USA. Caroline Bedell Thomas was investigating whether we can predict who is going to get sick. If we knew that a certain person was at risk of heart disease or of breast cancer, that person could take particular care to observe the precautions relevant to that particular disease. She found that the major predictors of cancer, suicide and mental illness were hostility to family and lack of closeness to family.[30]

Studies of chronic stress in families have yielded some fascinating insights into family factors and physical health. Hamilton McCubbin and associates in Minneapolis have established a world-wide reputation for their studies of families and stress.[31] Not only have they shown that some families develop (or naturally possess) patterns that lower the stress endemic to coping with a chronically ill member, but that stress experienced by one family member can be detected in the physical health of the patient, *even though the patient is not the member exposed to the stress.* Stressful but not traumatic experiences, such as starting at a new school, facing exams, starting a new job, which other family members were facing, could be clearly detected in the health measures of the chronically ill member. McCubbin studied families with a member who had cystic fibrosis, a disease that requires intensive treatment and measurement of body fluids and lung congestion. This study not only showed how stress can be detected as affecting physical health, but that family members are closely linked and each experiences stresses that, from an individualistic perspective, would be thought to apply to only the member experiencing the stress directly.

The renowned family therapist Salvador Minuchin has studied how psychosomatic illnesses (such as some forms of asthma and anorexia nervosa) can be triggered by family dynamics.[32] He has also described a study that shows how physical health can be affected by family factors.[33] In the family studied, two daughters suffered from diabetes, one more severely than the other. Dede, seventeen years old, had had diabetes for three years, and her sister Violet, five years younger, had suffered from the disease since her infancy. Dede was a 'superlabile diabetic', which means that her diabetes was affected by psychosomatic factors. She suffered from bouts of illness that did not respond to insulin administered at home and had been admitted to hospital for emergency treatment twenty-three times. Violet was under good medical control.

This family was studied using a technique that enables measures of individual physiological response to stress to be made.

During a structured family interview designed for this purpose, blood samples are drawn from each family member in such a way that obtaining the samples does not interfere with on-going interactions. The level of plasma-free fatty acids in the samples is later analyzed. Free fatty acid (FFA) is a biochemical indicator of emotional arousal — the concentration rises within five to fifteen minutes of emotional stress. By comparing the FFA levels at different times during the structured interview, the individual's response to stress can be physiologically documented.

Studies of the children's 'physiological lability' indicated that they had roughly the same individual response to stress, yet, with the same genetic defect, living in the same house with the same parents, they had very different forms of diabetes.

The family interview was structured so that in the first phase the parents were subjected to a stress-inducing discussion, while the children watched through a one-way screen. Even though the children could not take part or be involved in the stressful situation, their FFA count rose, indicating increased stress for them. Their parents also recorded increased levels of FFA. Later, the children were brought into the room with the parents and the discussion continued. At this stage the parents' FFA levels dropped, but the children's rose even higher. At the conclusion of the interview Violet's FFA count dropped to the baseline level almost immediately, but Dede's remained elevated for another hour and a half. It was noted by the team of researchers that the two children played very different roles in the family. Each parent tried to get Dede's support in the fight with the other parent. Dede could not respond to one parent without seeming to side with that one against the other. Violet was not pressured to take sides.

This experiment shows how conflict and stress between spouses can be 'detoured' through the children, and that, while the parents feel better, the children pay a price. It also shows that different children in the same family play different roles and can be very differently affected by the family dynamics. And it also shows how family dynamics can be involved in the development of psychosomatic illness or the psychosomatic components of genetically based illnesses.

Minuchin finds three factors common to the development of psychosomatic illness in children: a type of family functioning characterised by enmeshment, over-protectiveness, rigidity and lack of conflict resolution; involvement of the child in parental conflict and physiological vulnerability. This example illustrates how these three intra-family factors can combine to make a family member sick.

There can be little doubt that family factors are significant contributors to the health of individuals and communities. One of the most striking findings is the hard evidence supporting an observation family therapists have reported for years. What affects one member affects all. The dynamics within a family can either protect and heal or undermine and make sick. Social skills and competence is yet another area where the impact of family of origin and family of choice can be seen.

3
Social Skills and Competence

The children of superior competence studied by Burton White were not only intellectually, linguistically and creatively superior; they were a pleasure to be with. Ability to get along with others and to perform social roles is strongly influenced by family experience and is evident in the areas of parenting ability, the ability to create and sustain supportive networks, moral development, social concern and action, and social status.

The inter-generational factor

Parenting ability
The patterns of parenting that characterise any particular adult and child's relationship are strongly influenced by the parents' experience with her or his own parents. This has been most strongly evident in a number of case study reports of distorted parent-child relationships. Studies of school refusal on the part of children find that quite often a parent had refused to attend school. Investigation often reveals evi-

dence of distortions in the parent's own development and the parenting she or he received that makes sense of the child's seemingly irrational refusal to attend school.[1]

Bowlby cites examples where refusal to attend school was based on the child's fear that something dreadful would happen either to the parent or to the child herself/himself if the child left home. Bowlby further stresses that these fears are usually not irrational, but are provoked by the parent's behaviour.

In the case of Susan, thirteen, and Arthur, eleven, Susan had been refusing to attend school for eighteen months, and all attempts by her mother (her father had recently died) and social workers to alter this pattern had failed. Further investigation with all three members of the family present revealed that for over a year the children had been taking it in turns to stand guard over their mother. Susan stayed home from school during the day and visited friends during the evenings. Arthur went to school and stayed home after he returned. It also emerged that, in an attempt to discipline the children, the mother would blame them for the father's death and threaten that she too would die if they did not behave. She also threatened to desert them, adding force to the threat by putting on her coat and leaving the house. As an older son had been forcibly evicted from the house, and as the father had in fact died, these threats had more than usual terror for the children. Once it became clear that Susan's refusal to attend school was a response to mother's threats to desert her, and the children were able to express how these threats affected them, more or less regular school attendance was re-established.[2]

Bowlby also cites the case of Stephen, who at eighteen months refused to eat and was seriously underweight. His mother was found to be constantly depressed and anxious, and his refusal to eat was made worse by her frantic efforts to force him to eat. Further investigation revealed that his mother, Mrs Q, had been reared in a family torn by constant quarrels and dissension. Her father was a shell-shock victim of the 1914–18 war. The sole survivor of his section, which was wiped out when a bridge was blown up, he became subject to long phases of depression and bad temper in which he ill-treated his family. Mrs Q's mother was active and competent, working as a domestic helper. *Her* mother had been a chronic alcoholic.

Throughout her childhood, Mrs Q had witnessed the violent quarrels of her parents: crockery was smashed, knives were drawn and furniture set alight. Meanwhile, her mother still maintained the image of domestic respectability, insisting that Mrs Q not breathe a word of dissension to anyone. There were suicide attempts, some discovered by the child, and threats by the mother to desert or to commit suicide. The threats were made more terrifying by the daughter's discovery of the mother with her head in the gas oven and by the mother's occasional disappearance.

Therapy for Mrs Q enabled her to refrain from her constant urging of Stephen to eat, and he in turn began to eat and gain weight. However, at the age of seven his mother reported that he was afraid she might die and was again afraid to go to school. Despite her intense desire to give her son a better life than she had experienced, it was evident that Mrs Q had transferred some of the hostility and fear she felt towards her own mother onto Stephen. She later admitted that, even as an infant, and even after she received some therapy, she had occasional outbursts when she smashed crockery, dented saucepans and damaged Stephen's pram. As Stephen got older, she mostly succeeded in creating the secure and stable environment she desired for him. But there were still occasional violent outbursts, when she theatened to commit suicide or to abandon Stephen, saying, in fact, exactly the things that her mother had said to her and that had so terrified her.[3]

Evidence of inter-generational trauma is often found in cases where there are distortions of parent-child relationships. In the 1970s Bowlby called for further investigation of the parent and grandparent generation, in order to understand and treat stubbornly distorted patterns of family life. The growing field of family therapy, family life-cycle patterns and family systems theory has supported the clinical experience of earlier researchers on the strength of inter-generational transmission of family-patterns. In general, the researchers in these fields would support Bowlby's statement that:

Because . . . children tend unwittingly to identify with parents and therefore to adopt, when they become parents, the same patterns of behaviour towards their own children that they themselves have experienced during their own childhood, patterns of interaction are transmitted, more or less faithfully, from one generation to another. Thus the inheritance of mental health and mental ill health through the medium of family microculture is certainly no less important, and may well be far more important, than is their inheritance through the medium of genes.[4]

Violence of parents to children, sexual abuse of children, drug and alcohol addiction, neglect, rejection and emotional deprivation of children by parents have all been found to be linked to similar or to related patterns in the parental generation. Although it is certainly not true that all parents who were abused themselves as children abuse their own children, serious abuse and neglect of children, unless remedied and healed by more nurturing experiences, consistently impairs the later ability of those children to nuture their own children. As parents, those who were neglected or abused may not abuse their children, but they are unlikely (in the absence of other healing and nurturing experiences) to be able to achieve the confident, spontaneous, sensitive, responsive and loving relationship with children that characterises the most competent of families.

There is much evidence to suggest that healthy patterns are likewise transmitted from one generation to another, though the newer field of research into competence in family life has not investigated the inter-generational factors involved. That is, we really know little of *how* competence-creating families develop their powerfully health-creating patterns. Blum's study of high and low drug-risk and family factors included a discussion with family members, which was videoed to allow intensive analysis and re-analysis, and which provided an opportunity for researchers not only to question family members about family-patterns and dynamics but to observe these patterns directly.[5]

Their assumption that the family 'is an enduring entity which continues in a distinct way for many generations' was supported in a number of ways.[6] The strong family unity of superior and good familes was evident in the deliberate efforts made in these families to cultivate the extended family. Troubled and pathological families made little effort to keep up contact with extended family and also were less cohesive and united as a household than the other groups.

The researchers specifically inquired about grandfathers. In only one of the Group 1 families (those families rated superior or good by clinicians) did the father describe his own father in other than glowing ways. In this instance the grandfather, although an understanding, loving and generous man, was portrayed also as an alcoholic and a 'beast' when drunk. This family, more than any other family, taught its children that people are complex and can be simultaneously good and evil. They stressed forgiveness of others and of oneself. The father, too, had come close to alcoholism but had given it up.

Those families rated as having superior or very good family dynamics had a sense of family continuing over generations. The love, generosity, wisdom and strength they perceived in their own fathers they perceived in even greater measure in their grandfathers, and family tradition served as a reason to do as their parents had done.

By contrast, the Group 3 families (those rated troubled and pathological in their family dynamics and also rated as having children who were at high risk of destructive drug-use) had many more instances of the grandfather having died when the father was still young. In these cases the fathers tended to be chronically depressed and had married domineering women. There were also instances of divorce after much distress when the son was still young, and other instances of grandfathers who were autocrats or who were weak and afraid.

Blum and his associates concluded from this intensive study of thirteen families selected from the high and low drug-risk ends of the group of 101 families studied by interview and rating:

> Though the grandfather cannot be construed as the cause of the grandchildren's behaviour, our impression is that the grandfather is a critical element in the family mix, and, when he is missing, ill, or not a good father, that is a liability. If other liabilities are also present, then we have troubled or pathological family outcomes.[7]

In this study and many others, there are indicators that strengths in families are handed from one generation to another, as are weaknesses. But this does not happen invariably. For example, Lewis and Looney's study of low-income black families found that those with strong health-producing patterns did *not* always come from a healthy family system. How did they come from a markedly flawed family pattern, yet institute health-producing patterns in their own family? This is a vital area for further research.

Family networks
One of the characteristics of those families who create well-functioning individuals is that they are embedded in a supportive community and the ability to create and sustain supportive networks appears to be strongly influenced by experiences in the family of origin. Again, this intergenerational pattern is most obvious in the socially deprived families. Dr Don Edgar, Director of the Australian Institute of Family Studies, commented on Jean McCaughey's study of family support networks in Geelong, Victoria:

> As these case studies show, socially deprived families tend to reproduce their state of social and economic deprivation from one generation to the next. There is a black side to family life which should not be forgotten, and no amount of exhortation, certainly no policy dictates, can hope to turn every family into a mutual-help society.[8]

Among the one-parent, low-income families studied by McCaughey, none had grown up in warm or secure family relationships.[9]

> Their own attempts at family life were proving to be much the same: eight of the ten marriages (*de jure* or *de facto*) had ended in desertion or separation, usually culminating in divorce. In families with adolescent children, relationships between them and their parents were poor, providing little hope of breaking the cycle of unstable family relations in the next generation.[10]

On the other hand, the low-income, two-parent families described growing up in families that were poor, often isolated as a result of that poverty, but with visiting by the extended family and some giving and receiving of help by neighbours, friends and extended family. Almost all these families had a wide network of extended family and many friends who were of considerable help in providing child-care, setting up home, and at times of crisis whether due to financial difficulties, illness or personal upsets. This support enabled the families to maintain their fierce independence and dignity. On the whole, the parents of these low-income families themselves came from families that were economically poor and socially somewhat isolated, but able to provide a measure of support. The one-parent, low-income families lacked both economic and relationship resources.

Half the parents of the better-off sample came from working-class families (in many cases they were poor, especially if there were large families) and half from professional ones. All remembered their childhoods as happy and their families as closely knit. In all except one case these better-off families were happy and were based on stable marriages.[11] These families received a great deal of support from their extended families, even though in most cases these better-off families did not live close to other family members. Whether it was help to set up a home, emotional or practical help and support at times of crisis, or child-minding, there was a common theme: they felt their parents were always there and that they could ask for help if the need arose. 'We've always been able to rely on our families and it would be a reflex action to turn to them.'[12]

It can be seen that the attitudes and skills gained in a family with warm and secure relationships within the family and supportive, reliable relationships with extended family, friends and wider community constitute a resource that is just as real as economic resources and security. The ability to form and sustain these supportive networks is clearly related to experience in the family of origin and the lack of such ability is not easily remedied once it has been lost in a family. The Geelong study indicated two groups who were at risk in this area. Firstly, there were the low-income, one-parent families who by and large lacked this supportive network and seemingly the ability to recreate and sustain an alternative one. A second group at risk were the migrant families who had been radically removed from their family and friendship networks and who sometimes experienced real difficulty in establishing alternative supports in a new country. It is sometimes assumed that the ethnic groups automatically maintain strong links with family and ethnic community. The Geelong family-support networks study indicates that this is not always the case.

Families and the economy

While economic factors undoubtedly impinge on families, families also impact on economic factors. In the first place, family breakup is the major route into poverty and is the major cause of the trend towards women and children increasingly bearing the brunt of poverty. Australian research found that 75–80 per cent of women are significantly worse off after marital separation, and that the average fall in income is around $80 a week.[13] US research finds a 30 per cent decline in average incomes for women who are divorced or separated.[14] Parental disruption has been shown to be associated with lower socio-economic attainment[15] and with lower educational attainment,[16] which has obvious economic implications. It is also associated with higher marital instability for the children's future marriages, which again has further long-term economic implications. The US psychologist McLelland studied economic productivity in European countries from the 1920s to the 1970s. He found a correlation between economic productivity and the population's attachment to values and its readiness to be creative. The higher the motivation behind production, the richer the nation becomes. However there is an inverse ratio between economic production and family life: the more energy directed to economic productivity, the more the situation of the family deteriorates. The studies also indicated that certain conditions were essential to develop in a person the orientation to production. One condition was an education that leaves a reasonable degree of freedom to develop one's personality. However this education can only be effective when the child experiences the affection and care of others, especially the mother.

Hence McLelland claims that economic growth is always built on strong family life, but a decline in family life takes almost a generation to be reflected in reduced economic productivity.[17] More will be said later on the fact that the public world and the formal institutions, such as business and education, are built on the informal world, of which family is a major part. Unfortunately, economic decisions are often made as if this informal world is of 'no account'.

Other areas of family impact

Families have a greater impact on at least some areas of the moral development of adolescents than peers or school,[18] and are a major influence on the *style* of religious attitudes, practices and beliefs adopted.[19] The degree of social concern and willingness to invest oneself in social action has been shown to be influenced by experience in both the family of origin and the family of procreation.[20] Habermas claimed that (in reference to the student protest movement of the late 1960s) 'The protest potential is clearly generated in bourgeois homes',[21] and other analysts who came to the same conclusion claimed that the style of protest also derived from the styles of home backgrounds.[22]

There is overwhelming evidence that the family is the strongest factor building individual and communal competence, happiness and well-being. At the time of Coleman's research into Equality of Educational Opportunity, little was known of the family factors that contributed to educational success or failure. The EEO study, reflecting the understanding of the time, focused on easily measured status characteristics, such as marital status, family size, number of adults in the home, father's income and mother's educational level. The finding of the impact of parental interest was scarcely understood at all by some of the research community of the time.

Disappointingly, educational research has responded to the Coleman Report as if the findings were the opposite of what they are. Very little effort or resources have been devoted to 'how the parents treat the children at home', which was found to be the key to educational success; and escalating resources have been poured into those areas of class-size, curriculum, buildings, and so on, which were found to have little 'leverage' to create educational achievement.

In other fields, research into families has given us a much clearer picture of the factors that distinguish those families who create competence, spontaneity, self-esteem, confidence, energy, intelligence and co-operation from those where self-doubt, depression, hostility, aggression and failure prevail. The key lies not in the family's material resources, helpful as these may be: the distinguishing variable or variables reside in the way the family members relate to one another.

Part 2

Creative Family Processes

4

The Family as a System

Identifying healthy families

In view of the evidence of the impact of family factors on human competence, it is imperative that we know which exactly are the factors within families that create competence and which militate against competence. A major difficulty with such research is identifying the 'healthy' families so they may be studied. Researchers have devised a range of strategies to overcome this difficulty.

These research strategies include comparisons between families in which one member has been institutionalised and families without an institutionalised member;[1] comparisons of families with a child measuring high competence and families with a comparable member measuring low competence;[2] studies of communication patterns in families;[3] studies of families with and without drug-addicted and alcohol-addicted members;[4] and studies of minority-group families and low-income families.[5] Other evidence emerges from clinical experience,[6] from research into families experiencing severe stress, comparing high-coping families with low-copers,[7] and from the few national studies that have sought to analyse what makes families work.[8] A different approach was used by Curran in a survey of professionals from five different disciplines, all with a high level of contact with families.[9]

This spate of research into health in family systems may have been the outcome of the *No Single Thread* study. Before that time, there appears to be a paucity of research into health in families and a concentration on family pathology. In fact, the very concept of 'healthy' or 'strong' families is still occasionally ridiculed. As late as 1984, Gilbert Steiner, a leading researcher in family policy stated:

> The intangible sentiments that are the foundation of strong family relations are susceptible neither to legislation nor to executive order or court decree. Government has no mechanism to enforce love, affection, and concern between husband and wife, parent and child, or sibling and sibling. *Because intangibles are so important to family relationships, even identifying the characteristics of strong families and of failing families poses problems.* No one knows, for example, how many persons live together in family groups sharing resources and chores, nursing each other as necessary, and celebrating or commiserating with each other as the occasion requires, all as a practical adjustment to life demands rather than out of deep emotional attachment. Nor does anyone know how many superficially stable families are really composed of incompatible parents sustaining family life temporarily 'for the sake of the children'. And if they could be identified, it is a safe bet that one observer would characterize them as strong since they hold together, and another would characterize them as failing.[10] (Emphasis added)

Steiner implies that because it is difficult it is also impossible to identify the characteristics of 'strong' families. He states that even if certain characteristics can be identified as associated with strengths in some families, 'what is dysfunctional in one family may be quite tolerable in another.'[11] These views are widely held, yet nothing in the studies of health or competence in families supports them. Certainly there are differences in family contexts and these affect family interactions,[12] but not in the sense that 'what is functional in one family is dysfunctional in another.' It is astonishing that the views expressed by Steiner are so widely accepted in the field of family research. Is it possible that in an area of vital concern to the physical health of populations, leading researchers would be sneering at those who wish to know more of the cause of a certain disease and claiming that exposure or nonexposure to pathogens was equally likely to cause infection or immunity and that what would infect in one area would be a 'safe bet' not to infect in another?

Contrary to Steiner's conclusions, studies cited above of varied populations, using different methodologies, from different disciplines, seeking answers to quite different questions, *agree* on what factors characterise those families who survive the predictable and unpredictable stresses of family life and produce competent children and allow for the development and growth of adult personalities. The convergence of findings from such different perspectives and methodologies, and from varying socio-economic, ethnic and cultural groups strongly suggests the findings are sound.

It is not possible to review such a wide-ranging group of studies in detail, yet it is important to gain some sense of the strength of the evidence showing that we do know a great deal about the factors, processes, attitudes and skills that contribute to the development of human competence. Before discussing these factors further (see chapter 5), one study will be looked at in detail. Lewis's study was influential and something of a ground-breaker in its findings on health in family systems, so we will look first at its approach to studying healthy families and its findings.

No Single Thread: a pioneering study

This study was undertaken at the Timberlawn psychiatric centre in Dallas, USA. The report, *No Single Thread*, is particularly addressed to family therapists, but also to others in the helping professions, and to educators and interested parents. One motive in initiating the study was to provide a balance to the influence of the 'anti-psychiatry' school of writers who were so impressed with the family's ability to create madness and incompetence that they were happy to foretell the death of the family. Lewis and his team, while influenced by this earlier work, could find no alternative to families for the socialisation of children and the stabilisation of adult personalities, and hence they were motivated to study family well-being. They could see that the great methodological advances that had come from studying pathology in families had not been applied to the study of health in families. As a result, there were interactional measures of considerable predictive strength for identifying pathology in families, but no such norms for family health.

Lewis and his colleagues distance themselves from the belief that a child's fate is sealed by the time she or he is six years old and that severe damage in that period is irreversible. They take the more optimistic view that experiences all through life affect human development, and that while the early years are particularly vital, later experiences may remedy early damage. They were inspired, too, by a commitment to prevention, seeing the family, especially young families, as having similar potential for intervention to that of infants. Young families, because their patterns are not fixed or rigid, may be organisms particularly responsive to education and may willingly adopt those patterns that set up a 'benign circle' (as opposed to a vicious circle) of interactions.

Lewis's research team had previously committed themselves to a five-year longitudinal study of adolescent psychiatric patients. The goal of this study was to determine which patients had been successfully treated and to what degree the staff of a psychiatric hospital had provided this successful treatment. They studied the nature and seriousness of the illness, the form of the treatment and the patient's family and in doing so had developed instruments to measure aspects of the patients' psychopathology and the family functioning. In the latter case the then relatively new technology of video enabled verbal and non-verbal interaction to be recorded for repeated viewing and analysis. To enable data about families to be quantified, analysed and compared for research purposes, the research team developed a format for videotaped interview in which the family performed five tasks.

Twelve families of adolescent patients sequentially admitted to the psychiatric hospital for treatment became the patient component of the pilot study. A control group of another eleven families were recruited with the help of a local Protestant church. The only prerequisite for the control groups was that no member of the family was currently receiving any form of psychiatric treatment or was in difficulty with legal authorities. They were selected from a large number of such families so as to comprise a demographically comparable sample to the patient group.

This small sample of twenty-three families, each with a child in mid-adolescence, provided the initial data on which the schema of family interaction was developed. Each family came to the research centre and participated as a family in the five interactional tasks mentioned above.

Twelve raters, none of whom was involved in the research project or in treatment of any of the patient-containing families, independently assessed the video tapes. The raters included experienced psychiatrists, clinical psychologists, psychiatric social workers with less experienced professionals and two non-professional raters. Each rater individually rated five-minute or ten-minute segments of different parts of the video material, a segment on 'Family Strengths' or a segment of 'Family Pain', for example.

The researchers found significant correlation between the degree of family dysfunction and the severity of individual patient psychopathology independently assessed. The more severe pathology came from the families with the lowest form of family functioning as measured by the raters. Raters were able to discriminate reliably between patient-containing families and control families. They found that the quality of marital interaction was closely linked to the overall rating of family functioning. Family members' ratings of the strengths and weakness of their own families were in reasonable agreement with ratings by mental health professionals. There was a close correlation between ratings based on the five or ten minutes of family interaction and ratings by an experienced professional on the basis of examining the whole fifty minutes of each videoed interview, which suggests that family styles are consistent and, for good or ill, the impact of family functioning occurs reliably or relentlessly minute by minute and day after day.

The researchers describe their 'excitement, interest and pleasure' in studying the healthy families. They were interested in whether levels of health could be delineated, as had levels of pathology in families, and decided to extend their study of eleven healthy families by recruiting a new sample of healthy families for more detailed study. In addition to the recorded video interaction tasks, the study made use of clinical evaluation, established psychological rating scales and intensive analysis of recorded family data.

The theoretical approach for assessing family competence with which the researchers approached the study stressed five dimensions of family functioning: family power structure, degree of individuation, response to separation and loss, perception of reality, and family affect or emotional expression.

Family power structure

By power structure the Timberlawn researchers mean the hierarchy of power in the family and also the boundaries between members and sub-systems. They found that in healthier families there was a clear hierarchy of power and the children were learning competence in relating from the experience of generous and benign parents who acted as the family leaders. Where this structure was lacking, there were constant battles in an attempt to establish clarity. If boundaries between individual members were very weak, then members spoke for one another, imputed motives to one another and claimed to read each other's thoughts. When boundaries were closed or very strong, it was difficult for members to hear each other, to empathise and understand. The best structure was shown to be 'permeable' boundaries, which enables individual autonomy to develop with closeness and understanding between family members.

The sub-systems referred to are the parental and the sibling systems. In healthy families there is a clear generational boundary between the parents and the children. That is, *the parental alliance is the strongest alliance in the family.* It is not threatened by a close relationship of one parent to a child or a person outside the family unit, such as mother-in-law, lover or friend. Parents do not act as 'friends' to their children, or allow children to take over the parental role while the adults revert to sibling-like behaviour. In the least competent families, the father is very weak and the mother often has a close relationship with a particular child.

In reviewing previous research, Lewis and his colleagues reported that completeness is a factor in family structure: the loss or absence of a parent or child is associated with an increased rate of child-rearing failure. They also suggest that children are disadvantaged if they do not experience adults of both sexes functioning intimately within a framework of mutual commitment.

Degree of individuation in the family

Tolerance and encouragement of individuation basically means encouraging autonomy, which is essential to the development of a satisfactory ego identity, 'for one must be permitted to consider oneself a separate person, and to experience oneself as such, to find an identity'.[13] Individuation involves members speaking for themselves and taking responsibility for their own feelings and actions, respecting the unique experience of others and being able to hear and respond to others within the system.

Response to separation and loss

Separation and loss are predictable events in family life. Moving into each stage of the life-cycle involves leaving something behind so as to adopt the ways appropriate to the next stage. A mother must stop treating the baby as an infant and allow the toddler and then the young child to emerge, but it involves loss for her. Lewis and his colleagues found that loss was poorly handled by severely disturbed families, who tended to deny loss and protect themselves against the anxiety of death by bizarre behaviour. Mid-range families also found it difficult to accept loss. Therapists commonly find that when parents are battling with neurotic symptoms or behaviour disturbance in their children, the parents themselves are still caught up in conflict with their parents or are still mourning an idealised, long-dead parent.

The more effective coping with loss found in the healthier families is demonstrated in the parents having a strong spouse bond, which enables them to break excessive attachments to their own parents. This is also the precondition for appropriate generational boundaries in their own developing family. Lack of a strong spouse bond often results in the spouse seeking such a bond with one of the children.

57

Perception of reality

Some families have a perception of themselves that is congruent with the way others perceive them. Others seem to be quite out of touch with reality as perceived by outside observers. The most common example is inability to see that a family member is psychotic. The emotional pain and bizarre behaviour of that member is ignored, and the member simply declared 'obstinate'. In other words, healthy families have a strong reality base, a feature markedly absent from non-competent families.

Family affect or emotional expression

By 'family affect' the researchers refer to the mood and feeling tone of the family (whether it is one of warmth and affection, of stiff politeness, of depression and apathy, or of overt hostility with cynical and bitter interchanges). The range of feelings that can be expressed is also relevant. Healthier families feel they can safely express whatever they are feeling to other members. They also show a degree of sensitivity and responsiveness to others' feelings that is not found in less competent families.

Family categories

On the basis of this research, the Timberlawn researchers concluded that families that produce adaptive, well-functioning offspring have a structure of shared power, an appreciation of individuation, an ability to accept separation and loss realistically, a view of themselves consistent with that of outside observers, and a warm and expressive feeling tone.

They found it useful to categorise families in three broad groups: seriously disturbed, mid-range and healthy. While it is not possible to make absolute distinctions between families who produce schizophrenic, non-psychotic but limited, and normal children,[14] these broad categories help to define interactional norms of health and competence. Families rate differently on each dimension, but a family low on several of these variables is 'generally least successful at child-raising and their children are most vulnerable to social failure'.[15]

The major limitation of this study is the small sample of families. In all, forty-four non-patient families were studied. A second limitation is that all the control families were drawn from one large Protestant church. The limited size and range of the sample families limits the generalisations that can be made from the study. But it should be noted that in a later publication (*The Long Struggle*) Lewis and Looney reported on a similar study — of well-functioning, black, working-class families. The researchers found fewer differences in style between the white and black families than they had expected. Other studies support Lewis's findings both on the links between family pathology and children's psychopathology, and, as we shall see, on family dynamics and children's competence. Before turning to these other studies, it will help to view the three categories of family competence that Lewis and colleagues developed in *No Single Thread*.

Seriously disturbed families
In these families the parental coalition is weak and is replaced by powerful inter-generational coalitions. As noted above, the father is often passive and weak and the mother has a close tie to a particular child in a way similar to that described by Lidz as a skewed family.[16] The distortion may be so severe that the father's role is more like that of a sibling to his own children, and the chosen child has assumed (or been given) a status more appropriate to that of a father. The emphasis in reports on the powerful mother could be interpreted to mean that she is somehow 'to blame'. But the wife's dominance may be provoked by the husband's passivity, which may in itself be a powerful, non-negotiating stance. In other cases there was constant open war between the spouses over who was to have the power in the family, similar to Lidz's description of the 'schismatic' family.

Individual boundaries are blurred so that members often speak for one another and purport to know each other's thoughts, motivations and what others really want and feel. Gross inefficiency is the rule, with autonomy discouraged. The patient population involved in the earlier part of the study came from these severely dysfunctional families, and later work finds schizophrenia, alcoholism and drug addiction more likely in these severely dysfunctional families.[17]

The mid-range family

This family often has a rather rigid authoritarian structure, with power being exercised through dominance.[18] The generational boundaries are not openly breached, and any parent-child coalitions are covert and less powerful than in the severely dysfunctional families. There are often clear boundaries between individuals, but intimacy and empathy are rare. Blaming is frequent, as is external scapegoating, in order to sustain self-esteem. Conflict is not open, and there is little use of negotiation. Raw power is often used to settle issues.

Communication is clear, and there is an acceptance of responsibility for one's feelings and actions. These families solve problems well and have a base-line mood of affection, although the atmosphere is more often polite. The pain in these families seems to surface first in the wife, who more than any other member expresses dissatisfaction and disappointment. A strength of these families is their initiative and their involvement with the community, which opens the children to other sources of stimulation and adult modelling. Children are often autonomous and symptom-free. If they do display symptomatic behaviour, it is usually neurotic or behavioural disorders, rather than the psychopathology, which is likely in severely disturbed families.

Lewis and his colleagues note that this type of family, rather than the less numerous 'healthy' family, is the one used most often as a control group in research. As it displays significant dysfunction, its use in control groups obscures the findings of many studies. Lewis and his colleagues argue that the norm in family functioning should be positive health, not merely lack of pathology. Before their study, no standards, measures or indicators of health existed.

Healthy families

The families with the most effective pattern of relating to one another demonstrate a clear pattern of parental leadership. Leadership comes from the parents, who model a co-operative coalition. The father's leadership role is often stronger than the wife's, but he is closely supported by her, as a partner rather than a follower. Power is exercised in a non-authoritarian way, and the parents' sharing of power is the model from which the children learn their own developing ability to relate.

These families demonstrate effective problem-solving, and observers note a warm tone in family interactions. The frequency of sexual intercourse varies from couple to couple, but across the group both spouses expressed their high satisfaction with their sexual relationship. The husband in such a family is busy and successful, but despite his vocational success has energy and affect left over for his wife and children. The wife, too, is energetic and competent. (In Lewis's sample, almost none had a career outside the home. This may well be simply an artefact of the sampling and the time when the study was done.)

There is a high level of closeness, but no sacrifice of individuality. Expression of feeling often receives an empathic response. Humour is common, gentle and appropriate, and the families' view of themselves as a family is realistic. The strongest relationship in these families is the husband-wife coalition, which is the basis on which the strengths of the family are built. Members demonstrate an optimistic, outgoing attitude, and they approach human encounters positively, expecting acceptance and love.

Children in these healthy families show no clinical symptoms or free-floating anxiety. The interviewers found them open and trusting and their speech clear and spontaneous. They accomplish age-appropriate tasks and demonstrate high levels of initiative. Each parent's description of each child tallies. Parental values are being smoothly incorporated.

The family is alive and well

One of the major findings of this study was that 'the family is alive and well'. The researchers expressed pleasure at discovering that healthy families are not rare. They stressed that their data indicates that many, or even most, mental health professionals were raised in mid-range or severely dysfunctional families and, since they spend their time treating the products of such families, are rarely exposed to optimal health in family functioning. To them, the idea that much more is possible in family life seems a 'wistful fantasy'. It is important that this biased viewpoint should not be overly influential in developing public policy on families.

The finding by the *No Single Thread* team that healthy families do exist was particularly significant at this time. Only five years earlier, in *The Death of the Family*, Cooper had described the family as the ultimately perfected form of non-meeting. He listed four ways in which the family's destructive impact on people was achieved: firstly, 'glueing' people together, based on a sense of individual incompleteness; secondly, imposing predetermined roles rather than allowing free formation of identity; thirdly, imposing greater controls than children need; and finally, indoctrinating them with an elaborate system of taboos.[19] For some years afterwards Cooper's pessimistic view of families was very influential.

Lewis's study has been reviewed to indicate the way one group of researchers have studied health in family systems and to present in a coherent way one model of the family system. In the next chapter some of the key characteristics of healthy families are described, calling on the findings of a wide number of researchers on family well-being.

5

Creative Family Processes

The *No Single Thread* study was reviewed in the last chapter
as an example of a study that described health-creating families. It is one of many studies that have sought to answer the
question: what are the characteristics of those families that
create health and competence in their members? We shall
now consider some of the characteristics that have emerged
over and over again in studies of health-creating families. As
the title of Lewis's book, *No Single Thread*, suggests, there
are a number of factors promoting family health, but the
following are among the most frequently found and the most
significant: communication patterns, use of power, support
networks, family time, spouse bond, and religious and spiritual rituals. One of Lewis's major findings was of the prime
role of communication in assessing family function. Many
others agree with him so this is a good place to start.

Communication patterns

Communication emerges as the key to family satisfaction and
to the full human development of family members, according
to virtually every current study of families.[1] But this is a
relatively recent understanding. We do not know why there

has been this recent recognition of the importance of communication within marriage. One possibility is that previous generations relied on established roles within marriage. The weakening of these roles may have necessitated vastly increased communication skills, as so much that was accepted in the past must now be negotiated. Or perhaps previous generations were able to communicate better, since they did not have the time pressures and competitiveness of modern life.

Salvador Minuchin, the noted family therapist and researcher of patterns of behaviour in families, found that communication was the key to strategies to rehabilitate multi-problem slum families.[2] He and his colleagues found that 'the entire process by which our family members relate to each other is affected by the characteristics and quality of their communicational system'.[3] Minuchin stresses the need for the family to accept certain rules of 'communication traffic'. The members of chaotic slum families he worked with had frequently given up all hope of being heard or understood. Instead they shouted over one another in spasmodic attempts to make contact, to make an impression, or to be assured that they counted. Minuchin helped family members learn to listen while others spoke, and to respond to significant communications from others rather than showing no interest or changing the subject.[4]

Epstein defines communication as the exchange of information within the family.[5] He finds it relates to two main areas, the instrumental or task area and the affective domain of feelings and emotion. Communication may be clear or 'masked' (vague and confusing), direct (messages are directed to their appropriate target) or indirect (messages are deflected to someone other than the intended recipient or addressed to the open air). At the healthy end of the spectrum, families communicate in a clear and direct manner in both the instrumental and affective areas.

The Scandinavian researcher Blakar has studied the patterns of communication in families in which a member displays symptomatic behaviour.[6] He reveals the importance of family members being able to 'take the perspective of the other' or to 'decenter' as he calls it. Another aspect of good communication, according to Blakar, is being able to recognise when a communication difficulty has occurred and to alert the partner to the breakdown. Blakar found that families with a pathological member were much less able (or possibly less willing) to take the perspective of the other or to make a clear statement when it was obvious there was a confusion or problem in the communication. In relation to this latter failure Blakar draws attention to the fact that in order to communicate there must be confidence in oneself and in the other. Unfortunately, some people's experience, either in family or elsewhere, leads them to conclude that they cannot trust themselves or others.

Blakar also demonstrates how even a relatively simple exercise in instructing another concerning a route on a map involves the establishment of a 'contract' for the communication. Of course, this is done in an informal way, but participants initially establish the purpose of the conversation, the topic, the perspective and orientation to be adopted, the roles of each of the participants, and the strategies by which they will achieve their shared purpose. Blakar found that the adequacy of this initial contracting was a 'relatively good' predictor of the participants' later success in unravelling an induced communication conflict.

In healthier families, members make frequent use of 'I' statements, feeling free to declare their individual wants, needs and opinions.[7] Individual differences are respected, explored and even encouraged, compared with less healthy families, where members speak for one another and where the emergence of differences results in hostility and defensiveness.[8] However, teenagers' moral development is enhanced when parents make judgements of the relative value and validity of actions, attitudes and events, and when these value judgements are supported by reasoned arguments calling on principles and norms.[9] Such judgements seem essential to teenagers' moral development and are compatible with the development of individuality and autonomy.

The range of feelings permitted
Some families readily express hostility and anger, but fail to express tenderness, love and appreciation. Other families

appear to have unwritten rules that allow the expression of kindness, concern and positive feelings, but then suppress irritation and exasperation, shame, self-doubt and expressions of disagreement, dislike and requests for what one wants for oneself.[10] The healthier families were able to express a wider range of feelings.[11] In the Bells' study of the ego-development of adolescent girls, for example, the girls who were developing very well came from families where a wide range of feelings could be expressed. Blum, in his studies of drug-risk and family processes, found that in the lowest drug-risk families, members felt free to be themselves and to express their innermost feelings without fear.

> Genuine laughter shared, humor, affectionate teasing, matter of fact comments which lacked the sting of personalised criticism, all these made it safe to express one's true feelings, made it possible for superior families to tolerate divergence without disruption.[12]

Blum gives an example of this ability to express feelings without attacking or criticising. One component of his study of families involved the whole family in a videotaped discussion with a police officer (narcotics), a hippie and a minister present. Blum gives the example of a family that had had differences with police in the past. One of the children inadvertently mentioned a taboo word, saying, 'I've met some real pigs and some good ones.' His mother immediately and gently reprimanded him saying, 'When we talk at home we don't refer to police as pigs. It's a nasty word and lacks imagination.' She addressed herself to the whole group in apology to the police officer present. The father, feeling the son was now in an exposed position, moved quickly to explain why the son felt the way he did. Further discussion of some experiences of peace marches and some fierce police responses followed in which the children described how the police seem to be expecting something criminal. Blum comments that during this discussion 'the speaker was uncommonly attractive, the tone was firm, explanatory, yet jolly; and there was no hint of personal criticism'. As a result the police officer present did not feel personally attacked, but rather that he had been included in the family despite some very real differences of opinion.

By contrast, Blum describes a family's response to being asked what not to do in rearing a child. One mother in a family rated as 'average' in the Blum study seemed worried about what her children might reveal in answer to this question. She turned to them in an anxious, pleading, yet threatening tone, saying,

> 'Are you secure? Would you prefer to belong to another family?' In view of the mother's concern, what child could deny his security and affirm a desire to be elsewhere? Sensing the mother's need for reassurance, the child calmed her fears: 'No, I know someone who would like to belong to ours.'[13]

Blum goes on to describe how this mother suppresses every hint of strife. No child disagreed with her on any topic. At one stage, when asked what he thought of a statement of his mother's, a child quickly said, 'Oh, I agree', but when he was asked to explain what he meant, he had to admit that he had not understood the content of the discussion. While the children in this family had a very low drug-risk, the mother was concerned about the tenseness and insecurity of the eldest child, who appeared to the researchers and clinicians as over-conforming, unemotional and too set in his ways at an early age.[14]

Lewis describes the pattern of evasion of feelings and of refusal to own feelings, beliefs and opinions in the following extract from a family containing a schizophrenic offspring. The mother was asked how she felt about her pregnancy. She completely ignored the question and changed the subject. On another occasion she said, 'I was really happy. I was sick all the time.'[15]

While finding that the ability to express all feelings is a characteristic of those families where children are developing a high level of competence, the research is not recommending 'letting it all hang out.' It is the *range* of feelings that can be expressed *without attacking other members* of the family that seems to create human development and intimacy. It may be because the family members can modulate the intensity of their negative feelings that they are able to express whatever they wish. In fact, the modulation of intense feeling is one of the prerequisites of effective conflict management. Blum contrasts the unbridled aggression of some 'confrontation groups' with the 'politeness of the heart' that enabled the best-functioning families he studied to live together joyfully. These families exercised that self-discipline that forbade unkindness or destructive frankness. In other places Blum reports that these superior families never attacked the inner selves of other family members. In any case, members were warm and happy inside themselves, with no volcanic destructiveness seeking an opportunity to explode. 'Politeness of the heart' differentiated the best-functioning families from those less competent families who could muster only a drilled and rigid politeness. The least competent families displayed a lack of interest or studied rudeness, hostility, cynicism and social mayhem.[16]

Empathy

Empathy is the ability to respond to another so that the other feels deeply understood. It is a feature of communication in healthy families and markedly absent in unhealthy ones.[17] Men's frequent inability to communicate at an emotional level has been shown to be a critical factor in creating marital stress,[18] and to be a barrier to effective fathering. Jackson speaks of the need to release men's tenderness, so that children have the double engine of mother and father propelling them to develop their own competence.[19]

The loneliness a woman feels in a marriage where her spouse seems unable to communicate at a feeling level is a major cause of marriage breakdown. In two-thirds of divorces in Australia, the decision to end the marriage was made by the wife, in only one-sixth of cases did the husband make this decision and in the remainder the decision was made jointly.[20] Similar figures have been reported in the USA and the UK.

There is some evidence that women are better able to communicate at a feeling level than are men. Whether this is genetically based or due to experience over generations in feminine roles is not clear. Certainly there is no evidence that men are biologically incapable of empathy. It seems that men are more socialised into technocratic modes of relating through their exposure to norms of the world of work, especially the mode of the corporation.

Patterns of turn-taking

A number of studies found correlations between health and competence in families and patterns of turn-taking in conversation. Analysis of recorded family conversations while the family attemped to solve a problem or reach agreement on an issue indicated that the healthy families interrupted each other *more* that the less healthy families, but that all members were interrupted equally. Less healthy families had a victim who was routinely interrupted and thwarted. [21] Interruptions can function in different ways. Sometimes members interrupted because they had caught the drift of the other's statement and were rushing on with the dialogue. In this case, the interruption actually facilitated the communication between the partners. In other cases, interruptions functioned to block and thwart certain family members, to discount their contributions and, in the worst cases, to convince some members that they did not count, they were not valued and no one cared about them.

In comparison with families in which one member is a drug addict, normal family communication is characterised by relatively flexible patterns of 'who follows whom' and 'who sides with whom'.[22] Rigid or stereotyped patterns of certain members opposing certain others or siding with others are indicators of 'alliances' and 'scapegoating' within the family. More healthy families ensure that all members are equally valued and equally part of the family.

Communicating about communication

The ability to communicate about the communication process has been called 'meta-communication' by Watzlawick, one of the pioneering family therapists and developers of the theory of family systems.[23] Like Blakar[24] and Miller,[25] Watzlawick finds the ability to communicate about the communication process a key factor in establishing satisfying relationships. Because breakdowns in understanding constantly occur, partners in dialogue need to be able to return to base and sort out the communication tangles. In this process two difficulties are common. One is failure to be able to 'meta-communicate' at all. The other is a tendency to get stuck in meta-communication sequences and to be unable to get back to the content of the discussion. Blakar's induced conflict situation (the map-reading exercise, page 26) provoked a situation therapists frequently describe: couples who seem unable to perceive problems or to take steps to solve them. The pretence of understanding despite evident lack of understanding seems to be similar to what other writers have described as pseudo-mutuality.[26]

In other studies, less happily married couples tended to get stuck in the meta-communication sequences more often than did happily married couples.[27] Brandt gives the following illustration. If one spouse comments, 'You're shouting at me. You don't need to do that.' The other might respond, 'I'm not shouting. You're much too sensitive.' 'Too sensitive, huh? What would you know about being sensitive?' and so on. More happily married couples are able to extricate themselves more quickly, 'You're right. I was shouting. I'm sorry.' They can then get the conversation back on the rails of its original purpose.

> . . . it seems that the more spontaneous and 'healthy' the relationship, the more the relationship aspect of communication recedes into the background. Conversely, 'sick' relationships are characterised by a constant struggle about the nature of the relationship, with the content aspect of communication becoming less and less important.[28]

It can be seen, then, that not only does communication emerge as central to the well-being of families, but that it involves a range of issues and skills from the acceptance of basic 'traffic rules' to the quite complex skill involved in the establishment of intersubjectivity.[29] Communication is also linked closely to other issues, such as acceptance of differences in family members and willingness to make judgements based on reasons or norms. The ability to express a range of feelings, to empathise and to meta-communicate are correlated with well-being in families, while rigid, stereotyped or unbalanced patterns of turn-taking in conversation tend to be found in families with indicators of dysfunction. One particular aspect of communication, communicating appreciation to other family members, deserves a separate comment.

Appreciation

Of three possible responses one person may give another (confirmation, rejection or disconfirmation), the response with the most negative effects is disconfirmation.[30] Confirmation gives the assurance that one's perception or experience has been heard, is valid, and, possibly, that another shares the experience or perception. ('Yes, I loved that program, too. I was glued to the set the whole time.') Confirmation validates not only our perception and experience, but our being. In fact, studies of sensory deprivation indicate that it is impossible to maintain emotional stability for long periods without communication from others and the validation and confirmation this brings.

If someone disagrees with our perception or opinion, the *rejection* at least implies one has been heard, even if one's viewpoint is not supported. The clear rejection of another's viewpoint is not as damaging as *disconfirmation*, the failure even to acknowledge the other's presence, contribution, perception, experience or being. An outright rejection implies a limited recognition of the other. Disconfirmation leads to loss of self. Disconfirmation involves such responses as ignoring the contribution of another and changing the subject or continuing to speak as if the other had not even spoken. Where rejection says, 'You are wrong', disconfirmation says, 'You do not exist'. Yet disconfirmation is routine in particularly unhealthy families and appears to be especially damaging when directed to one member specifically, especially if that member is a child or an adolescent.[31]

Confirmation or validation is the response chiefly associated with the growth of competence, initiative and self-esteem: a response to members that tells them that they are noticed, recognised and valued.[32] Studies of conflict in happily and unhappily married couples[33] and of couples' decision-making patterns[34] demonstrate the importance of validation. Gottman describes how unhappily married couples during the build-up to an argument can only complain to each other, while more satisfied couples say things like, 'Yes, I can see you're tired' or 'I know you like to go out on a Saturday night', or they nod agreement once in a while or say 'uh-huh' or 'yeah' in response to the other's complaints.[35] This different pattern seems to be associated with a much more satisfactory solution of differences. Studies of decision-making patterns reveal the same importance of validating the other's statements, agreeing where possible and keeping calm in order to maintain the co-operative framework in which the decision-making process can continue. It seems that agreement and validation operate as a 'glue' holding the conversation together while the partners search for a solution to their difficulty.[36]

Confirmation and validation are two responses that affirm family members' being. Positive appreciation is another. It, too, is associated with greater self-esteem and self-confidence in children. In fact, positive perception of one another is more important to family satisfaction than is accurate perception,[37] though accurate or realistic perception of other members and the family as a whole is also associated with health in family members.[38] However, the positive perception needs to be expressed if it is to increase satisfaction and competence.

Blum describes a family in which the father is portrayed as 'the one who soothes the wounds of each', the one who breaks up the 'crab-in' with a 'love-session', the one who 'is there, binding us all together'. The father, quick to sense any hurt, even the self-inflicted hurt of the mother mentioning her tendency to crabbiness, immediately intervened, 'Mama makes the kids do their work. Mama really makes the kids come through.' This pattern of constant appreciation and praise was obvious in the healthiest families studied by Blum, and was associated with low risk of destructive use of drugs.

Another family described their belief in praise: 'Parents should praise children at many points. Later on they will be better able to withstand criticism. If a child is getting love and understanding at home, he does not have to get acceptance in his peer group.'[39] The researchers note that the parents who made this comment did not once criticise their children during the session, and in any case the children did nothing to offend.

In fact, other research shows that there is a correlation between the amount of praise children receive and their school achievement. Teenagers were asked if their parents had done any of the following in the past twenty-four hours:

helped with homework, given praise for something done, hugged or kissed the teenager, said they loved her or him, talked with the teenager about activities during the day. The better students, regardless of background, answered yes to the five questions in greater numbers than did those of average or below-average academic standing. The greatest difference between the groups was in relation to praise. The more students received praise from their parents, the better they were able to achieve.[40] Most studies report on praise for genuine achievement.[41] Praise given indiscriminately is probably not associated with competence.

It is clear that not all parents in the USA and Europe give their children the praise they need,[42] and it is likely that those Australian parents who fail to spend time with their children or to show an interest in them also praise less than is desirable.[43] The Finnish educator, Toiva Ronka, comments: 'It is difficult for at least a Finnish parent to give recognition for fear that it does not feel genuine or that recognition will make the recipient proud: "pride comes before the fall".'[44] It seems that many Australian, UK and North American parents would share these sentiments, though praise and affirmation seem to be much more culturally accepted activities in North America.

Conflict
Neither absence of conflict nor pervasive conflict are associated with health in families. Blakar found that families containing certain types of pathology were much more likely to avoid conflict, to the extent of pretending to understand or to agree when it was clear that understanding had broken down. Families with borderline psychiatric patients as members, on the other hand, were hostile and suspicious towards the researchers and constantly fought among themselves, as if fighting was their main activity in common. Minuchin, too, describes chaotic families in which conflict was endemic and family functioning virtually paralysed by conflict without resolution.[45] In Lewis's study, the least healthy families operated on either a system of domination and the exercise of raw power, or there was constant war over power and control.[46]

The healthiest families demonstrate established ways of handling problems efficiently and easily,[47] which obviously lowers the amount of conflict. While they acknowledge the need to confront conflict, they do not believe in heightening it or 'letting it all hang out' as many therapists have been perceived to have recommended in recent years. (Therapists are often confronted with families pathologically unable to face or deal with conflict. They attempt to teach these families to bring conflict out in the open. When already conflictual families adopt this advice, they go from bad to worse.) Curran's healthy families believed, rather, in choosing 'the right time' to raise the issue, and most had their own techniques for keeping the conflict within bounds while it was negotiated. Many had specific ways to ensure conflictual issues were brought to a close and family harmony restored.

An OECD study found that the most competent families expressed strong feeling towards children when they transgressed parental demands, but that harmony was quickly restored.[48] Blum describes the ability of the 'superior' families studied to be frank with each other without destroying the relationship, and Lewis found that being able to express feelings reduced the amount of conflict. There was much less conflict in families where feelings could be expressed, and no unsolvable conflict.[49]

Use of power

The use of power is critical to family functioning. In the healthier families, power was shared, but not equally. It was shared first between the spouses. Lewis and his colleagues stress the positive effects of the spouses having equal power in the relationship. They found that the intimacy that grows from communicating at many levels and being able to express one's individual needs, wants, opinions and feelings was found only between spouses who were equals in the power relations in the family. These researchers found no examples of intimacy between spouses where the power relationship was one of domination and submission. The sharing of power did not necessarily take the form of doing away with traditional gender roles. In some families, the parents followed the traditional allocation of roles according to gender, but there was a genuine sharing of power in decision-making over all aspects of what was to happen in the family.

Epstein and his colleagues put less stress on the need for leadership to be egalitarian (equally shared between the parents) and emphasise only that there should be *clear* leadership patterns within the family and that these patterns should be *perceived as fair and reasonable* by family members.[50]

Power in healthy families is shared with children, but the parents are clearly in control.[51] Well-coping families seem to combine high control of children with high support and nurturance plus assistance in enabling children to understand and internalise the standards set.[52] Carew describes an incident observed in a low-income family with those patterns that create competence in family members. The mother offered the toddler a glass of milk. The toddler refused it and pushed the glass away. The mother then offered the drink to the four-year-old, who promptly accepted it. The toddler screamed for the drink. The mother calmly explained that you must not say no unless you mean no. She then hugged the child and drew his attention elsewhere to distract him from the incident. In a few seconds this mother had set a very high standard for her toddler, 'Don't say no unless you mean no.' She had refused to allow the child to set the standards, but she had helped the child cope with the intense feelings of being refused. This is what is meant by assistance in enabling the child to understand and internalise the standards set.

In the healthiest families there is a minimum authoritarian use of power, the least use of threats and punishments. Parents effectively set limits to their younger children[53] and allow their older children an increase in freedom and decision-making.[54] Australian research found that closeness and firm control was associated with high levels of competence in young children but not in adolescents, where more separation and less control seemed associated with optimal development.[55] However, studies of high-achieving, low-income ethnic families in the USA seem to find a greater stress on high control of adolescents. This may be related to the severe economic constraints these families experience and the influences of peer group and neighbourhood, which are inimical to success in school and to family values.[56]

Clark confirms Baumrind's[57] finding that high parental support and high control, when that control is internalised and based on reasoning and accompanied by a child's sense of power, result in academic achievement. He found, however, that for the low-income, inner-city black families he studied power on the part of the offspring was conducive to school achievement only when it was power in the intellectual sphere; for example, power to inform and influence the parents in intellectual matters. Those teenagers who had power to go out indiscriminately or to miss school at whim, were not successful at school. Clark stresses the centrality of parents and other authority figures and the way parents capitalise on the child's emotional dependency to delegate responsibility, to exercise control over home learning activities and to transmit parental values to children. In these ways parents enable their children to learn and achieve at school.

Blum finds that the ability of the parents to allow an increase in freedom to adolescents is predicated on the adolescent's successful socialisation at earlier ages. He gives the example of bathing. The superior families he studied did not allow their little children to bathe according to their whims and desires. The children followed a regular bathing routine. The less competent families allowed their little children much more freedom to set their own standards of cleanliness. Later, parents found themselves arguing constantly with their adolescents over routines of bathing, as the adolescents, to the parents' horror, now failed to conform to cultural norms of cleanliness. This is not what the parents had intended, but they had not made it clear earlier. When researchers report only the finding that more competent adolescents come from families where the parents do not constantly nag over bathing, church attendance, homework and curfews, without understanding the genesis of these differences, they give young parents the impression that it is damaging for parents to set limits and to guide and restrict children's behaviour. Nothing could be farther from the truth.

A number of researchers have commented on the frequency with which parents seem unable to accept their authority role within the family. Blum finds that parents are unable to act authoritatively if they have never had a loved and admired authority figure in their own childhood. If they have only a negative image of authority, they cannot accept the authority role.[58] Blum describes families in which the parents try to escape from the obligations of authority. One way to do this is to concentrate on moral or social issues in the wider community — the ecology or nuclear war, for example — and escape from confronting issues within the family that involve interfering in what the child wishes to do. Blum speculates that if a father has an unresolved dislike of his own father because of his father's authoritarianism, he expects his children to feel the same way about him. Such a father or mother lives in fear of the child's censure. Blum found that frequently such parents say they want their children to like them and that they would do nothing to alienate their child. On the other hand, an authoritative father speaks humorously but genuinely about how his son must learn to get along with him and not vice versa. 'A father with authority ambivalence, however, cannot accept unequal or hierarchical parent-child relations.'[59]

The least effective families studied by Blum 'were mired in self-doubt and deferred to their children as authorities on major matters such as sexual activities and drug use'. Some attempted to hide behind intellectualisations, or giggled inappropriately and avoided important topics. They seemed unable to respond with genuine, positive emotion and with a clear stand on issues. Their children, in turn, evaded issues and avoided commitments.[60] By contrast, the parents in the superior families were 'unflappable', which allowed the children to turn to them in any case of need, knowing nothing too bad would happen. The parents likewise were free to be themselves. They were comfortable with their roles, felt no fear of their children, and did not worry that the children might not love them. They did not ingratiate themselves with the children, assume superior knowledge on the part of the children, or attempt to be their children's 'friends'. They seemed to sense when trouble was in the air, and moved to prevent it, protecting their children from ultimate folly. While giving strong leadership, these superior families were in no way autocratic and in fact allowed a great deal of leeway for experimentation.[61]

Blum finds that in the superior and good families the fathers were dominant and authoritative. In fact, a strand running right through the research on healthy families is the need for fathers to be authoritative and involved in family life. These findings should not be over-interpreted. In this case dominant does not mean dominating. In fact, a number of studies use the word to describe the parent who is 'dominant in drawing out the child'. In other words, in healthy families the father is active in the relationship and nurturing aspects of family life, and also the limit-setting and standard-setting. The men are assertive, decisive and involved, and the women confidently play an equal role.

The consistency with which fearful, weak, passive and uninvolved fathers are found in dysfunctional families alerts to the essential role men play in families. When men are absent, passive, withdrawn or authoritarian, the effect on the family is destructive. It seems it is quite common for men to behave in these ways and rare to find mothers who are absent, uninvolved, withdrawn or passive. Hence the stress on the positive effect when men are involved.

The frequent findings of the negative effect of dominant mothers is linked to the father's withdrawal and passivity. If the father persistently withdraws and refuses to participate, the mother has two choices: to withdraw also, or to try to compensate. Faced with a non-involved husband, *any* action on her part makes her 'dominant'. Blum found a pattern where men who had been deprived of a father in childhood, whether through bereavement, separation or father's withdrawal, were often depressed and adopted this passive, withdrawn role.

The healthiest families demonstrate that both men and women can, and do, have authority in families.

Making authority palatable

It may be worth reporting Blum's description of how these superior families made authority palatable. In the first place, authority was equated with protection. Fathers encouraged and protected their whole families. For example, a father would urge the youngest child to speak, and then he, with the rest of the family, would listen respectfully. If the conversation carried the child in over his head, the father would immediately intervene and rescue the child. (Incidentally, this is the behaviour to which Blum applies the word 'dominant'.)

In Blum's study, the superior families all accepted a religious faith. Authority was seen as held on trust from higher authority, allowing the father to 'ground his strength on sources that are greater than himself' and also to make mistakes.

A third source of palatable authority comes from the sense of a family tradition that creates an historical equality. The child becomes the father who becomes the grandfather in a process in which all have their place. Finally, authority in superior families was exercised discreetly, with humour, flexibility and affection, and with children learning early that they are to share in it as they grow to deserve it.

Several issues arise from this research into leadership, authority and power in families. One is the widespread lack of appreciation of the value, the essential nature of authority in families. Consequently, we have the all-too-frequent phenomenon of parents who themselves have no positive notion of authority. Parents need a positive view of authority; that is, authority that is neither authoritarian, autocratic, punitive, nor capricious, but it seems it is difficult to develop this if one has not had the opportunity to experience it.

One study indicated that some social welfare professionals did not appreciate the role of authority in family life and were unable to tell a healthy family from a dysfunctional one. They tended to see parental action to set limits and guide children's behaviour as 'hostility' and see endless 'meta-communication' about roles and relationships as evidence of health.[62] In *Haven in a Heartless World*, Lasch argues that there has been an attack on authority from 'the helping professions', aided and abetted by many social scientists. He argues that Adorno and his colleagues analysed *The Authoritarian Personality* at the moment of its demise. They found only 10 per cent of the American population fitted the profile of the authoritarian personality. Lasch argues that the personality style of the current age is not authoritarian, but narcissistic. Narcissism is said to develop when children are indulged but denied genuine warmth. One of its major characteristics is a refusal to accept responsibility and a pervasive jealousy and rage.

Coleman links the attenuation of authority to increases in child suicide in the USA and other industrialised countries.[63] Durkheim found that suicide is strongly related to social isolation, which emerges, not from *anomie* as is so commonly thought, but from *egoisme*, which could be translated as individualism. To Durkheim our youth suicide statistics would be of the greatest significance, indicating disturbing trends in society. Coleman links these trends to the changed relationship of authority between young people and their parents, suggesting that when the authority is attenuated, the relationship weakens, because children and parents are not peers, which is the only alternative relationship possible. The increase in suicide is not caused by authoritarian parenting but by 'relaxed and inattentive parenthood'.

Family educators find that power is a key area for family learning. Blum suggests that the main thing is to ensure that well-functioning families are not mis-led by 'experts' who do not understand the role of parental authority. Ronka reports European research, which indicates that parents have rejected permissiveness as an alternative to authoritarianism (which they have likewise rejected). However, Ronka finds that parents are not always able to develop an alternative 'authoritative' or 'firm but not harsh' style, if they have never seen it in practice.[64] Yet there is considerable evidence that parents *can* learn these authoritative styles of family leadership if a learning opportunity is presented to them.[65]

Support networks

Many studies have found evidence of a correlation between the health of the family system and the existence of a supportive network for the family. The more isolated a family becomes the more likely it is to have serious problems.[66] Hansen notes that when families have a trusted confidant outside the family, it seems to help the family to function better. McCubbin found in studying families of cystic fibrosis sufferers that families who are able to cope with the severe stress of this illness can elicit support from the community. A Sydney church consultation with families found parents strongly expressing their need for more community support.[67] A study of one-parent families found that it is not the size of the network that indicated greater health in the family, but the extent to which the network supported the mother.[68]

For married mothers, larger networks and greater access to instrumental and emotional support from relatives, neighbours and friends are associated with more positive views of self as a parent and of the child, and of the reporting of greater amounts of joint mother-child activity.[69] Relatives play a key role in how the mother perceives herself.[70] Networks, then, seem to supply a number of vital provisions for the family and its members.

Family time

Curran[71] places control of family time as one of the key indicators of health in a family system, as without time it is impossible to communicate, negotiate conflict, make joint decisions, notice and appreciate each other, or be able to switch off from work and relax and enjoy one another. The professionals she studied, each of whom belonged to a profession such as medicine, education or youth work, which gave them a high exposure to families, gave high ratings to families having a sense of play and humour (which can only develop when there is time to relax) and to sharing leisure time together.

The professionals rated volunteering for community organisations very low as an indicator of health in families, and many of those seventy professionals (out of a total of 551) who chose it as a sign of health in families themselves worked for voluntary agencies. Curran's interviews with families indicate that pressure to be involved in community organisations can be detrimental to family life. She writes of 'the tyranny of youth leagues':

There's a long overdue need to study seriously what effects these leagues and practices have on family life, and if there's no alternative to infringing upon the one time sacrosanct to the family as a unit — the dinner hour — then we need at least to teach families about their potential cost to family health. It may come as a sobering revelation to thousands of parents that contrary to the positive image fostered by these organised activities, the family, in fact, suffers from them.[72]

The healthier families in Curran's study were aware of these time pressures and able to make the hard decisions required to cut down on organised activities for their children and themselves. Many of the healthy families have a rule that a child should not have more than one activity that requires practice. Her interviews indicated that parents, too, can become over-involved in volunteer activities or work commitments that seriously usurp family time. Lewis found that the healthy families in his study, while not isolated, spent most of their leisure time in family activities.

Curran concludes that control of family time involves a willingness to put limits on the amount of time spent at work, an ability to gain control over TV, and an active and intentional monitoring of time so that the family makes time for family time. Curran and Bronfenbrenner both draw attention to the effects of institutions on family time: work, sport, schools, and churches can all invade family time. The demands of work and other interests can seriously restrict family time. Educational deficits are being increasingly attributed to this lack of time with parents and other significant adults, leading to what Coleman calls lack of 'social capital'. By this, Coleman means that if the parents have high educational and other attributes, these can benefit the child only if the parent spends time in joint activity with the child. Schools and churches have the option of re-arranging some of their programs so that family time can be increased: that is, occasionally a 'whole-family' component can be included. Some examples will be given in chapter 11.

Concern has been expressed in Japan over the effects of Japan's industrial style on family life, especially the curtailment of family time involved in a corporate structure that demands enormous commitment to work. Japanese workers are expected to move away from their families for periods of two years without relocation expenses being paid. Extremely long work hours followed by socialising in the work environment to build up commitment to the corporation undermines family life. Researchers write of 'hotel families', because of the external pressures that make home nothing more than a place to eat and sleep.[73] A major form of violence in Japan is violence of young adults and older adults against their parents. Japan's economic miracle is having a significant impact on families.

Spouse bond

The spouses are the architects of the family system. Their relationship is the predictor of the health of the whole system. The marital relationship is the measure of the socialisation of the young.[74] The mother's healthy communication in a laboratory setting with the father present and the parents' communication and ability to function as a couple are the most consistent predictors of their children's performance on a whole array of school measures.[75]

Jerry Lewis writes at some length on the special relationship between the spouses in the healthier families in his study.[76] It was a relationship of trust, shared power and close communication, which formed the basis of the health of the family system. Lewis talks of the impression given of 'two strong partners pulling together'. Other studies show that even when one or both parents exhibit indicators of emotional disturbance, some couples still manage to develop this positive relationship, which seems to insulate the children from the emotional deficits of the parents.[77] In other words, the *relationship* between the spouses seems to be more significant for child well-being than the emotional health of the individual parents and can compensate for emotional disturbances severe enough to warrant hospitalisation.

Elder's research on children of the Great Depression of the 1930s was referred to earlier. Elder found that the negative effects to be expected from the Depression experience on families with very young children were modified and even avoided completely in those families in which, prior to the Depression, there was a strong bond of harmony and love between the spouses. This bond prevented the father losing status in the family because of his damaged bread-winning role, and preserved his relationship to wife, sons and daughters, a relationship vital to the children's developing social competence.

Few social scientists would expect the supposedly fragile, private, personal bond between husband and wife could match in power the massive social impact of the Great Depression. Yet Elder's research shows that, indeed, this private, personal bond did have the power to protect the family from the Depression's negative effects and enabled the children to extract a positive benefit from the experience of stress and privation.

Religion and spiritual values

Many US studies find that the attachment to spiritual values and the celebration of the rituals associated with the family's spiritual tradition are associated with health and well-being in the family.[78] Lewis and Looney found religious beliefs and practices to be the core of black, low-income, competent family life. They underlay and supported the family's commitment to each other and their resilience in the day-to-day struggle to survive physically and emotionally in an often hostile environment. Both *No Single Thread* and *The Long Struggle* argue that mental health professionals as a group under-estimate the adaptive value of religious beliefs and practices.

Four factors linking family well-being with religious beliefs have emerged. One is the role of spiritual beliefs in enabling family members to deal with loss and grief, and another is the links to a supportive community that many religious groups provide. A third element is the role the spiritual traditions play in providing a coherent rationale to support a communal way of life rather than individualism. Yet another factor explaining the positive correlations of church-membership or spiritual tradition is the church's role as a mediating institution.

Lewis found that realistic acceptance of loss, as indicated by the ability to speak about death in the family, was the factor associated with markedly lower rates of illness in families.[79] He finds that ability to deal with loss is an essential ingredient of family life, because death enters every family sooner or later, in due course or prematurely. Loss is a constant theme in family life and is an element of every transition, developmental stage and achievement. Lewis reports that, in his experience, it is impossible for family members realistically to accept death and loss without the support of a transcendent belief-system. Hence he finds a core of transcendent beliefs are essential to superior family competence.[80] Coleman also reported the lack of spiritual beliefs as contributing to the unresolved mourning so often found in the families of heroin addicts.[81]

Caplan studied families in Israel during the Six Day War. He was struck by the vital resource spiritual or patriotic values were for families at this critical time. Especially for families facing the shock of bereavement, these transcendent values were a strength and source of meaning. Caplan speculates on the value of any spiritual or values commitment that gives an added level of meaning to family belonging and offers hope or meaning in times of tragedy or loss.[82]

Lynch's research into the effects of loneliness on physical health indicates another dimension to explain the positive correlations found between church-membership and family well-being.[83] Firstly, Lynch finds physical health to be strongly supported by an intimate network of love and support. In fact, family status is a strong predictor of physical health. Lynch found that church-membership provides networks of relationships and belonging. Many people do not belong to a church, but few alternative structures have arisen to replace their community-building role. Hence church-membership can positively influence family life by providing the network of support that all families need. In *Habits of the Heart*,[84] the influential study of how individualism has undermined the very notion of commitment in American life, Bellah finds church-membership to be the major way, apart from work, that North Americans are linked into the community and contribute to the life of the community. Of course, Bellah's study draws attention to another factor, which may be the major contribution of church or other spiritual or values allegiance to family life.

The major spiritual traditions of the world attest to the folly of individualism and selfishness, and to the wisdom of a life based on commitment to others, loyalty, forgiveness and love. Bellah shows that Americans from a broad spectrum of society have lost a language of commitment. They can no longer explain why they should be committed to another person, beyond the fact that it feels good at the moment, or that it suits their current self-interest. Of course, commitment implies that it is good, even when it doesn't feel good and doesn't seem to promote one's current self-interest. Apart from the republican tradition, the spiritual traditions (and for most Americans that means their church tradition) are virtually the only coherent alternatives available to the endemic doctrine of individualism.[85] It is not surprising, then, that maintaining the spiritual links and traditions emerges as a strength in family life and that partaking in the religious rituals also strengthens family rituals, family cohesion and family commitment. For many families, the recurring cycle of baptisms, first communions, weddings and funerals, or their equivalents, are the high points of family life. The meaning of these events is inextricably interwoven with personal, family and religious associations.

Blum is yet another researcher who reports that religious beliefs were intimately linked to the attitudes and patterns of behaviour that characterised the superior families he studied. The families' religious beliefs underlay their insistence that the core of family life was love, respect, forgiveness and understanding. The average and poorly functioning families studied by Blum wanted information and educative programs to help them guide their children away from drugs. The superior families placed no faith in such programs. They insisted that their children's resistance to drugs was based in love and respect and family values. They placed virtually no faith in information as a deterrent. As mentioned earlier, another area where religious faith emerged as significant is in enabling family members to accept authority.

Brigitte and Peter Berger have drawn attention to the role of 'mediating structures', those ethnic, racial, neighbourhood and voluntary groups that give meaning to private life and mediate between individuals and the large public institutions.

They show that the churches are centrally important among these mediating structures, especially for many lower-middle and working-class Americans.

> We believe that many of the problems of the modern welfare state would be greatly mitigated if not eliminated if public policy would favor and even utilize these mediating structures more, instead of ignoring and even running over them, as has been the tendency to date. This is particularly important for family policy.[86]

However, in the Berger view, one obstacle to the above policy in the US is a 'narrow, indeed sectarian (the sect being secularism) interpretation of the First Amendment', which leaves unused the vast capacity of churches to perform societally important services. They continue:

> If one respects the communities in which people live and from which they derive meaning, then one must also respect the fact that many of these communities are religious. Public policies that do not do this are not only exceedingly abstract and remote from social reality, they will inevitably (and, we think, needlessly) offend and polarize people.[87]

Evidence of the significance of the churches for families indicates that they, and perhaps alternative groups, may play an important role in providing the network of support that families need. One implication is that churches may have the potential to play an even more important role in relation to families than they have to date.

The church has access to the internal life of the family at those critical moments in the family life-cycle known as 'rites of passage'. Today, it is within churches, in the main, that these key moments in the family's life-cycle are celebrated. This means that churches still have access to families and considerable credibility with families. This is evident in the number of studies that were able to find non-client, community families to study only with the assistance of churches, who extended their access to and credibility with families to researchers.[88] The churches' unique access to and credibility with families may mean they can play a vital role in mediating the public-private split that is the source of the denial of public resources to families.

Evidence of the family's vital role in making human beings human is overwhelming. A number of implications follow from the realisation of the impact of the family and from the fact that the family's power derives from its own internal processes: the way the members relate to each other and the outside world.

6

Policy Implications

The unanimity of findings from studies of family health calls into question the belief of family policy experts that characteristics of health in families cannot be identified. This has implications for family policy and research.

Research studies converge

In chapter 4 I quoted a statement by Gilbert Steiner, probably the leading family-policy researcher in the USA, whose work is internationally known and respected. Steiner asserted that 'Because intangibles are so important to family relationships' identifying the characteristics of strong families or of failing families 'poses problems'. He went on to declare that, even if they could be identified, 'it is a safe bet that one observer would characterise them as strong since they hold together, and another would characterise them as failing'.[1] Steiner's views are widely shared, not only by researchers, but also by many people throughout the community. Steiner is unusual only in having committed his opinion to writing. Yet, despite the prevalence of the belief, there is nothing in all the research reviewed to support it.

It seems it is *never* functional in families for members to routinely discount and ignore one another; to fail to listen; to fail to respect one another's wants, needs, concerns and individuality; to fail to accept or even notice one another's differences and to insist that all are the same. There are no studies that report that it is effective for families to be unable to solve problems, or to be unable to negotiate with each other. Not one study has reported that the domination of one spouse by another has led to spouse satisfaction and the development of optimal competence in the children. There have been no instances where parental authoritarianism and the refusal progressively to share power and responsibility with children has been associated with positive outcomes in the children's growth and development. Nor have any cases been reported where the practice of parents disclaiming their adult status and rejecting or neglecting to exercise leadership in the family and to guide and restrict children's behaviour has been shown to be functional.

Researchers in many countries are concerned about the erosion of family time and about absent parents, usually fathers, but increasingly mothers. When parents fail to spend time with their children and fail to take an interest in them, it is invariably damaging to the children's confidence and development. It is generally agreed that the more isolated and excluded a family becomes, the more likely it is to have serious problems. No cases have been reported in which the spouse relationship is one of constant conflict, mutual antagonism and misunderstanding, and yet the children are developing competence and self-esteem. In fact, several studies find the spouse relationship a reliable predictor of the health of the whole system, and of children's schooling achievement and social competence.

The belief that 'what is dysfunctional in one family may be quite tolerable in another'[2] is totally unsupported by research data. It raises the question of why this belief is so commonly accepted in the family-policy field. Such contradictions are often pointers to the operation of ideology. Allan Bloom opens his *Closing of the American Mind* with the statement that, today, 'almost every student entering university believes, or says he believes, that truth is relative . . . The relativity of truth is not a theoretical insight but a moral postulate, the condition of a free society, or so they see it.'[3] He goes on to assert that 'The purpose of their education is not to make them scholars but to provide them with a moral virtue — openness'[4] (hence the title of the chapter, 'Our Virtue'). It can be seen, then, that Steiner's beliefs about there being no 'strong families' is a particular example of this moral virtue of openness. As Bloom notes, however, this belief in openness means that 'indiscriminateness is a moral imperative because its opposite is discrimination'.[5] Bloom criticises current conceptions of openness because they are closed to the truth: 'To deny the possibility of knowing good and bad is to suppress true openness.'[6]

Need for non-material family policy

Steiner's belief that 'what is dysfunctional in one family may be quite tolerable in another' *may* apply to those 'surface status characteristics' such as the family unit's composition or economic standing. However, these are the family characteristics that, though commonly measured and quoted, have been shown *not* to be the source of children's developing competence.[7] Recognition that intra-family factors *can* outweigh factors such as socio-economic status, neighbourhood and school in the development of competence in children leads to the notion that the development of family policy should focus on *economic* opportunity, *and* public support services, *and* creative family *processes*. Yet, in fact, public policies have concentrated on economic factors, and public services such as the provision of institutionalised childcare. *There has been an almost complete neglect of non-material family policy to support these non-material family factors that are so vital to family well-being and through which families make their best contribution to society.*

Need for more research on family well-being

Researchers who have explored the characteristics of healthy family systems are unanimous on the need for more research of these areas, firstly because many parents experience a degree of confusion over aspects of child-rearing and seek information, understanding and skills in this area.[8] Ronka reports European research indicating that from 50 to 90 per cent of parents are uncertain about how to bring up children.[9] At the same time, therapists have been shown to be at times unable to identify better-functioning families from dysfunctional families, confusing parental setting of limits to children's behaviour and insistence that tasks be completed as expressions of 'hostility' and 'autocratic control'.[10]

Secondly, while they are confident they are clarifying significant relationships between family processes and family well-being, many researchers comment that it is one thing to elucidate such relationships: it is quite another to discover *how* well-functioning families developed the attitudes, activities and overall cultural style that creates competence and well-being in their members. Longitudinal studies are needed to provide an understanding of how well-functioning families developed their effective style, which, in turn, can lead to an informed development of policies to encourage those positive family attitudes, practices, beliefs and relationships.

Family is part of our humanness

The convergence of findings on research into the characteristics of well-functioning families raises the question of whether there are some universals in the environment needed for the social development of humans, or whether well-functioning families are merely those who fit in best with the social structures of society and submit to producing and reproducing the personality features needed by industrial societies in the phase of late capitalism. It seems unlikely that the latter is true, in that superior families are slightly counter-cultural rather than super-conforming, at least in that they resist the perpetual seduction of TV and other culturally accepted values such as the work ethic, consumerism, sports ethic and (in the USA) volunteerism.

Not one study found family well-being associated with super-wealth or super-status, and at least one researcher has found a negative correlation between marital satisfaction and husband's success in his occupational pursuits.[11] The mere valuing of family life above work is a non-conventional and counter-cultural stance.[12] Families may be the most persistent resisters to the power of the state and the dominant élites and the most successful buffer between the individual and the naked power of the state.[13] For these reasons, attacks on the family in the name of increased liberation and autonomy are misguided and can lead only to a loss of freedom for all individuals in the society.[14]

The similarity of findings on the characteristics of health in families calls into question current demands that the word 'family' should be shelved for the word 'families' on the ground that there is no such thing as 'the family' but only many different varieties of family. The foregoing research indicates, instead, that family may be part of our humanness and that the aspects that families have in common outweigh what divides them. It was argued earlier that the outlawing of the term 'family' was part of a struggle over the role and status of families within the public realm. It is no coincidence that this 'denial of the family' occurred concurrently with the removal of financial supports from families in a number of countries.

Edwin Friedman, a North American who has been both a rabbi and a family therapist for twenty-five years, insists that family is the truly ecumenical experience, that family dynamics are the basis of the dynamics of organisational life, and that in pastoral experience those who emphasise the discontinuities between family dynamics in different ethnic or racial groups are not only mistaken but frequently have ulterior motives.[15] For example, he finds that when parents refuse to attend a wedding because their offspring's spouse is the wrong religion or cultural group they are using the religious issue as a weapon and disguise. The problem nearly always lies in distorted family patterns.

It seems that the belief that child-rearing is totally culture specific is overstated. Certainly there are cultural patterns, but there are also species-wide similarities.[16] For example, Rainwater's study of the Pruitt-Igoe estate demolished the myth that Negroes[17] in the USA prefer single-parent family life.[18] They valued the same qualities in family life that white, middle-class Americans valued at that time. They wanted stable relationships between the parents, the father to earn an income and the mother to mind the children.

The insistence that the 'nuclear family' is a creation of capitalism is not historically based. In English-speaking countries the two-generation household has been the norm for centuries, though industrialisation, the growth of huge urban centres and the corporation have certainly stripped families of the supportive network of wider family and neighbourhood. It is strange that two relatively recent institutions, school and the corporation, are often seen to have eternal status in human life, and the one pan-historical grouping, the family, is declared to be the invention of capitalism.

Family is irreplaceable

The studies of the impact of families and the characteristics associated with a positive family impact indicate that it is the unique interest, commitment and love and the informal structure of families that provides the key to their power. It is unlikely then that families can be replaced by any alternative social group, and it is already proved that institutions are not able adequately to replace the intimacy of family life.

New criteria for quality family life

In Steiner's statements about family life (quoted in chapter 4) it is implied that the only criterion we have for quality of family life is stability; that is, whether the couple stay together. The problem with stability as the sole criterion is that it is always easy to find examples of family life where people stay together in situations of human depravation, such as violence, incest or psychosis. Then one is forced to accept that in some situations it is better if families are not stable (that is, if they separate), which leads to the conclusion that we have no criteria at all for quality family life. The research into the characteristics of health in families creates criteria additional

to the criteria of stability and enables a more nuanced judgement than those based on stability alone. The studies of
health in family systems also balances earlier research into
family pathology. It at least reveals that not all families make
people sick. Some, in fact most, have the reverse effect.

Disturbed families are 'systems-stunted'

From the *No Single Thread* study and previous research and
clinical experience, Jerry Lewis concludes that disturbed
families are 'systems-stunted', not 'biologically stunted'. By
this he means that most schizophrenia, psychopathology,
neurosis and behaviour disorder are due to the way the families of the sufferers function. Sometimes the disturbance was
initiated in events of earlier life. Sometimes the current
organisation of the family is causing the problem. In the past,
the observation that such disorders seemed to run in families
was attributed to 'bad blood', or in other words to genetic
factors.

There is both good news and bad news in Lewis's finding.
The bad news is that it places a high responsibility on families
for the pathology that develops within their boundaries. If
Lasch is correct in saying that the characteristic personality
profile of our age is narcissism, and the narcissist refuses to
accept responsibility, this is very bad news indeed. The good
news is that if awareness is created of the patterns that have
led to the problem, if healing and learning are provided and if
responsibility is accepted, families can change.

Vicious cycles can be turned into positive ones. We know
that various forms of therapy are able to achieve this transformation. We know that many individuals, without therapy
and without formal intervention, break out of a family with
dysfunctional patterns and establish positive patterns in the
next generation. But we know virtually nothing of *how* they
are able to do this. We know that the family life-cycle provides some key transition moments when members are open
to new learning and new patterning. It seems that the rituals
of passage were designed to enable individuals to pass from
one stage of life into another and for their families and com-

munities to adjust to and support these changes.[19]

Friedman maintains that these rites of passage still provide opportunities for healing and growth in individuals and families at a time when distorted family patterns are particularly open to re-alignment;[20] and he contributes the convincing insight that rites of passage are primarily *family*, not individual, events.

Conclusion

In all, there is overwhelming evidence of the impact of families in shaping individual and communal competence, happiness and satisfaction with life. We know that families are the most powerful influence in shaping development in many areas of human competence. We know a great deal about what it is that distinguishes health-creating families from families that undermine and destroy human competence. We know that it is in the informal realm of family interaction and family relationships that the difference lies. It follows that we have no substitute for families. It is in the 'irrational', compassionate love members have for one another, in their enduring ties, in the informal organisation of family life, that the family's unique strength lies.

In view of the impact of families on human competence, the role of the internal family processes in creating this competence, and that there is no way to replace the unique role of families, it is to be expected that family and family issues will have a prime place in public policies. Many think this is a fact attested to by the rhetoric surrounding motherhood, family and home. Unfortunately, while families are honoured in rhetoric, in reality they are ignored, neglected and undermined by aspects of public policy.

Part 3

The Family Ignored

7

Lack of Resources to Support Marriage

No group or institution outweighs the influence of the family in creating human competence and in contributing to satisfaction with life. In fact, we do not know of any way of making human beings human other than by rearing them in a family. Yet there are many signs of the public realm's failure to recognise the importance of families and of the unique and irreplaceable role they play. This failure is evident in the disparity between the enormous costs of family dysfunction and high rates of marriage breakdown compared with the meagre resources allocated for supporting and enriching family environments.

The costs of family breakdown

The statistics paint a paradoxical picture of evidence of a high incidence of marriage and family breakdown and distress, and of high levels of satisfaction with marriage and family. In the 1950s in the UK, Elizabeth Bott published her classic study of family networks.[1] In her preliminary interviews she discovered that older people were convinced that family life had deteriorated, but that those who were themselves parents of young children considered that *their* family life was an improvement on family life as they had experienced it as children. Her finding is a warning against tendencies to see nothing but gloom and doom in statistics of family life. In the USA, family is reported to be the major source of satisfaction with life.[2] The Australian Institute of Family Studies' national survey of eighteen- to thirty-four- year-olds revealed a similar affirmation of the satisfaction to be derived from family ties:

> Eighty-five per cent agreed that 'marriage provides love, warmth and happiness', 75 per cent agreed that 'marriage is for life', and 81 per cent of men and 74 per cent of women agreed that 'marriage develops a sense of responsibility in you'.[3]

High rates of marriage breakdown

During the years 1982–86 in Australia the number of divorces has declined. This is the first time the rate has shown any sign of abating since the end of World War II. Yet, while reviewing their predictions of future divorce rates downwards somewhat (from a projected rate of 40 per cent of all marriages to around 30 or 35 per cent), the experts are not yet interpreting this as a reliable sign of greater stability in family relationships.

Australia has a high divorce rate (somewhere between that of the USA and the UK) and the costs of marriage breakdown are of increasing concern to governments and communities. We know that the time preceding, during and following a divorce is intensely painful for most family members. We also know that some families who do not take the option to divorce or separate live continually in a similarly painful atmosphere. Therefore, the following research on the costs of family breakdown is intended to be read as indicating the costs of separation and divorce *and* of distress and dysfunction in some intensely stressed families who choose not to divorce.

Some US research suggests that the children from the least happy (that is the bottom 3 per cent) of two-parent families are more distressed than children of divorce. Children of happy two-parent families were happiest and least stressed.[4] Australian research finds few differences between children of divorce and children of non-divorced two-parent families, and also that adolescents' adjustment is related more to whether they have a good relationship with at least one parent than to whether the parents are together or not. Yet, despite some ambivalent findings on the effects of marriage breakup, there is strong evidence that our current high rate of marriage breakup incurs heavy costs financially (both personally and communally) and exacts further tolls in emotional pain, in physical health and in social cohesion.

The financial effects of divorce on families

Most women and some men are worse off financially after divorce.[5] Women are usually so much worse off that it is appropriate to speak of the 'feminisation of poverty'.[6] It is even more chilling to realise that, as well as women, it is children who are bearing the brunt of poverty in Australia and the USA.

Australian research used equivalence scales to enable comparisons to be made between the actual standard of living before and after separation. The research took into account the different needs and household compositions at these two points of time. It was found that some years after divorce many men and some women were actually better off. The new family structure, especially the presence or absence of children and whether the woman had remarried usually indicates the financial position of the post-divorce family. The incomes of single women were only 50 per cent of their pre-separation, household-income level.[7] Bumpass reports that in the USA, on average, women's incomes decline by 30 per cent following divorce or separation.[8] Weitzman reports *divorced women and minor children suffer a 73 per cent decline in their standard of living and their former husbands a 42 per cent rise.*[9]

In the USA in 1979, the median per capita income of divorced women who had not remarried was $4152, just over half of the $7886 income of divorced men who had not remarried. The median income of families headed by women with children under six was only 30 per cent of *all* families with children under six.[10]

In 1984 in Australia 14.3 per cent of families with children were headed by a single adult. There was a 57 per cent increase in the number of one-parent families between 1976 and 1981, and the number doubled between 1969 and 1986.[11] Most of these one-parent families rely for financial support on the Social Security system.[12] The poverty of one-parent families compared with two-parent families can be seen from the fact that, in July 1985, 83 per cent of one-parent families were receiving a pension, benefit or family income supplement, compared with 9 per cent of married couple families with dependent children.[13]

In the USA one-parent families now total 20 per cent of all families with dependent children, and by 1990 it is expected that there will be more one-parent families and step-families than intact nuclear families.[14] Over 50 per cent of children born in the 1970s in the USA will experience life in a one-parent family, and US Census Bureau data show that almost 60 per cent of US children born in 1983 would *not* spend their entire childhood living with both natural parents.[15] One-third of US children will experience what it is to live in a family on welfare before they are eighteen years old. The most recent projections in the US are for two out of three marriages to end in breakdown.

The financial costs to governments of marriage breakdown

The financial consequences of marriage breakdown at a personal level are most distressing, but the financial implications for governments are just as serious. The Australian National Marriage Guidance Council has attempted to estimate the costs of family breakdown to the Australian community.

They took into account the costs of maintaining the family courts, providing mental health services used by those who are not coping with the crisis of divorce and separation, treating the physical health problems that so often accompany the emotional crisis of separation or divorce, and running youth refuges (there are 25,000 young people homeless in Australia). Absenteeism from work increases during traumatic separations and is also taken into account. In this manner, in 1985, the Council estimated the annual cost of marriage breakdown and divorce in Australia to be in the realm of $1900 million. When it is realised that this staggering figure represents a new Parliament House *every year*, it makes one wonder why so little is done either to prevent it, to understand it or to take it seriously as a social issue.

Despite the lack of realistic response to these figures, there are signs that government is becoming concerned at these increasing financial costs to the community stemming from family dysfunction and family breakdown. In 1985 the family courts in Australia cost about $15 million to administer. Another major legal item is government Legal Aid in courts, around $25 million in the same year (63 per cent of the Legal Aid budget goes to lawyers in connection with family law matters). Yet this sum of $40 million is dwarfed by the cost of the Supporting Parent Benefit, $1173 million in 1984–85, up $91 million from the previous year.[16] The budget estimate for the Supporting Parent Benefit 1988–89 is $2541 million. It is estimated that 70 per cent of the Supporting Parent Benefit is allocated to parents who are single due to marital breakdown or divorce. This means that the current cost of the Supporting Parent Benefit due to marriage breakdown is $1.7 billion.

The Supporting Parent Benefit represents a heavy cost that not all in the community bear willingly, especially when it is known that 70 per cent of non-custodial parents fail to pay child maintenance either in whole or in part. This is an international trend. In the UK, 80 per cent of maintenance orders are not complied with,[17] and 2000 men are in prison for non-payment of maintenance. In the USA between 60 and 80 per cent of orders are not complied with[18] and 7,000,000 children over ten years of age are not getting the support from their parents (mostly fathers) to which they are entitled.[19]

There is reason to believe that the Supporting Parent Benefit is of the utmost importance to families and to the community as a whole. Australian researchers find less difference between children of divorce and children who have not experienced the divorce of their parents than do US researchers. One possible cause of this is that Australia has a better level of financial support for one-parent families than does the USA. It is also known that families cope with one problem, such as death of a parent or a parent's absence, quite well. But when such a problem is combined with another (such as poverty or illness) undesirable effects are *much* more likely. Hence the importance of the provision of the Supporting Parent Benefit to families.

While the costs of marriage breakup make problems for governments in balancing their budgets and for citizens in paying their taxes, the most serious problem is the effect on children of the resulting poverty. Some families lack the bare essentials of adequate food, heating and shelter, and many more are deprived of opportunities for social contact with others and become increasingly isolated. It is known that the effects of economic deprivation can be traced to the next generation, especially when it leads to social isolation,[20] and the socio-economic achievement of young adults is reduced if they experienced divorce during their childhood.[21] Higher marital instability[22] and lower educational achievement[23] have also been reported for the children of divorce. In Australia one family in five has an income low enough to require Family Income Supplements, and this rises to between 48 and 60 per cent of one-parent families.[24] One-parent families are six times as likely to be living below the poverty line as are two-parent families.

Funds allocated to resource marriage and family

In view of the magnitude of the financial costs to families it is to be expected that vigorous efforts are being made to prevent or mitigate these rising expenses. Instead we find that where the direct and easily accountable costs of divorce and marriage breakdown amount to around $1.8 billion each year, and they are rising rapidly (in 1986 they were estimated at $1.5 billion), funds devoted to marriage education and marriage counselling amount to only $6 million. Obviously, marriage counselling is a remedial rather than preventative measure, as people present for counselling only when there are serious problems. Research in the UK finds that marriage counselling organisations are consulted by only 5 per cent of those with serious marital problems. Pre-marriage education is budgeted to receive only $205,000 for the whole of Australia in 1988–89.

It is instructive to consider how far $205,000 would go to provide basic education in one primary school. How pre-marriage educators, over the whole of Australia, can be expected to develop courses and programs, provide materials, train leaders, professionally supervise the work done and evaluate both process and outcomes on $205,000 is a mystery. Yet a surprising amount is being done by highly qualified people who consider that the task is too vital to be left undone. At least 6000 couples receive pre-marriage education from organisations registered with the Attorney-General's Department.

Yet, even if we include marriage counselling as a preventive measure, it means that the direct and easily accountable costs of marriage breakdown and divorce cost every Australian man, woman and child $175 a year, and we allocate no more than 44 cents per head to our entire effort to understand, prevent and remedy this. If we count only the truly remedial aspect of the pre-marriage education, we find that only one cent is spent on prevention for a problem that costs us $175 per head and which increases every year. (See Tables 1 and 2.)[25] It is commonly believed that funds for marriage counselling and premarriage education have increased dramatically. In fact, over four years they increased by almost $2 million. In the same period the costs of marriage breakdown increased by $639 million!

The financial costs of the rate of marriage breakdown are enormous. However, family members themselves rate the emotional costs, especially those associated with the loss or attenuation of valued relationships with other family members as the highest cost.

Table 1. Government funds allocated to prevention of family breakdown compared with costs of breakdown 1984–85

Prevention	$000
Marriage counselling services	$5000
Costs of breakdown	
Family courts	$15,000
Legal aid for family courts	$25,000
Supporting Parent Benefit due to family breakdown	$1,173,000
	$1,213,000

Table 2. Government funds allocated to prevention of family breakdown compared with costs of breakdown, 1988–89

Prevention	$000
Marriage counselling services	$6960
Costs of breakdown	
Family courts	$39,600
Legal aid for family courts	$34,000
Supporting Parent Benefit due to family breakdown	$1,779,260
	$1,852,860

Emotional costs of family breakup

The results of the quite extensive research into the emotional effects of family distress and family breakup are paradoxical and difficult to summarise. The Australian researcher Ailsa

Burns stresses the positive outcomes she found in a study of divorced and separated Australians responsible for 469 children under the age of thirteen years.

The vast majority of parents (87 per cent) considered their children had now adjusted to their situation. In addition almost three quarters felt that the children were now emotionally better off than they would have been had the marriage remained intact.[26]

Wallerstein and Kelly approached their investigation of the effects of divorce on adults and children with the conviction that 'divorce is and should remain a readily available option to adults who are unhappily married'. While maintaining that stance, their conclusions stress that the choice to divorce is one with serious implications for all involved.

There is considerable evidence in the study that divorce was highly beneficial for many of the adults. There is, however, no comparable evidence regarding the children. There is, in fact, no supporting evidence in this five year study for the commonly made argument that divorce is overall better for children than an unhappy marriage or, for its opposite argument . . . neither unhappy marriage nor divorce are especially congenial for children; each imposes its own set of stresses.[27]

Divorce, a stressor of the first magnitude

Despite ambiguous findings on the emotional effects of divorce, no one would deny that it is 'a stressor of the first magnitude'.[28] There is agreement that, at least in the short term, marital breakup is intensely painful for all, or most members of the family. It affects the children's development, and causes symptoms of physical distress in both adults and children. It interferes with work, parenting ability, school and play.[29]

Marriage breakup means that a 'whole subjective world has been destroyed', so that the participants report they are 'shattered', 'devastated', 'broken up' and that 'everything is falling apart'.[30] A two-and-a-half-year period of distress is common for children, and this period can often be much longer.[31] Some children never adjust,[32] and children of divorce appear for admission at psychiatric hospitals at higher rates than the general population.[33] However, other researchers indicate that a significant number of children who lose or are separated from their parents later achieve eminence. Those who achieve this positive resolution of the loss do so through a 'creative mourning response' that very much depends on the way the loss is mediated by the family.[34]

Mothers' reports of the effects of divorce

Some studies have been based on reports by mothers of their children's adjustment. However, other studies have found that while two-thirds of children report being distressed by their parents' separation, only one-third of parents were aware their children had been distressed in any way. There was a tendency for mothers to assume that the children experienced the same relief that they themselves felt. However, this was quite often not the case. Adults have reported later in the divorce process that during the intensely painful period of separation they had been absorbed by their own grief and the multitude of decisions to be made. They were not aware of how their children were reacting. It is also evident that often the children perceive their parents' distress and deliberately hide their own grief to avoid distressing the parent further.[35] The courage of these children who reverse the parent-child roles in order to care for a parent suffering severe distress is admirable. Unfortunately, they do so at a high cost to their own maturing process. There are likely to be future symptoms arising from this distortion of parent-child roles. Family therapists speak of the 'parentified child' in describing the character defences that can arise when children attempt a maturity for which they are not yet ready. If children are forced to repress the grief they are experiencing in order to care for their grieving parents, they are prevented from achieving a resolution of their own grief.

Divorce and unresolved grief

Unresolved childhood grief manifests in many ways. Behaviour disorders and depression are the most frequent, the latter being a particularly frequent side-effect of divorce. 37 per cent of children have been found to be suffering from some form of clinical depression five years after their parents divorced, more than were depressed eighteen months after the divorce.[36] Divorce is probably the major cause of childhood depression.[37] Case study researchers often find well-masked depression or anger in children of divorce. Sometimes large-scale statistical surveys find few differences between these groups, but they are not designed to identify masked depression or anger. Researchers also point to the significant rates of depression present in control groups, which obscures findings. For example, some researchers are concerned at evidence of delayed depression surfacing in adolescents or young men some years after the divorce.[38]

Loss of a parent in childhood is a common predisposing factor in the development of depression in later life,[39] but depression is also related to separation from a parent for a period of at least a year, when this separation occurs before the age of seventeen years.[40] To lose a parent through separation may be more likely to lead to later depression than loss through death.[41] Four studies found that loss of a parent through divorce is more likely to result in psychological distress and symptoms than is loss through bereavement.[42] Both Burgoyne and his colleagues and Wallerstein and Kelly find that divorce can be compared more accurately to parental suicide than to parental death.[43] As has already been mentioned, the loss of a parent can be associated with the development of superior competence, but it is at a cost that a child cannot lightly be asked to pay.

Burgoyne finds that the common belief that children blame themselves for the divorce is misplaced. They find this applies only to very young children, and even so is quite rare. They suggest that parents would prefer to believe that their children are upset because of a childish misunderstanding than because they are very hurt by something the parents are choosing to do.

Wallerstein compares the child's experience of divorce to the stress experienced by a child who loses a parent through death or who loses her or his community following a natural disaster. (These are scarcely instances in which one responds with the saying, 'Don't feel the world is caving in', which is in fact the title of an Australian study of divorce.[44]) Wallerstein claims this comparison is valid because in each case the event strikes at and disrupts close family relationships and weakens the protection provided by the nuclear family. Each begins with a time-limited crisis, but is followed by an extended period of disequilibrium, which may last several years or even longer. Each introduces a chain of long-lasting changes that are not predictable at the outset and that affect many domains of family life.

Phases of adjustment to marriage breakdown

Judith Wallerstein and Joan Kelly conducted a longitudinal study of sixty families going through the crisis of separation and divorce. They studied the families for five years, starting with the crisis of separation. They then extended the study to a ten-year follow-up. The research took place within the context of a counselling agency, which offered counselling to the family members in return for family participation in the study.

The combination of longitudinal research with case study methodology provides a particularly interesting insight into the separation and divorce process. Caution has been expressed about Wallerstein and Kelly's work because no control group was included in the study. (Whether such a thing as a true control group exists for such a study remains a point at issue in the research community. Qualitative research is a different methodology to the experiment. We don't criticise questionnaire-type research because the respondents were restricted to answering focused questions and could not define the situation in their own way.) But no other study has provided the five-year follow-up, later extended to ten years, of Wallerstein and Kelly's work. This longitudinal approach, combined with the understanding that emerges from intensive interview material throws a unique light on the divorce process. Their research also included observation of play, verbal fantasy, and child behaviour at clinic, school and home. The strengths of Wallerstein and Kelly's methodology justifies the wide readership and influence of their study.

Wallerstein finds that the adjustments the child must make following divorce extend from the time of the divorce through adolescence and culminate in late adolescence and young adulthood. She outlines a series of coping tasks that the child of divorce must master, and which 'represent a major addition to the expectable customary tasks of childhood and adolescence in our society. In this view, the child of divorce faces a special set of challenges and carries an extra burden.'

The phase of separation

Wallerstein found that the acute symptoms of separation anxiety, sleep disturbances, regressive behaviour and acute mourning reactions usually came to an end within a year or eighteen months of the decisive separation. But this is merely the first phase of the adjustment completed.

> But the feelings aroused by the separation, the anger at one or both parents, the profound and sometimes pervasive sorrows, the sense of vulnerability, the concern with being unloved and perhaps unlovable, the yearning for the departed parent, the intense worry over the parents, the loyalty conflict, the general sense of neediness and being overburdened, the nostalgia for the intact family — these were more likely to remain in place and endure long after the symptomatic responses and regressions had disappeared.
>
> Indeed, it is strikingly clear that five and ten years after the marital rupture the divorce remains for many children and adolescents the central event of their growing-up years and casts a long shadow over these years . . .
>
> We have been startled to find young adults at the ten-year follow-up who remain intensively occupied with a parent's infidelity ten years earlier or other youngsters, who were age two or three at the time of the marital separation, who seemed unable to leave our office, where they cried for an intact family they had hardly known and for close contact with a father they had encountered over the years as a capricious or disinterested parent.[45]

The first two psychological tasks confronting the child of divorce, acknowledging the reality of the marital rupture and disengaging from parental conflict and distress and resuming customary pursuits, need to be addressed immediately at the time of the separation and hopefully brought to resolution within a year or so. Most children of divorce show a dip in academic achievement during and after the crisis of separation, but if these two tasks are mastered, results start to improve along with other developmental agenda. However, the resolution is not achieved easily. Wallerstein describes children of all ages who for months stayed at home or close to home, too dispirited, wretched or worried to take an interest in their ordinary pursuits. Many youngsters paced the floor nervously when the parent was late in returning home. Others begged the custodial parent to give up smoking saying, 'What will happen to me if you get cancer?' Yet others experienced despair due to a parent having confided their suicidal preoccupation to the child and the child being aware that her or his presence was needed to help ward off suicidal impulses in the parent.

Eighteen months after the separation, most of the children in the study had re-established their earlier levels of learning and regained their relationships with friends driven away by earlier moodiness and irritability. However, a significant number of children of every age, but especially adolescence, did not find their way back to age-appropriate activities after the trauma of the family crisis.

Absorbing the loss of a parent
In the second phase the task of absorbing the loss of the parent or the intact family must be addressed. This phase is probably the most difficult. It involves the child overcoming a profound sense of rejection, of humiliation, of unlovability and of powerlessness. 'He left me', they say, and are likely to conclude, 'He left because I was not lovable.' Wallerstein and Kelly find some indications that feelings of unlovability, unworthiness and rejection are even stronger where the mother has relinquished or abandoned the child or is an irregular visitor. It is easier for children and adolescents to achieve a resolution of the loss if it is only partial and if the

non-custodial parent and child can establish a loving relationship within a reliable visiting parent.

Wallerstein reports that many children fail to negotiate a resolution of the loss they have suffered. They remain trapped and disappointed by unreliable, uninterested or absent father or mother, unable to renounce the vain hope for better things. A sub-group of youngsters, spurred by anger during adolescence, break their ties to a rejecting or uninterested parent and choose to identify with another adult. It is too early for the researchers to be able to report how this affects future development.

Resolving anger and self-blame

In the third phase the task identified by Wallerstein's team is to resolve anger and self-blame. Unlike bereavement or natural disaster, divorce is made by human beings. Wallerstein comments that 'children are aware that divorce is not inevitable, that the immediate cause is the decision of one or both parents to separate and that its true cause is the unwillingness or failure to maintain the marriage'. The researchers find that, as far as children are concerned, there is no such thing as no-fault divorce. They blame one or other parent and they blame themselves for not being able to hold the marriage together. The anger engendered by the divorce of their parents is intense and often little allayed by time. A fourteen-year-old boy wrote in a school composition five years after his parents' separation: 'My father picked up his suitcases one day and walked out because, as he said, he wanted his freedom. We thought we were a close-knit family, and it was an unexpected shock. It was the death of our family.'[46]

When the anger remains intact over time, it contributes to acting-out behaviour in the adolescent, including delinquency, poor school achievement and other schooling difficulties. It keeps the child alienated from one parent, and it blocks the way to acceptance and forgiveness. As the adolescent gets older, there is sometimes a greater understanding of one or both parents and of the reasons for the divorce. This paves the way for forgiveness of the parents and of themselves. Wallerstein finds a growing closeness at the ten-year mark between parent and child, often based on a mutual mastery of the anger engendered by the divorce. Barbara, aged seventeen, reported ten years after the marital rupture:

> My Mum and I are real close now. I stopped being angry at her when I was 15 when I suddenly realized that all of the kids who lived in tract houses with picket fences were not any happier that I was. It took me a long, long time to stop blaming her for not being in one of those houses.

Accepting the permanence of the divorce

Wallerstein finds that it is one thing to achieve some resolution of the loss of divorce. It is another to accept that the divorce is permanent — the fifth task. The researchers have been astonished at the persistence of the children's belief that the family will be reunited, and even the remarriage of one or both parents does not destroy this dream.

> We have concluded that the child of divorce faces a more difficult task in accepting permanence than does the bereaved child. The bereaved child, despite intense hopes to the contrary, knows full well that death can never be undone, whereas the living presence and availability of two parents gives continuing credence to the child's wish to restore the marriage.[47]

The researchers conclude that the fantasy of reunion is so strong that it 'taps deep well-springs within the child's functioning and yields to reality only very gradually', probably when the child makes a clear psychological separation between self and parent in adolescent years.

Achieving realistic hope regarding relationships

The final task, achieving realistic hope regarding relationships, is one that Wallerstein judges 'perhaps the most important both for the child and for society, namely the resolution of issues of relationship in such a way that the young person is able to reach and sustain a realistic vision regarding his or her capacity to love and be loved.'[48]

While stressing that the results of this ten-year study are still preliminary, it seems to the researchers that this final task confronting children of divorce is particularly daunting, and that youngsters who have successfully negotiated previous

114

tasks often founder on this one. Many had soberly measured their parents' behaviour and found it wanting. A twenty-six-year-old man who had chosen a quite different lifestyle to his father commented, ten years after the separation, 'Some day I will say to my dad, "Are you proud of what you have done with your life?" But . . . what can he answer me?'

Others had attempted to assess what had gone wrong so as to evolve strategies that would safeguard them from a similar failure: 'My parents cheated and lied, but I decided never to do that.' 'They should both have been more considerate. My mother is selfish and my father should never have married.' 'The trouble with my parents is that they each gave too little and asked too much.'[49]

The researchers found that at times the self-awareness of the youngsters was startling and cynical. A fourteen-year-old boy commented: 'Dad left because Mom bored him. I do that all the time.' Apparently he meant that often people bore him too, in which case he breaks off the relationship. There were youngsters who intended never to marry because they were sure their marriages would fail. There were others caught in a web of promiscuity and low self-esteem without hope of ever achieving a loving relationship. And there was the emergence of acute depression during adolescence, especially delayed depression among adolescent girls, many years after the marital rupture.

Even when there is a successful resolution by the young adult in their experience of their parents' divorce and they have achieved a feeling of independence and pride and an ability to love and to trust, there will still be a residue of sadness, of anger and of anxiety about the stability of relationships. This uncertainty may re-appear at critical times during their adult years.

It is a matter of concern, then, that family dysfunction — whether parents choose not to divorce and continue in unresolved pain and conflict or whether divorce ensues — is a serious social problem. Divorce is not a solution free from side-effects. It causes massive dislocations in the links between parents and children, with the majority of children seeing the non-custodial parent rarely or never. In an Australian investigation of the Brisbane family law courts, Hirst and

Smiley found that three years after separation in one-third of cases the non-custodial parent had ceased contact altogether and had only very irregular contact in another third.[50] Another Australian researcher, Ailsa Burns, reported that 52 per cent of the children in her sample saw the non-custodial parent rarely or never and that the loss of contact is more likely in a one-child family. She comments: 'All in all, then, the exodus of non-custodial parents from their children's lives was truly massive.'[51]

Research in the UK finds a similar number of children losing contact with the non-custodial parent after divorce. In a nationally representative sample of children in the USA, 52 per cent of children of divorce between ages eleven and sixteen had had no contact with their non-custodial parent within the past year. Ten years after the divorce the proportion of fathers who had had no contact with their children for at least a year had risen to 64 per cent. Only one child in six saw her or his father once a week. The principal researcher, Frank Furstenberg, concludes: 'a divorce not only severs the marital bond, but often permanently ruptures the parent-child relationship, especially if the child is living apart from the father'.[52] These findings on the dislocation of the links between parents and children are particularly disturbing, as it is agreed by all that the children's competence and adjustment after divorce is related to their having an ongoing relationship with *both* parents.[53]

There is no lack of evidence of the severity of the emotional anguish surrounding marriage breakdown and divorce, a pain that far outweighs the financial losses, severe as they may be. But, despite the many difficulties accompanying divorce in the USA, 83 per cent of divorced women and men report their own personal functioning to be better than when they were married, and that they have derived certain personal benefits, such as confidence and self-esteem, from the divorce.[54] This is a sobering statistic indicating that many families function in a way that undermines their members' sense of confidence and worth.

In view of the severity of the emotional pain, and in the light of recent appreciation of the links between emotions and health, it is not surprising to find that both dysfunctional marriages and marriage breakup are accompanied by a deterioration in physical health.

Physical health costs of marriage breakdown

Illness frequently accompanies separation and divorce,[55] and Holmes and Rahe found divorce was second only to death of a spouse as a cause of stress and a contributor to physical illness.[56] The divorced have a worse health outlook than those who are married, single or widowed. It must be remembered that there are marked health differences between well-functioning and poorly functioning families, so it is clear that dysfunction imposes a health toll, just as family breakup does. In those cases where divorce leads to a better adjustment within the post-divorce family, it can be expected that family health will also improve.

Social and communal costs of marriage breakdown

There is no doubt that the current high rate of stress and instability in family life incurs a high social cost. For example, the Ministry of Education in the state of Victoria, Australia, released figures reporting that for each divorce, five school moves resulted. The resulting counselling and interviewing of parents and the disruption to classes and school routines had been identified as a major source of teacher stress.[57] Little attempt has been made to calculate the social and communal costs, but it is known that family breakdown is associated with alcoholism, suicide and mental illness.[58] In Australia there has been an unexpected eruption of violence in connection with the family courts, with the murder of a family court judge in 1980 and the bombing of the homes of two family court judges in 1984. This is the first time in the history of Australia that any such violence has been directed towards law courts. This violence is an indication either of the intense emotion surrounding issues of family life, or the intensity with which some people react to the dissolution of their family or to the judge's failure to agree with their perception of the issues. Whatever the cause, the eruption of such violence against the courts and judges is an alarming event. It is a sign of the disruption in marriages and families invading other vital social institutions.

The public response to breakdown of marriage

In 1985 there were 39,830 divorces in Australia. It is currently estimated that around 35 per cent of all marriages taking place in the 1980s will end in divorce. The number of one-parent families doubled as a proportion of all families from 1969 to 1986, from 3.4 to 6.9 per cent. The cost of the Supporting Parent Benefit has risen dramatically in the last decade. In one-third of new marriages at least one spouse has been married before.

In the USA, the rate of marriage breakup is even higher and at least one in two marriages are expected to break-up. There, 50 per cent of children born in the 1970s are expected to spend time in a one-parent family (the average time being six years) and many have the experience of living in a step-family. In 1980 in the USA 66 per cent of white children lived in the simple family structure of their natural parents who had each been married only once. This situation applied to only 27 per cent of black children.

Marriages do not break down over night or without considerable stress and conflict. The high rates of marriage breakdown indicate high levels of stress in families. In view of the vital roles families perform, this level of stress and breakdown indicates serious social issues. Yet the major public response has been a divorce response only.

The major public realm response has been to provide easier, speedier, more dignified divorce procedures. The imbalance between what is spent on divorce and what is spent to inform, support, resource and strengthen marriages can be interpreted only as a 'divorce solution'. Few in the community would wish to return to a situation where couples who are irrevocably estranged are forced to continue to live together in the empty shell of a marriage. It is no longer acceptable to use legal coercion to force people to remain in demeaning, often violent situations. Yet we do not have to go to the other extreme of assuming that all we need to do is provide easier, smoother, faster divorce and everything else will take care of itself. In fact, new problems are emerging with the new family law acts that were introduced in most states of the USA, beginning with California in 1970. The UK had accepted 'irretrievable breakdown' as the basis of divorce in 1969, and Australia introduced similar laws in 1976. In a recent book Leonore Weitzman has drawn attention to the consequences of these changed laws.

The unintended consequences of the new legislation

In outlining the 'unanticipated, unintended and unfortunate consequences' of the no-fault divorce laws,[59] Weitzman points out how the reformers have recast the psychological context of divorce, but they have also recast the economic consequences of divorce and redefined marriage. She finds that the new approaches have reduced some of the hostility and bitterness surrounding divorce (the psychological context), but the other changes embody some serious difficulties.

Women's economic difficulties increased

One problem is that whereas the new family law acts were intended to do away with bias against women, in fact, at least as far as the Californian Act goes, and there is reason to think the findings apply to other acts, the effect has been that women are worse off. Weitzman describes how in her ten-year study of the new Californian Family Law Act, when she first started coming across cases where women were very poorly served by the new act, she assumed these cases were exceptions. Gradually she came to accept that women were not better off. They were worse off. One reason for this was the tendency of judges to insist that the marital home be sold so that the assets of the marriage could be split. For most marriages, the assets are small and entirely held in the marital home. This meant the woman lost her home, her neighbourhood, her access to friends and her established social life. She could not afford, with her share of the home, to be re-housed at the same standard and had to move to a different and less desirable neighbourhood.

Weitzman coins the term 'new property' to draw attention to the fact that property has changed and that the most valuable assets of a marriage are not in bank accounts and the family home. Women's contributions to their husbands' career were rarely fully recognised. Hence, the 'new property' (superannuation and husband's earning capacity) were considered 'his' assets rather than joint assets for retirement security. It was also assumed that women were able to earn an equal income to the male, and this was simply not the case. Women who for twenty or so years had devoted themselves to making the home and supporting the husband in his career had very little chance of getting any sort of job and absolutely none of a job that supported a standard of living comparable to the pre-divorce standard.

For these women, as Weitzman points out, the rules have been changed in the middle of the game. When they entered marriage it was understood by them, their husbands and the whole society what the contract was: the wife gave up her own career and concentrated on making the home, rearing the children and supporting the husband in his career. The husband concentrated on his job or career and was the major bread-winner. They shared the financial security that he primarily created and the secure and harmonious home life that she primarily created. Suddenly the rules were changed, without warning, so that the wife's right to a share in the husband's financial security was denied. By then it was too late for her to create a career of her own. She was stripped of her assets and left to make it as best she could, while her husband's earning power, if he was a professional man, increased. Treating women 'equally' when they are not equal in the economic world meant women were worse off. The combined effect of the increased number of divorces under the new laws and the economic effects on women led Weitzman to link these laws, as currently administered in the USA, to the increasing poverty of women and children and the widening economic gulf between the sexes.

The redefinition of marriage
Weitzman argues that the new laws have radically redefined

the rights of husbands and wives in marriage. When half of new marriages are expected to end in divorce, the rules for ending marriages affect the rules for contracting marriages. Under these new laws the legal criteria for marriage has moved from fidelity to the traditional marriage contract to individual standards of personal satisfaction. Marriage has been redefined, at least as far as legal dimensions go, from a lifelong commitment to a contingent, time-limited arrangement. The state's role has moved from protecting marriage to facilitating divorce. The no-fault provisions enable a unilateral decision to terminate the marriage. They have moved the power from the one who wants to stay married to the one who wants to divorce.

Weitzman finds that, under these new laws, even parenting is becoming increasingly optional. The lax enforcement of alimony or child maintenance has resulted in the severing of bonds to children and the financial as well as personal abandonment of children. If that phrase seems too harsh, Weitzman would point to the fact that 52 per cent of the children of divorce have not seen their non-custodial parents for over a year. Ten years after the divorce, this rises to over 60 per cent.

Weitzman warns that women's commitment to children has been assumed or taken for granted. But she suggests that as the new laws contain incentives for women to lower their investment in children, women may join men in the flight from children. She warns that as women realise they will not receive preference in custody decisions, that nurturance of children receives no protection in the law, as women face the realities of a competitive job market and the impossible situation of having custody of children but insufficient financial resources to care for them, they may choose to become less invested in children.

A woman who chooses to be a housewife or to put family before work takes a grave risk. She has a 50 per cent chance of being divorced, and without marketable skills. In these ways, Weitzman outlines the powerful disincentives for women, or men, to invest in the partnership or the family or the children.[60] She contrasts two concepts of marriage: a temporary alliance of two separate individuals or a unified partnership where the individual interests and identities are fully merged.

> . . . the new laws confer economic advantages on spouses who invest in themselves at the expense of the marital partnership . . .
> The traditional law embodied the partnership concept of marriage by rewarding sharing and mutual investments in the marital community. Implicit in the new laws, in contrast, are incentives for investing in oneself, maintaining one's separate identity, and being self-sufficient. The new stress is on individual responsibility for one's future, rather than the partnership assumption of joint or reciprocal responsibilities.[61]

She suggests that both women and men may well conclude that one's own career is the only safe investment.

What is most concerning about this trend is that altruistic, 'family-first', co-operative and sharing behaviour is penalised. Individualistic, selfish, personal aggrandisement is rewarded. Further, the whole nature of marriage is changed. For couples beginning their marriage, the co-operation and sharing that were assumed to be the basis of marriages of twenty years ago becomes more difficult. Instead of being able to assume that the fruits of their shared labours will be shared equally, it is all too evident to them that, should serious conflict arise, the one who has guarded his or her private interests best will come out on top. The norms of co-operation, loyalty and sharing that used to apply to marriage and family relationships have been weakened by the technocratic, individualistic bias that underlies these new laws.

The irony of this failure of the new laws to protect marital ties and responsibilities is that at the very time that the law is withdrawing its support for marriage bonds, it is increasingly intervening in work relationships. It is less and less possible for an employer to terminate a person's employment for an arbitrary or unfair reason. The employer must give a series of warnings to the employee and state clearly the nature of the complaint and give the employee help and time to rectify behaviour. The employer's complaints must be of a serious and relevant nature. She or he can no longer dismiss without grounds. At the same time, it is being made increasingly easy for one marriage partner to dismiss the other without reason and without serious negotiation. Nor is such capricious behaviour on the part of one spouse, where it does exist, in any way taken into account in the allocation of the marriage assets.

Until recently, in Australia at least, there was no serious requirement that the non-custodial spouse even pay maintenance to support the children. Financial settlements were routinely made on the basis that the tax-payer would be the prime supporter via Supporting Parent Benefit. The custodial parent, usually the mother, was expected to shoulder the care and supervision of the children, and the non-custodial parent would give minimum support, if he felt like it. If he did not feel like it, the wife and children went without, but the husband was free to start another family and assume extra financial obligations, which would then become a valid reason for not contributing to his first family.

The attempt to solve the very real problems of distress, dysfunction and dissatisfaction in marriage by a divorce policy only is inadequate. To assume that all one needs to do to solve problems of conflict or stress in marriage is to enable the couple to split up and eventually remarry is a mechanistic approach. It assumes that the relationships between family members can be replaced, just as the components of a machine can be replaced to repair faulty functioning: a new set of gears is just as good as the old set, even better if they work properly. This denies the enduring and unique nature of the bonds between human beings, especially the bonds between spouses and between children and parents. It replaces a human approach to life with a technocratic one, reducing individuals to disposable objects.

A child does not want 'a father' she or he wants 'my father', and, as Wallerstein and Kelly document, the longing for the father, even when he has been inattentive and capricious, can persist for many years. There is evidence that the mother is even more significant and irreplaceable.

In 1988 Australia introduced laws that enable child-maintenance payments to be garnished directly from salaries. It is one of the first countries in the world to take such an action. It is a radical change of direction, in which, once again, the law is playing a role in requiring the ties and responsibilities assumed in marriage and child-bearing be honoured. With this law, the community is giving an entirely different message to parents, especially parents contemplating divorce, but in fact to all parents. It is saying that the obligations of parenthood are serious ones and, even when it is inconvenient and difficult, they will be expected to fulfil those obligations.

Weitzman's research indicates how the laws affect, or may affect, couples' commitment to marriage and family. It follows from her work that to assume that tendencies to withdraw investments in marriage and family are inevitable and must continue unabated, without observing the pressures that may be being applied to force this withdrawal is naïve. To proceed to plan future policy as if these forced or incentive-led withdrawals are totally free choices that are insensitive to information or altered incentive is to be worse than naïve. It betrays a lack of reflectiveness, a lack of awareness of the public realm as an active and not always co-operative player in the private choices made by individuals and groups.

The discrepancy between what is spent on the costs of marriage and family dysfunction and breakup and the meagre resources allocated to prevention cannot be understood in any rational allocation of resources. Mr Jim Crawley, director of the Marriage Guidance Council of Western Australia, gives the following example of how ludicrous is the current lack of funding for this area.

> The direct cost of marital breakdown to the Commonwealth Government is such that if my organisation succeeds in helping only 1 per cent of the people who approach us for assistance each year to avoid separation and the need for supporting parent benefits, then we have saved the Commonwealth more than the total amount we receive by way of an annual grant. It costs approximately $70,000 per annum to maintain a branch in a country town; and to offset that amount of government grant three couples would need to be helped avoid separation and Supporting Parent Benefit. These figures are only crude and indicative, but they are sufficiently startling that it is demonstrably irresponsible of the Commonwealth Government to continue to stonewall in the face of the National Marriage Guidance Council of Australia's repeated calls for a thorough and independent review of government policy and practice in this area.[62]

In other words, as the marriage counselling organisations help at least 20–30% of their clients avoid the need for the Supporting Parent Benefit, the government nets a return of $20–$30 for each $1 of the annual grant to these agencies. Crawley objects that in these circumstances it is crazy that his agency has to beg for funds, operate with waiting lists, and cannot service many areas of the state due to lack of funding. The same applies to other states. Despite the significant rises of funding for marriage counselling agencies in 1987/88 and 1988/89, Crawley sees no sign that the government has altered its attitude to the marriage counselling agencies and is developing a reasoned policy initiative in this area. He points out that the increased funds are due to the fact that marriage counselling agencies had reached a crisis point in funding by 1987. The eight constituent organisations of the National Marriage Guidance Council of Australia had closed 25 per cent of the counselling centres they operated due to lack of funds. Further closures were immanent and would have resulted in 40 per cent of all N.M.G.C. centres closing. Hence the 20 per cent increase in funding for 1987/88 was a band-aid measure not a reasoned policy initiative. Crawley finds the refusal of the Commonwealth Government to initiate an independent review of policy in the area of marriage education and marriage counselling (which the N.M.G.C. has been calling for for three years) as further evidence of the Commonwealth Attorney General's Department's complete lack of overall policy in this area.

Crawley cites two other examples of government failure to support marriage and family. One is the Western Australian government's glossy brochure 'Putting families first: a social strategy for WA'. The document does not once mention marriage breakdown as a problem for Western Australian families, though it does contain a great deal about services to help those affected by family breakdown. Several pages are devoted to the needs of women, but none to the needs of men. Numerous references to children appear, but none to the problem of marriage breakdown that 40 per cent of children worry about. There is nothing resembling a comprehensive strategy to *prevent* family breakdown.

Crawley's second example is the story of a couple who

came to the Marriage Guidance Council of Western Australia after experiencing a crisis in their marriage. They had separated and gone to the Family Court for help with the children's custody arrangements where it was suggested to them that in their case it was worth attending counselling to see if a reconciliation was possible. The couple were incredibly angry to discover that to get help to achieve a reconciliation they would be charged a fee whereas the services of the Family Court Counsellor with the process of divorce had been free. The wife protested 'What on earth is this situation saying about the value Australian society places on marriage compared with divorce?'

Further evidence of the need for a more appropriate balance between prevention and attempted band-aid solutions after the problem has escalated comes from the Queensland Task Force on Domestic Violence. Its recently released report included a cost analysis of 20 cases involving domestic violence. The result was a staggering $1.6 million spent on those 20 cases. The N.M.G.C. is trying to arrange the same research to be done on a sample of cases of 'ordinary' marriage breakdown.

8

The Family's Role as Educator Ignored

In chapter 1 the findings of the Coleman Report into Equality of Educational Opportunity were discussed. Apart from finding that schools in the USA did *not* create equality of educational opportunity, the major finding of this major research effort was the weakness of school factors and the strength of family factors in deciding educational success. Yet little has been done to further investigate or utilise the family potential.

The Report inspired a wealth of research and experimentation. Several strands can be discerned. Some teachers and researchers sought to find better ways to make real to poor and minority-group children the ideal of equality. Unfortunately, the UK Educational Priority Areas (EPA) scheme came to little due to lack of finance.[1]

Many accepted Coleman's own conclusion that a new definition of equality of educational opportunity was needed. Equal inputs to schools or groups or individuals could no longer be accepted as a measure of equality of opportunity. Only when schools achieved equal output or achievement for different groups could true equality of educational opportunity be said to be achieved.

Another response was to question whether schools should have any role in levelling out inequalities.

> The strong relationship between the average scores of entering and graduating students suggests that the principal function of the schools is to serve as an allocation and selection agency rather than as an equalizing agency.[2]

A strong debate ensued over whether schools are in fact merely agents to select who will have the opportunity to access the coveted positons in society and who will be allocated to factory fodder and unemployment. Considerable research and debate was provoked by the charge that, in reality, this selection is a major function of schools and that in performing this function schools are agents of social reproduction and supporters of the status quo rather than liberalising agencies. Investigation of how poor students and minority-group students are discriminated against in schooling increasingly included the element of gender as feminist research raised awareness of girls' handicaps in education.

Yet another response was to contest that schools 'achieve nothing'. This, of course, was not what the Coleman Report and other studies had found. In fact, they found the reverse. The evidence indicated that virtually all schools were competent, but that who succeeds and who fails in schools was being decided *outside* the school, especially by family factors.

This response leads to the most amazing outcome of all this research and debate. The factor that was identified over and over again as the key factor, the only factor that had the potential or 'leverage' to lift the achievement of students who were not benefiting from school, the family factor, was completely ignored. The reasons for this remarkable lack of response to such a significant body of research are discussed in a wider context in chapter 10. But before leaving the Coleman Report and its re-analysis, it is important to note several issues that were raised by the original researchers.

Smith used the term 'leverage' in referring to the factors that have the potential to help those who do not benefit from schooling.

With regard to the differences among schools in resources that we conventionally measure and consider in making policy, there are few that give us any leverage over students' achievement. Within the fairly broad boundaries of existing variations, the simple manipulation of per-pupil expenditure or the hiring of more experienced teachers or the instituting of a new curriculum does not lead to dramatic changes in students' verbal achievement. The myth that the reallocation of conventional inputs will lead to a redistribution of achievement outputs can no longer be accepted.[3]

The area where 'leverage' does lie is in the area of family. Families do have potential to enable or to thwart their children's educational achievement. Coleman, in referring to similar data, comments that 'much more radical modifications of the environment are necessary in order to greatly increase achievement of presently low-achieving groups'.[4]

The whole tenor of the Report and its re-analysis was to throw doubt on the possibility of bringing about improvement and change 'within the present framework'. The re-analysis, instead, raises the possibility of influencing home and family contexts. Mosteller and Moynihan summarise the findings of one of the re-analysts (Jenks) as follows:

> ... the least promising approach to raising achievements is to raise [school] expenditures, since the data give little evidence that any widely used school policy or resource has an appreciable effect on achievement score ... radically different policies and approaches might have an impact on achievement ... Although Jenks does not specify, presumably such devices as giving parents funds that can be spent on the private education of their children, or the removal to boarding schools of children from family situations that are unsatisfactory for the purpose of academic and citizenship improvement, or the development of new kinds of schools, would fall within the framework of such radical developments ...
>
> A more promising alternative ... is socio-economic integration.
>
> The most promising alternative would be to alter the way in which parents deal with their children at home. Unfortunately, it is not obvious how this could be done. Income maintenance, family allowances, etc., seem a logical beginning.[5]

These few passages are virtually the only ones in the re-analysis where 'doing something' at the home and family level is mentioned, and then it is raised and dropped within the space of five lines. It was not even suggested that perhaps we needed to understand more about what were the family factors that enabled some children to succeed in school. It was not suggested that, as some parents seemed to know something that the whole educational and research established did not know, perhaps it would be an idea to consult parents. What do the parents who enable their children to succeed in school understand of why their children succeed? What do they see themselves to be doing and to be trying to achieve? What help do they want from schools or from other institutions? What difficulties do they experience? And what of those parents whose children are failing: what are their understandings and difficulties? What help or changes do they want? And what exactly is going on in the homes where children develop educational competence that is not going on in other homes?

There seems to have been a complete failure to *imagine* any way of altering 'the way parents deal with their children at home'. The only suggestions are to revert immediately to the public sphere, 'Income maintenance, family allowances, etc.', or even more dramatically to ignore and bypass families, 'the removal to boarding schools of children from family situations that are unsatisfactory'.

The failure of imagination is partly explained by the references to the need for 'much more radical interventions'. It seems as if there was a brief moment of recognition that things needed to be done differently, and then a flight from such a notion as being 'radical'. It did not seem to occur to anyone to search, not for 'radical' interventions, but for simple and effective ones. It may in fact be that what is needed are relatively simple modifications of schooling and other formal programs plus *a major change of attitude within our institutions to the significance of families and family factors*. Indeed, it seems that this very lack of appreciation of family factors (or possibly the denial of the private realm) in the research community prevented them from being able to respond to or accept the major finding of one of the most significant and expensive research projects of the last quarter-century.

It is important to discover what it was that made the whole research establishment shy away from the significant discovery they had made, because children's futures depend on a better response. One reason is that the researchers saw themselves as researching on behalf of schools and having no responsibility beyond that arena. They therefore looked for correlations related to school factors and failed to notice correlations beyond that realm. Another way of conceiving this is that there is a split between the public and private realms.[6] It seems that the researchers could not comprehend that the factors that determined a child's success in school did not lie in the formal, public institution with responsibility for education, but in the informal, private domain of families. Secondly, it was unthinkable, apparently, to breach the chasm dividing public and private and to 'do something about the way parents deal with their children at home', even something as simple and unthreatening as attempting to understand what were the family factors that facilitated or thwarted the ability to benefit from schooling. Whatever the explanation, it indicates a powerful ideology is operating to blind serious and thoughtful researchers to such obvious data.

Families and alternatives in education

An example of the tendency to focus on the public and ignore the private can be seen in a recent article by James Coleman in which he returns to some of the themes of his earlier research on the impact of families on education. Coleman himself focuses on the public aspects of the phenomena and opts for a solution in the public realm. Before exploring this further it is necessary to outline his argument about the relationship of families and schools.

Social capital
A major theme of Coleman's article is his proposed concept of 'social capital'.

> What I mean by social capital in the raising of children is the norms, the social networks, and the relationships between adults

131

and children that are of value for the child's growing up. Social capital exists within the family, but also outside the family, in the community.[7]

Coleman gives as an example of social capital the case of a school district where parents buy the books for their children's schooling. It was found that some Asian families bought two books: one was for the mother so that she could help the child with schoolwork. The mother is usually not well educated: hence there is little 'human capital'. But her intense concern for the child's schooling and her willingness to put time and effort into helping the child succeed means that she is creating a high level of what Coleman calls 'social capital'. So Coleman is extending the original notion of 'capital' meaning physical or financial resources to 'human capital' meaning human resources, especially the developed human resources of education, creativity, leadership and entrepreneurship, and finally to 'social capital'.

Social changes and schools
Coleman outlines the social changes that have affected families and schools over recent centuries: especially noting that mass formal schooling is less than a century old and apparently arose concurrently with the movement of productive activity from the home, farm and local shop to the office and factory. This was accompanied by the movement of men from the homes and the growth of public schooling, presumably to replace the role played by men in socialising youngsters and teaching them trades and skills. Another 'constructed' entity also arose in this process, the modern corporation. More recently women have begun an exodus from the home, which parallels that of men, almost a century later in time (see Figure 1). As the modern corporation has absorbed the energies and activities of men and women, the family has become a kind of backwater of society, cut off from the mainstream.

Figure 1. Percentage of Male Labour Force in Agriculture
1810–1982 and Percentage of Women Not Employed in Paid
Labour Force 1890–1982

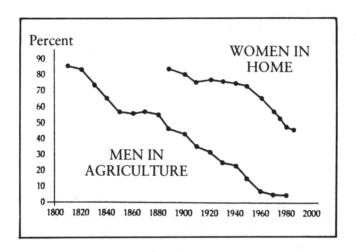

Source. Based on data from US Bureau of the Census 1975,
Table 182–282, for proportion of labour force on farms
1900–1970 and proportion of labour force in agriculture,
1800–90; and table D49–62 for proportion of females in
labour force 1890–1970. US Bureau of the Census 1984 is
used to bring series up to 1980.
Table compiled by J. Coleman. Reprinted with permission,
Educational Researcher.

The world of 'corporate actors' has become the 'real world', but it does not include children, the old, the sick or those we call dependants. As families have become less capable of being the primary welfare system (due to lack of finance and lack of adults in the home), welfare has been moved, not to the corporation but to the state. The problem is that the state is not good at humane welfare, and it is almost impossible for the state to be involved in welfare without creating an incentive for the problem it is attempting to solve. Coleman outlines a number of areas where state involvement has meant reduced incentives for parental responsibility and weakened parental and family ties and responsibilities.

We now have the opportunity to develop another constructed institution, analogous to the school, to replace the (possibly even more fundamental) vacuum left by the absence of mothers from children's lives. Coleman notes that an awareness already exists for such an institution in calls for full-time, year-round child-care. He sounds a note of warning that what is demanded and what is needed may not be quite the same thing. In particular, Coleman is aware that the kinds of inputs that this new social institution will make need to be different from those made by schools and similar to those made by homes in that they will create attitudes, effort and conceptions of self that enable youth to succeed in school and as adults. These attitudes, efforts and conceptions of self are built through attention, personal interest, intensity of involvement, persistence and continuity over time, and intimacy.

Weight given to the private realm

Most of Coleman's analysis is convincing and sound but, finally, he fails to give sufficient weight to the factors in the private realm. His analysis is marred by a bias towards the public realm as the only 'real' realm. He has assumed that the only solution will be one that is centred in the public realm and that strengthens the public realm. He fails to see the positive possibilities within families. There is a tendency to assume that families are passive and unintelligent non-actors in these massive social shifts, and their decisions are not amenable to reason or information.

Coleman fails to explore those *family factors* that his own research has highlighted. How and why are Asian families so much stronger than non-Asian families, in the USA at least, in their capacity to create the attitudes, effort and conception of self that leads to high educational achievement? Are these Asian families going to adapt to the individualism that has weakened the social capital in so many non-Asian families? Is it possible that, given information on the effects of excessive individualism on their children's development, parents may choose to re-order their priorities and give time with children a greater value?

Another weakness of Coleman's analysis is the failure to consider consulting families on these issues. How is it that, often with low educational levels themselves, without government incentive or expert guidance, in competition with the seduction of TV and despite social pressures that are thought to be invincible, some families have discovered and developed the ways to create 'social capital' and enable their children to be successful in school? We should be studying these families. We need to learn from them.

A few small studies indicate that families do not wish to choose the future that Coleman outlines (another institution, analagous to the school to replace the place of mothers in the home).[8] Perhaps the studies, being small, are quite out of touch with the mainstream, but where is the large-scale research into family opinion on these vital issues?

The 'inevitable' future?

Yet another weakness of Coleman's analysis of families and education is his acceptance that current trends must continue unchecked, and that the future will be determined by market forces and new technology rather than by the decisions of human beings made in the light of shared information and mutual interests. One writer has parodied this common attitude by saying: 'it is time now to conform to the future.' Under old ideologies, people accepted misery and oppression 'as the will of God' or as only right and just for people in their social position. The critical sociologists have identified the 'conform now to the future' position as modern ideology. It assumes that the future is in the hands of the 'gods' of technology and market forces, and humans can do nothing but submit. An alternative view is that the future is created by human decision and will.

Coleman's own research offers alternative lines of investigation. He gives the example of the Catholic high schools, where significantly higher social capital exists than in most public or other private high schools (see Figure 2), but again he fails to explore the implications of this data. In the USA, Catholic high schools have slightly higher achievement rates than either public or private high schools. More significantly, they have much lower drop-out rates. Those most likely to benefit from the lower drop-out rates are those most likely to drop out in other schools, such as black students and children from one-parent families. (The only other schools that compare with the low drop-out rates being achieved in Catholic high schools are those schools run by other religious groups.) Coleman attributes this lower drop-out rate to 'a different relation of the school to the parental community'.

> We concluded that the community surrounding the Catholic school, a community created by the church, was of great importance in reducing the dropouts among students at risk of dropping out. In effect this church-and-school community, with its social networks and its norms about what teenagers should and should not do, constituted social capital beyond the family that aided both family and school in the education of the family's children.[9]

The Catholic high schools (and the non-Catholic religiously homogeneous schools) are characterised by much closer links between the school and the parents and by closer links *between* the parents. The most significant factor related to the lower drop-out rates was that if teenage students were friends, it was likely that their parents knew each other. The Catholic schools supported the parental values and attitudes.

The fact that some schools have lower drop-out rates than others suggests how all schools may be more effective. All schools have a great potential to encourage and facilitate networks among parents. Parents have a great potential to

Figure 2. Drop-out Rates (Spring of sophomore year to spring of senior year)

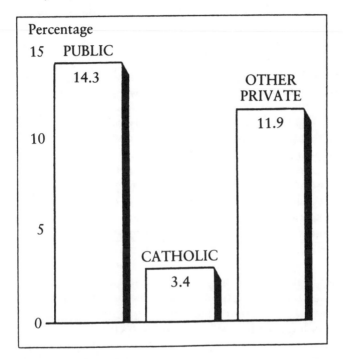

Reprinted with permission, *Educational Researcher*.

develop such networks when they are aware of their importance. It is the overlooking of such simple applications of Coleman's research and the too ready acceptance of the need for a new public institution that I question. It is possible that the essential features, the type of community around the school, are acceptable to — even desired by — parents in the public schools, and capable of reconstruction in a different setting.

The limits of the public institution

In proposing that we may need a new institution to take over the role of child-care and child-rearing, Coleman warns of the danger that these consciously designed institutions may be inferior to those they replaced. Another danger he foresees is that nothing will replace the old 'institutions' of family and neighbourhood, and 'children will grow up in an environment consisting primarily of commercial recreation (music, clothes, thrill-generating activities) and populated primarily by other children'. However, Coleman presents the opportunity facing society of creating a new institution, or institutions, designed expressly for child-rearing, which can do 'better than a system in which most childrearing occurred as a by-product'.[10] He refers back to the findings of the Equality of Opportunity research that the vital inputs that come *only* from homes, *attitudes*, *effort* and *conception of self* cannot be compensated for by more school-type inputs: *opportunities*, *demands* and *rewards*. Hence the new institution that is created must be able to provide the home-type input.

The question is, of course, whether a public institution can deliver the qualities that create the home inputs: 'attention, personal interest, some persistence and continuity over time, and a certain degree of intimacy'. Personal interest means the 'irrational' bond that links family members to one another. Parents have an interest in their own child that is unlike the interest that teachers can develop for their students. Persistence over time implies loyalty and commitment. Certainly teachers love their students and show interest in them. But no one expects teachers to forgo promotion to stay with a particular class. Persistence over time is possible only with a different form of rationality to that of the public, institutionalised world. The rationality of family life is based on a lifelong commitment of love. The rationality of the public world is based on the 'contract', and Durkheim has doubted whether the purely contractual society can survive, because it reduces society to a 'dust' of individuals. The private world says, 'till death us do part'. The public rationality says, 'This is all very good. But you understand that if I get a better offer, I owe it to myself to accept it.'

Blum reported that love is the most important factor

stressed by superior and good families.[11] In this they were referring to the heart of this different rationality that predominates in the private world of the family, one quite at odds with the 'value-free' rationality of the public world. So in advocating the creation of a new institution to replace the social capital that is leaching out of families and neighbourhoods, Coleman assumes what is at issue: whether public institutions can provide the inputs that have, in the past, been made only by the private realm.

Failure to note the intrusions into the private world

In his 1987 article, Coleman, in predicting the growth of a new institution, nowhere shows any awareness of systematic pressures on the private world. It is premature to predict the demise of the private world without analysing whether it is being assailed by forces that could be modified or transformed. An alternative approach is to demand that the public world be accountable to the values of the private world. Coleman's own research in the 1960s showed that there is a limit to the power and efficacy of the public realm. There is real power and influence emanating from the private realm. There are inputs from the private world that the public world cannot replace. The public world must take cognisance of the private realm and be open to adapting its own rationality to the demands of the private, rather than insisting always that the private adapt to the public.

There is room to study and experiment with different relationships between schools and families, churches and families, neighbourhood groups and families and local government and families and to discover whether social capital can be recreated without inventing a new institution. Perhaps a different organisation of the schools can strengthen the family and community links that Coleman has reported as being so vital to school effectiveness.

Twenty-three years later, it seems as if the whole EEO research project may as well not have happened, at least as far as the major finding is concerned. Despite the clear statement that the answer to the major problems of education (the children who resist learning) does not lie in increasing school expenditures or in manipulating factors such as class sizes, curriculum, teacher-pupil ratios, these very factors have continued to command an undiminished share of resources and of psychic and research energy. Despite the finding that we need to do something about the way parents deal with their children at home, there has been little interest from the educational research community in this area.

9

The Family and Poverty — the Links Denied

In the same year as the Coleman Report was published another report appeared linking family factors to poverty. A comparison of these reports reveals some interesting parallels.

Family factors and the war on poverty

Daniel Patrick Moynihan, now the senior US senator for New York, was a member of the cabinet or sub-cabinet of presidents Kennedy, Johnson, Nixon and Ford. He is the only person in US history to have served in four successive administrations. In 1965 he raised the issue of family as a factor in the economic and social disadvantage of black Americans. Basically, Moynihan was pointing to evidence that increases in unemployment were associated with increases in measures of family dysfunction such as rates of separation and divorce and numbers of families on welfare. More recent research has shown similar correlations for the state of the economy and rates of child and wife bashing. Moynihan noted that from the early 1950s through to the 1960s, the link between the state of the economy and family factors at first seemed chained together with remarkably high correlations, then in the 1960s the correlations weakened, disappeared and finally emerged as their own opposite. As he says 'the data went blooey'.[1] It was as if a drug tested to be effective worked for ten or fifteen years and suddenly did not work at all.

> This came to be known as the 'scissors'. Plotted on a graph, the various rates would go up and down as if chained together, but then the relationship weakened, disappeared, and reappeared as its own opposite. Without exception the indicators of social stress — separation, welfare — would go *up* while the economic

indicator — unemployment — would now go down. These patterns were to be found both for whites and blacks, but most strikingly for blacks.

I thereupon moved to a large, and obviously debatable, hypothesis. Employment, in a sense, was an easy answer to what social problems we might have. Full employment was then thought a feasible goal and was on display in just about every nation of Western Europe. But what if employment had lost its power to determine social arrangements? What if deprivation, discrimination, had gone on too long? What if disorganisation now sustained itself?[2]

Kenneth Clark, a noted black scholar, had recently published his study of ghetto life, *Dark Ghetto*, which supported the line of thinking Moynihan was developing.

Not only is the pathology of the ghetto self-perpetuating, but one kind of pathology breeds another. The child born in the ghetto is more likely to come into a world of broken homes and illegitimacy; and this family and social instability is conducive to delinquency, drug addiction and criminal violence. Neither instability nor crime can be controlled by police vigilance or by reliance on the alleged deterring forces of legal punishment, for the individual crimes are to be understood more as symptoms of the contagious sickness of the community itself than as the result of inherent criminal or deliberate viciousness.[3]

This was the background to what came to be known as the Moynihan Report: *The Negro Family: The Case for National Action*. In a brief document, a mere forty-eight pages in length, Moynihan argued that the gains of the Civil Rights era were in danger of being eroded. Even while the nation was making triumphant progress in securing the Civil Rights of black Americans, dismantling the segregation of the mainly rural South, there were signs of growing social disorganisation in the North and elsewhere. Moynihan pointed to the main indicator of this social disorganisation as the growth of one-parent families living on welfare and claimed that if this trend was not halted and reversed, it was likely that the Civil Rights revolution would be aborted.

My hypothesis was that a group in which a very large proportion of children are raised in the generalized disorder of welfare dependency will have a disproportionate number of persons not equal to their opportunities. In consequence there would not be equal results [from equal laws or equal opportunities].

Absent equal results it would be judged that there never had been equal opportunity or, alternatively, that equal opportunity did not work. Either way, the historic achievement of that moment would be in jeopardy, could be lost.[4]

The report went to the White House on 4 May, and a month later it provided the basis of a presidential address at Howard University. The President spoke on the theme that it is not enough 'just to open the gates of opportunity. All our citizens must have the ability to walk through the gates.'[5] To pursue these issues, President Johnson declared a White House conference of scholars and experts, outstanding black leaders and government officials. The theme was to be: To Fulfil These Rights. The conference was held in June 1966, but events in the meantime so altered the proposed thrust of the gathering that Moynihan declared it a 'no-conference'. The delegates never even met in plenary session, and the topic of the family had been struck from the agenda.

President Johnson's address at Howard University in June 1965 had been followed by the signing of the Voting Rights Act of 1965 on 6 August. The Watts riots in Los Angeles took place in August of that same year, adding a new dimension to the Civil Rights struggle. Rebuttals of the Moynihan Report appeared. Moynihan was declared to be operating out of a new kind of 'subtle racism'. He was accused of having demeaned and stigmatised the black family and having failed to recognise its strengths as a healthy adaptation to the situation of black Americans. He had imposed, or so it was charged, a middle-class, white model of family onto the ebullient, matriarchal families preferred by blacks. Moynihan reports that 'point by point the propositions were considered and rejected as not true or at best not proven and that was the end of the matter'. By the time the White House conference was convened, both the White House and the Civil Rights community were determined that nothing should come of it.

The suddenness of the change of attitude is particularly

evident in light of the fact that prior to the presidential address the report had been read to the principal Civil Rights leaders of the time. Moynihan narrates that 'Each in turn was quite transported by propositions that a year later, each, save one, would quite reject'.[6] Martin Luther King Jnr, the exception referred to above, disliked the turn the conference took and retired to his room. Moynihan discloses that 'he was personally gracious to me at a time when this could be done only at some risk'. King spoke publicly several times on the issue of family, agreeing with Moynihan that family issues were central to Civil Rights issues and to the future well-being of the black community. Specifically excluding King, Moynihan narrates that there was 'seemingly no untruth to which some would not subscribe if there appeared to be the least risk of disapproval from the groupthink of the moment. This was notably so among the churchmen.'

Subject dropped but trends continue
In 1972 Moynihan returned to his theme that the historic achievements of the Civil Rights era were in danger of being lost. He noted a strange paradox, a movement both forwards and backwards for blacks in the USA. First he drew attention to a significant achievement. One cohort of black families (two-parent families outside the South where the head was under thirty-five years) were earning incomes equal to white families. This was a magnificent achievement for the Civil Rights movement. It was the first moment of income equality in three centuries. Yet the achievement was undermined because the number of black families on welfare had also increased rapidly. It became evident later that, as a group, blacks were worse off in relation to whites at the end of the 1970s than at the beginning. Moynihan reports this as another first. It is probably the first decade in which income equality between whites and blacks actually *went backwards*. In his 1972 article, Moynihan declares that this downward movement of blacks on welfare was being denied with fury, and he asserted that it was evident that 'poverty is now inextricably linked with family structure'.[7]

By 1981 it was becoming clear that half the children then being born were likely to live in a female-headed family before their eighteenth birthday. The rate of single parent-hood was expected to be higher in low-income and minority groups. In fact it was expected that 75 per cent of children from deprived minority groups would have the experience of living in a one-parent family, while 'only' 40 per cent of majority children would be affected in this way. One third of all children being born were likely to live in a one-parent family receiving welfare payments before their eighteenth birthday (precisely the figures estimated by Moynihan in 1965, but which were rejected at the time as being 'stupefy-ing' and, presumably, therefore also stupid).

In 1984 Arthur Norton and Paul Glick made independent estimates of rates of single-parenthood and forecast that 60 per cent of children born in 1984 can expect to live in a one-parent family before the age of eighteen years, a marked rise in only three years. At the same time Mary Jo Bane and David Ellwood calculated that one-third of white youths and three-quarters of black youths then aged seventeen had spent some time in a single-parent family. They projected that in ten years these proportions will likely rise to 46 per cent for white youth and 87 per cent for black youth.

In other words, the data that had indicated to Moynihan that the war on poverty would be thwarted by family dys-function in the black community came to be the statistics of the *whole* American population. Meanwhile, the black com-munity's figures deteriorated to be five times worse than they had been in 1965.[8]

In 1983 a report of the Civil Rights Commission expressed concern over the number of one-parent families and the num-ber of teenage illegitimate pregnancies, 'of children having children'. Moynihan sees this as a sudden emergence of the topics of family and 'children having children' as acceptable in general public policy discussions.[9] However, he is clearly disappointed that in the meantime, 'not only did we do noth-ing, we learned nothing'. As the black scholar Eleanor Holmes Norton, of Georgetown University, commented, 'the search for workable solutions' was delayed 'for a generation'.[10]

Moynihan is particularly distressed at another result of the denial of those trends that were apparent in 1965, and which he identified as inevitably leading to the creation of an urban minority under class if they were allowed to continue. It is now claimed by some 'small government' proponents that welfare programs inevitably create a demand for the services they provide. They are an incentive to increase the problem they are supposed to alleviate. Hence Charles Murray attributes the growing urban under class to government welfare. The truth is (and it is documented by Moynihan's contentious report) that the trends were evident *before* these programs were introduced or even thought of.[11]

The silencing of debate

Moynihan's perception that his report created a flurry of comment that quickly subsided, although the trends he reported did not,[12] is supported by Mary Jo Bane. In a 1984 paper on household composition and poverty, Bane reported that in the early 1980s half the population of poor were women living alone or members of households headed by women. She traces the development of this situation from Moynihan's original report in 1965 and finds a process of denial, encounter and *flight*. The controversy over the Moynihan Report 'led to the avoidance by scholars and policy makers of the whole problem, which has gotten steadily and dramatically worse since the time of the report'.[13]

In agreeing that the issue was barred from intellectual debate, the black scholar Glen Loury wrote, 'It is hard to overstate the significance of this constraint on discourse among blacks.'[14] Other black scholars, Wilson and Aponte, write that Moynihan's earlier analysis was prophetic, but that 'serious scholarship was curtailed during the aftermath of the controversy'.[15]

Re-opening the family issue

At the time of the Moynihan controversy, Martin Luther King spoke publicly on the issue saying:

> It is appropriate that a Negro discuss the subject [of the dignity of family life] because for no other group in American life is the matter of family life more important than to the Negro. Our very survival is bound up with it.[16]

Suddenly, in the 1980s, black scholars are returning to this theme. In 1983 Benjamin Hooks, Executive Director of the National Association for the Advancement of Coloured People, stated that, 'finding ways to end the precipitous slide of the black family is one of the most important items on the civil rights agenda today'. He went on,

> We can talk all we want about school integration; we can file suits to have more black role models in the classroom and in administrative positions to have a cross-fertilization of ethnic cultures and background. But if the child returns home to a family devoid of the basic tenets necessary for his discipline, growth and development, the integrated school environment must fail.[17]

In 1985 Loury wrote that 'many people now concede that not all problems of blacks are due to discrimination, and that they cannot be remedied through civil rights strategies or racial politics'.[18] In the spring of 1985, Eleanor Holmes Norton wrote in the *New York Times*

> Some argue persuasively that the female-headed family is an adaptation that facilitates coping with hardship and demographics. This seems undeniable as an explanation but unsatisfactory as a response. Are we willing to accept an adaptation that leaves the majority of black children under the age of 6 — the crucial foundation years — living in poverty?[19]

It also leaves women with an impossible task of being the sole income-provider and attempting also to provide adequate nurture for young children.

William Raspberry noted the temptation of the black middle class to abandon the growing under class. Declaring that the middle class are 'helpless, idea-less witnesses to a near-total social breakdown', Raspberry outlines the problem of unsocialised youngsters:

> The youngsters most in need of help seem least ready for it. They lack the basic skills and, more dismayingly, the basic attitudes that would make them attractive even as entry-level employees. They don't know how to seek the help they need, and worse, they positively frighten those who feel the urge to offer help.[20]

147

In 1985, Dorothy Height, president of the National Council of Negro Women, published an article in *Ebony*, 'What must be done about children having children?' She reported that it was common in former times for girls to marry early and to have babies very young. The current situation is different in that *now the majority of black children are born to single teen mothers*. She supports Eleanor Holmes Norton in saying that the situation is a crisis. 'It must be regarded as a natural catastrophe in our midst, a threat to the future of the Black people without equal.'[21] Moynihan also reports a black publication arguing that 'we cannot wait for the larger society to act . . . The black community has to push society and its youth and itself'.[22] Such an attitude is required of all groups wishing to live by their own values rather than those imposed on them by the public and technocratic realms.

The similar fates of the Coleman and Moynihan reports
The reason why a short article by Moynihan, intended for a readership of about two dozen people, should first have gained such public exposure and then should have aroused such controversy is cause for some speculation. Why it was universally rejected, and then twenty years later found to be 'prophetic' both in its accuracy of prediction and in directing attention to a vital area of concern for public policy is puzzling.

Moynihan himself quotes Mary Jo Bane's interpretation that the educational and employment efforts required in response to his analysis were 'just too hard'.

> The programs that do seem to work for the chronically poor, like supported work, are very expensive and their successes have been small. The programs that work . . . also seem to require a degree of discipline and motivation that liberals have been unable to enforce and clients to demand; it is, after all, easier for both sides to slack off.[23]

Moynihan seems to accept this as a reasonable explanation, but it hardly fits. If the problem was merely that the issues were too hard to address, why was that never claimed?

Such an explanation fails to account for the vilification to which Moynihan himself was subjected. He was smeared as a racist, which is a patently untrue accusation, for his writings are marked by a consistently democratic spirit and wide compassion. Yet, in the sense that the vital issues raised by Moynihan were universally avoided by the research and academic communities, it can only be concluded that these communities accepted the charge that Moynihan *was* a racist. Further, they accepted that it was racist even to explore the issues he had raised of family factors, family structures and poverty. Or perhaps they were merely aware that to explore these issues laid one open to similar vilification.

When the fate of the Moynihan Report is placed alongside the Coleman Report of the same year, 1965, some striking parallels emerge. The reports are on similar topics, in one case the salience of family to education, in the other the salience of family to the economy. In both cases the reports indicate that major public programs will be ineffective without certain inputs from the private sector, especially families. In both cases it seems to have been the finding of the salience of family that was either enraging or unacceptable.

In both cases the findings were avoided. In the case of the Coleman Report the findings received immense publicity and discussion. It has been called 'a contribution to the study of American intergroup relations second only to Myrdal's *American Dilemma*.[24] Yet its major discovery, of the links between family factors and educational achievement, was ignored. In the case of the Moynihan Report the findings first aroused furious controversy, then were quickly agreed to be in error, and immediately forgotten. As if by unspoken agreement, the subject was not raised again until Moynihan himself returned to it twenty-one years after the original report. By this time it was evident his projections were correct. In view of these similarities it seems unlikely that the fate of the two reports is totally unconnected.

The failure of the public policy and research communities to respond to these reports is actually the most interesting aspect of the whole saga, and one most likely to throw light on the processes that currently determine social policy, in particular the contradiction between clear evidence of the significance of families and the failure of the public realm to accord them that significance.

It is now agreed that family breakdown is one of the main contributors to poverty, but there is little more interest in investigating ways to prevent family breakdown as one of the strategies against poverty than when Moynihan first issued his report. At a recent Melbourne conference on child poverty, prevention of marital breakdown was not even mentioned in reports of the conference. Another aspect of the link between family issues and poverty is the withdrawal of economic support for families.

Withdrawal of economic support from families

In Australia, declining economic and government support for families over the last fifteen years is evident in the falling values of family allowances. Bettina Cass, who headed the Commonwealth Government's Social Security Review in 1986, found that families with dependent members were significantly worse off compared with single and 'unencumbered' persons than they had been ten years previously. This is largely due to the deterioration in the real level of family income support that resulted from failure to index family allowances and made them 30 per cent lower in real value in 1986 than they were in 1976. Despite the fact that in the 1930s Australia was a world pioneer in introducing Child Endowment (payments to parents to assist them in the expenses incurred in child-rearing), by 1986 Australia had fallen to being the third lowest of eighteen OECD countries in terms of the value of tax-relief and cash transfers made to families to support them in their child-rearing work.[25]

In the USA economic support for families has likewise fallen. Daniel Patrick Moynihan points out that in 1948 in the USA three-quarters of the income of a family of four on a median income was exempt from federal income tax. The amount of income not subject to income tax was roughly equal to the cost of rearing one child for one year. In 1983 less than one-third of the median income of a family of four was tax-exempt. In 1948 the US tax-exemption threshold for a family of four was $600. If that tax-exemption was to have the same value in current-day terms it would now equal about $5600. In fact, the personal exemption level has risen only to $1000. A US treasury official, Eugene Stuerle, has commented, 'By any measure, this decline in the personal exemption has been the largest single change in the income tax [structure] in the post-war era.'[26]

Moynihan draws attention to a flattening of the tax structure in the US. In 1948 upper-income families paid marginal tax rates of 80 per cent and more, rising to 92 per cent in 1952, but these were down to 50 per cent in 1982. Meanwhile, inflation had pushed more and more low-income families into the taxable range, and the percentage of Social Security tax (for which there are no personal exemptions) rose steadily. An American family of four on a median income paid about 4.4 per cent of its income to the federal government in tax in 1948 and 18 per cent in 1982.

In Australia, likewise, the tax system has been changed over the past decade to favour individuals rather than families.

> The tax system penalises families with children at every level of income, particularly single income and large families . . .
> The amount of income tax imposed on a family with four children living on average weekly earnings increased 435 per cent over the last ten years while wages have increased only 135 per cent.[27]

Because Australia has no provision at all for income splitting, a $40,000 single-income family pays 30 per cent more tax than two $20,000 incomes. Between 1981 and 1986 the value of payments to average families (Family Allowance, Dependent Spouse Rebate and Dependent Child Rebate) fell $417 for a two-child family and $648 for a three-child family. The situation of large families is quite severe. 79 per cent of Australian families with four children have equivalent incomes less than average weekly earnings.

Proposals to index family allowances were opposed by the Australian Institute of Family Studies, which showed that a family of four (two parents and two children), needed an income of $42,900 to have a similar standard of living to a single person on $24,000. A family with three children would need an income of $50,000 to equal the living standard of a single person on $23,500. Hence it was argued that the proposed levels of indexing were far too low, and that, in any case, compensation for the costs of child-rearing should be a right of *all* parents. The Institute considered that such compensation should definitely not be seen as part of the welfare package, nor carry any implication of being a 'handout'.

In fact, indexation was introduced, but with a higher ($50,000) threshold. This was in line with what the majority of Australians thought fair according to a poll conducted by the Institute. It seems Australians believe that compensation for the costs of child-rearing is essential, but it would be unjust and wasteful for a rich man to receive the same benefits as poorer families. This is particularly so when much of society's wealth is inherited and largely untaxed.

It comes as a surprise to realise that in spite of rhetoric about families, and despite the fact that they are supposed to be an election issue, the trend to remove financial supports from families has not yet been reversed.

Although the *Fair Go for Families* document of 1986 won wide support the authors insist that in the intervening years things have become even worse for families and hence *Fair Go for Families II* is in preparation. The authors lay the blame first on the inequitable tax system, then on the escalating cost of housing and rent (housing having become an investment commodity), the high interest rates on houses, the rising costs of caring for children (only a small part of which is covered by the Family Allowance) and the tax traps that make it so difficult for families to get off welfare once they have been forced onto it. They point to current rates of child poverty as evidence that, economically, matters continue to deteriorate for families.

Perhaps the greatest indicator of the public realm's overlooking of families is the failure to count work in the home as part of the national economy. The major work of the nation just doesn't count, and the people who perform it are deemed to be 'not working'.

Failure to recognise work in the home

More work is done in the home than in the entire workforce, yet it is not counted as part of the national economy. Dr

Duncan Ironmonger, director of the Centre for Applied Research into the Future at Melbourne University, bases this finding on surveys undertaken in the late 1970s in which it was found that within households an average of fifty-four hours was spent in cooking, cleaning, laundry, shopping and child-care. Over all the households in Australia this totalled over 200 million hours of housework being done each week. 'The evidence is that Australian households supplied more work for their own purposes than they supplied for the whole economy', Dr Ironmonger said. Dr Ironmonger calculated a monetary value for this work at the rate of $2.80 per hour, the average wage per hour for a woman in the workforce in 1975–76, plus the costs of materials used. In this way he values work in the home in that year at $47 billion dollars. The Gross National Product for that year was only $60 billion. It can be seen that 30 per cent of the Gross Domestic Product is contributed by the household, yet this contribution is not included in the national statistics.

In more recent research Dr Ironmonger has calculated the value of work in the home based on the actual value of production that occurs there. This is more accurate and shows that production in the home is worth at least 50 per cent of the market economy and possibly outweighs the total productive activity of the latter realm. He writes, 'Collectively the household is a far larger industry than any other sector of the "market" economy. Australian households actually produce about three times the output of Australia's manufacturing industry; or ten times the GDP of Australia's much publicised mining industry . . . How can such a vast amount of production be omitted from our National Accounts?'[28]

Obviously, using the model of the market economy as the whole economy is wrong, as Dr Ironmonger has so clearly demonstrated. On what 'rational' basis can it be right to fail to count the major work of the nation and to deem those performing it to be 'not working'? It is a particularly ironic oversight by economists who are expected to be able to count. It is doubly ironic when we recall that the word economy derives from the Greek word for 'management of the household'. Unpaid work in the home, carried out on the basis of altruistic motives of concern, love, care for others has just as much effect on the whole economy as work done for money. But if it is never counted, its contribution cannot be acknowledged or valued, nor will it be noticed that the contribution is being withdrawn until such gross damage is done that it may be difficult to repair.

Failure to count work in the home is an appalling and embarrassing oversight by economists and it has resulted in a totally deficient image of the economy and has contributed to the inadequate view of society discussed in chapter 10. Once the productive activity of the home is taken into account, the dominance of the formal sector recedes and it can be seen that the market economy is in fact only one part of the whole, and a part that depends utterly on the informal sector and on the natural world. Henderson has suggested a much more accurate image of the total productive system of an industrial society as a three-layer cake with icing. (See Figure 3.) Each layer of the economy is seen to rest on, and to depend on, the layers beneath it. The monetarised economy can be seen to be only the top two layers of the cake and to depend utterly on the non-monetarised 'counter-economy' of the family and neighbourhood which in turn rests on nature's layer — the basis of all.[29]

The failure to consider and calculate the value of work done in the home, in the private informal realm, means that there is no status for that realm or that work. It also means that the public realm assumes that the private realm, or aspects of the private realm, can be done away with and nothing will be lost. Basic errors can be made and are being made because the contribution of the private realm was never accounted for and placed on the balance sheet for all to see. The deficits becoming apparent in the public educational institutions are an example of precisely this type of failure to take into account.

No public recognition or image of family

Failure to count work in the home as part of the national economy is only the tip of the iceberg of the many ways we ignore the contribution of the informal, private domain. The American researcher and expert on child development Urie

Bronfenbrenner has been urgently stating that we need more status for parenting. He notes, for example, that an experiment in the provision of more flexible work hours has not resulted in parents using the added time in parenting roles. The added time was devoted instead to gym and similar pursuits. Bronfenbrenner perceives that a change in such trends can come only from added status for parenting. The lack of status is directly tied to this tendency of the public to ignore the private. Status is visibility in the public domain. Yet we rarely see on the media anything of the sensitive, complex, amusing, thoroughly challenging process of rearing a child. It is difficult to have status for family life when it has such little visibility in the public realm. And without status it is difficult to see how it can achieve increased priority.

Feminism and work in the home

All too often, feminists have joined the male, public, disparagement of child-care and work in the private sphere and have embraced the current perception that work (paid work in the public sphere, even if it is tedious, menial, frivolous or exploitative) is of greater value than work in family and neighbourhood. However, increasingly, the ignoring and denigration of work in the home is being perceived as a feminist issue.[30]

Failure to count work in the home as part of the national economy and failure to distinguish between the categories of child-care and housework are powerful ways in which the public realm ignores, fails to appreciate, denies status to and undermines the informal, private sphere. Families, as the major component of that sphere, are weakened by this manoeuvre. Women who share this relegation to the private and the denigration of the private are tending to respond by joining the males in the valuing of the public over the private and in elevating the public values of individualism, competition, material success over shared, communal well-being.

The failure of the public realm to understand, appreciate and support the family factors that are so essential to the well-being of communities and individuals can be seen in the withdrawal of economic supports from families; in the discrepancy between what the community is prepared to pay in

Figure 3. Total Productive System of an Industrial Society
(Three-Layer Cake with Icing)

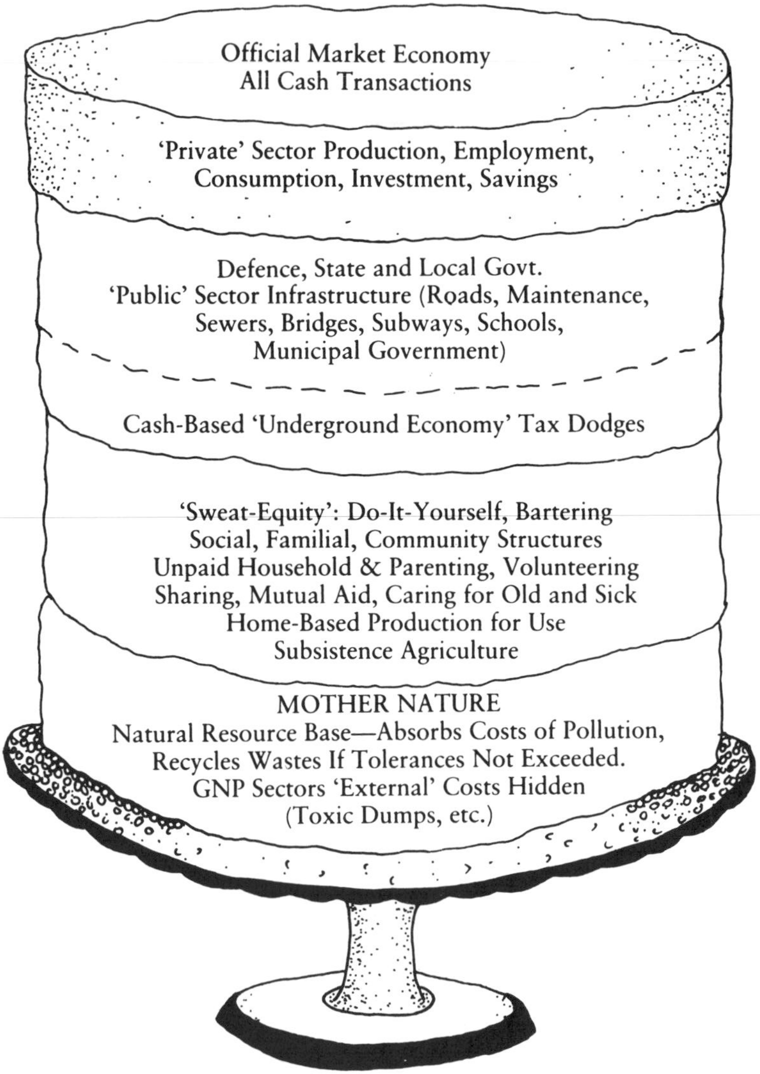

Official Market Economy
All Cash Transactions

'Private' Sector Production, Employment,
Consumption, Investment, Savings

Defence, State and Local Govt.
'Public' Sector Infrastructure (Roads, Maintenance,
Sewers, Bridges, Subways, Schools,
Municipal Government)

Cash-Based 'Underground Economy' Tax Dodges

'Sweat-Equity': Do-It-Yourself, Bartering
Social, Familial, Community Structures
Unpaid Household & Parenting, Volunteering
Sharing, Mutual Aid, Caring for Old and Sick
Home-Based Production for Use
Subsistence Agriculture

MOTHER NATURE
Natural Resource Base—Absorbs Costs of Pollution,
Recycles Wastes If Tolerances Not Exceeded.
GNP Sectors 'External' Costs Hidden
(Toxic Dumps, etc.)

GNP-Monetised
½ of Cake
Top Two Layers
Monetised, Officially
Measured GNP
Generates All
Economic Statistics
(15% 'Underground'
Illegal, Tax-Dodging)

Non-Monetised
Productive ½ of Cake
Lower Two Layers Non-
Monetised Altruism, Sharing
'Counter-Economy' Sub-
sidises Top Two GNP-Cash
Sectors with Unpaid Labor
and Environmental Costs
Absorbed or Unaccounted,
Risks Passed to Future
Generations

GNP 'Private' Sector
Rests   on

GNP 'Public' Sector
Rests   on

Social Co-operative
Counter-Economy
Rests   on

Nature's Layer

the costs of family dysfunction and family breakdown and the meagre resources allocated to understanding and preventing family dysfunction and family breakdown; in failure to recognise the inputs families make to education by creating the attitudes, effort and conception of self that enables youngsters to learn; and in the failure to recognise or to count the value of work in the home as part of the national economy.

10

Reasons for the Neglect of Family Issues

The influence and impact of families on human competence is nowhere disputed. The factors within families that create that human competence have been identified by a multitude of studies. There are no fundamental disagreements between the studies, which all agree that it is *the non-material factors of parental interest, time, love, attention, discipline, availability and stability that are crucial* to the growth of competence. These non-material factors outweigh in influence the material factors of income, social status and neighbourhood.

It would be expected, in view of the impact of families and the evident importance of the internal family processes, that these processes would be appreciated, studied and supported in every way possible by public policy. As the source of the human competence of the whole society, they are a vital asset. Their lack cannot be compensated for in any other way. The unique and irreplaceable roles played by families can be expected to be recognised by the high status families and family issues command in public policy. In fact, the reverse is the case.

Reasons for the neglect of family factors

Many reasons can be found to explain the current neglect of family issues and the failure to accord families the status and resources needed for them to perform their uniquely humanising roles. These reasons include the influence of the 'anti-psychiatry' movement of the late 1960s, the conviction that no such thing as a strong family exists, that family privacy precludes programs to enrich or resource family groups, and that it is impossible to learn in the area of family relationships. These all militate against research, development and policy in this area.

Feminism, too, is a factor bringing changed attitudes of women to families. In many cases it involves a hostility to family as a major source of oppression of women. Some influential social theorists have seen families only in deterministic and functional terms as inherently conservative and maintainers of the status quo. Family values have been recently associated with extremely conservative values, and earlier this century it was thought, in some circles, that the rise of fascism in Europe could be attributed to the bourgeois European family. This resulted in some suspicion and hostility to 'the traditional family'. However, this view has never been substantiated, and the poor case that has been mounted has been shown to be very weak.[1]

Some researchers have identified 'The New Class' as influential in policy and as hostile to family values. Even those who see the importance of families as a social group fear that there is no way to support or strengthen family groups without imposing one (traditional) model of family on the variety of family forms that currently exist.

Negative perceptions of families

Families as creators of madness
A major source of negative perceptions of families emerges from the anti-psychiatry literature of the 1960s and 1970s. The title of Cooper's book, *The Death of the Family*, vividly captured the public imagination and encapsulated the think-

ing of this group of thoughtful and radical psychiatrists who had noted that the families of many psychiatric patients seemed to exude a toxic influence that made the patients sick.[2] In fact, these psychiatrists emphasised that seemingly mysterious illnesses and bizarre behaviour were nothing more than the desperate attempts of children, adolescents and even adults to make sense of a meaningless world. Their mental illness was imposed on them by the crazy family environments in which they had been reared.

It has often been pointed out since that the radical psychiatrists had an excessively jaundiced view of families: after all they were dealing with the walking wounded from some of the most destructive families in the UK. They made the mistake of assuming that family life *of its very nature created mental illness:* hence the need for *The Death of the Family.* As Laing said, 'the initial act of brutality against the average child is the mother's first kiss.' The anthropologist Edmund Leach, took up the theme in his Reith lecture in 1968: 'Far from being the basis of the good society, the family, with its narrow privacy and tawdry secrets, is the source of all our discontents.'

The film *Family Life* and the TV series *Talking to a Stranger* made the thinking of the anti-psychiatry school widely known. The Beatles song 'She's leaving home' powerfully sold this concept of families to millions; and families came to be seen as typically oppressive, narrow, hypocritical and constrained, as presented by Laing and his colleagues, and as such the cause of mental illness.

One reason why this excessively pessimistic view of families gained such wide currency was that there was virtually no research into families that promoted high well-being to balance this research into destructive families. It may also be that the writings of Laing, Esterson and Cooper struck a painful nerve: there seems to be no doubt that, for many, the most painful experiences of life occur in the family context. All too often, people experience in their families the rejection, manipulation, hostility, fear and alienation that the radical psychiatrists described so brilliantly. (Fortunately, only rarely are such experiences constant and unrelieved.)

It was also a time of almost unprecedented questioning of

all of society's institutions: student riots on campuses, disillusion with government, opposition to the Vietnam War and so on. To question the goodness of family life and family love, to show how oppression within families mirrored oppression within society was a readily accepted message. And even now, over twenty years after the shocking discovery that families make people sick (the work of the earlier psychotherapists had, in fact, shown the same thing), we still have little idea of how many families fall into the range of dysfunctional families and how many create optimal health and competence in their members.

Feminism and families

Feminist analyses have successfully created a general awareness of the ways that traditional practices have allowed an exaltation of motherhood to disguise a denigration of women. But some feminist analyses have seen family as the major oppressor of women. For example, Firestone's scenario of a better world involves freeing women from the biological tyranny of their gender. This freeing will undermine all society and culture that is erected on this biological tyranny and the family. Finally, all systems of tyranny based on the family, including the economy, state, religion and law will erode and collapse. Firestone looks forward to an end to the 'barbarism' of pregnancy through test-tube babies becoming the major method of procreation. Firestone, of course, is an extremist. But much mainstream feminine debate has seen family as a major element in the oppression of women. This focus can be challenged on several grounds.

In the first place, to identify marriage and families as the primary source of oppression of women is an example of the 'politics of displacement'. The family unit, already vulnerable and weakened, is attacked as the cause and symptom of female subordination. In doing so, attention is diverted from structural and political contributions to female oppression.[3] There is no doubt that women have been forced to choose between the needs of their children for nurture and the family's need for economic self-sufficiency. In blaming only families for women's oppression and, to the extent that the economic structures that force this no-win situation on women escape attack, feminism can be accused of merely echoing the culture that it claims to criticise: work takes precedence over family.

In the second place, to perceive only families and marriage as the source of women's oppression can result in treating children as commodities. The feminist political philosopher Jean Bethke Elshtain has argued this case compellingly when she insists on the need for women to achieve their humanity without trampling over the bodies and futures of others. Claiming that human beings achieve their humanity only through personal, eroticised, emotionally charged bonds with the specific, intimate others who nurture them, Elshtain seeks a feminism that expands the human agency of women, men and children and forgoes apparently simpler solutions based on the denial of the human needs of either women, children or men. Elshtain acknowledges the achievement of feminism in dismantling the ideology of family. However, she sees the task of constructing a comprehensive alternative that adequately treats human sexuality, child development, kinship and familial ties and structures, and links these to political and educative theories and structures as one that remains to be achieved. Many women and men would agree with her.

Carol McMillan, another feminist philosopher, has described a masculine bias in our current notion of reason which gained ascendancy at the enlightenment.[4] Reason was defined according to what distinguished 'man' from the animal kingdom. As emotion was seen to be shared with the animals, it could not, in this scheme of things, be distinctively human. Only abstract, conceptual thought, the type of thought that emanates in the discovery of regular, unvarying 'laws' or principles could be included within the realm of reason. McMillan describes and analyses some examples of complex and sophisticated reason which do not meet these criteria, including the navigational processes of the Trukese, the aesthetic processes of artists and craftsmen, and the literary and philosophic reasoning process that cannot produce a 'law' or formula for all human problems or issues, but which must analyse each problem or theme in a different way according to its unique elements. Each of the above processes gives birth to beautiful, useful and human products and each deserves

163

to be acknowledged as reason. McMillan includes the ever-challenging, continually adapting response of parents to children and the task of child-nurture as an example of the highest human reason.

In this way McMillan creates a devastating critique of the current, widely accepted notion of reason, and at the same time shows that an anti-feminist bias lies within the very notion of reason. Deep-rooted and faulty notions of reason underlie and support women's low status and the low valuation placed on child-rearing, nurture and family ties.[4] To the extent that some feminists have been unaware of this bias, they have tended to share with sexists (and have failed to challenge) this anti-feminine bias within the very notion of reason.

Overly deterministic social theories and families

Elshtain finds a 'surprisingly hostile' attitude to families and family issues prevalent in the early 1980s, which she attributes, not only to the anti-psychiatrists, feminist influences and Marxist theories, but also to the dominance of functionalism in sociology.[5] Functionalism assumes that there is a stable congruence between the modern industrialised economy and the nuclear family. Therefore it is assumed that the function of the family is to produce and reproduce the physical bodies and the personality characteristics needed by the modern state. From such a perspective the family is seen to be an inherently conservative institution, a necessary accomplice to the industrialised state, an agent of social reproduction. Often this perspective is adopted so thoroughly that no positive possibilities can be envisioned for families.

A student proposing to write a thesis on family and education is given to understand that the whole proposal is suspect, because 'the family is an agent of social reproduction'. Of course the university (where this advice is being given to her) and the school are also agents of social reproduction according to this same wisdom, but they are not perceived as inherently conservative in the same way. No stigma seems to be attached to them. It is acceptable to draw a salary from one and to supervise research into the other. But even to research the area of family, especially if it is seen as a site of positive possibilities, is to risk being tainted.

An overly narrow and technocratic view of knowledge
The widespread opinion that it is impossible academically to investigate the area of family relationships, or that knowledge of human relationships is a trivial, mickey-mouse affair, not to be included in the 'real' body of knowledge, is quite at variance with the work of one of the century's greatest sociologists, Jurgen Habermas. Habermas identifies such opinions as typical of those under the sway of the domination of technological reason. In fact, many of the stances associated with the falling fortunes of families are identical with what Habermas sees to be the core of modern ideology, that one branch of knowledge (technical knowledge) has abrogated to itself the whole field of knowledge and in the name of a growing rationalisation of life is turning the direction of human affairs over to a growing irrationality.

One aspect of technocratic thinking is the conviction that values fall outside the realm of science, even of social science. A positivist philosophy of knowledge underlies this belief. To even consider the question of the need for support for families involves placing a certain value on families. But since the time of Weber it has been assumed that social science is incompatible with values and norms. The social scientist assumes that to adopt a values stance is to fall into the realm of the irrational. However Habermas has argued that a social science based only on a positivist understanding is hopelessly irrational. His ambitious project has been to lay the foundations of a social science which retains the classical aim of politics (to maintain an order of virtuous conduct among the citizens of the polis) and combines it with the study of society using to the full the methodological rigor which is the great strength of modern science. In Habermas' view the primary problem today is 'the reconciliation of the classical aim of politics — to enable human beings to live good and just lives in a political community — with the modern demand of social thought, which is to achieve scientific knowledge of the workings of society'.[6]

Positivist philosophy set out to combat pseudo-science in

all its forms. It unmasked the normative and hence 'non-cognitive', 'subjective' and 'irrational' basis of those global views of persons and society that were used to justify particular ethical and political systems. Yet, if all values are subjective, as the positivists claim, then the positivist commitment to science and technology and opposition to dogmatism and ideology is itself subjective and rationally indefensible. Positivism needs to call on forms of reason beyond those it recognises in order to defend its own methodology and its claim to be a reasonable approach to truth.

Habermas does not deny, in fact he strongly affirms, the remarkable contribution to knowledge achieved through empirical methodology based on positivist premises, referring to it as the 'irreversible achievement of modern science'[7]. His argument is that positivists have limited the whole field of reason to the observation of facts based on sensory data. Habermas labels the area of knowledge shaped and determined in this way, technical knowledge. Technical knowledge can answer questions such as, 'What is most efficient?' 'What is most expedient?' It can choose between strategies to a given objective, but it cannot address itself to what the objective should be. The refusal to recognise forms of reason over and beyond that of the technical he refers to as the domination of technical rationality.

Habermas would consider that to treat the future as if it were an aspect of the external world of nature over which humans have no control is to be subject to a form of ideology more pervasive and irrational than earlier ideologies in which it was considered that human misery was the will of God and could not be avoided. Yet it is increasingly common for people to accept that what is technically possible is 'inevitable', whether it is good for human individuals and communities or not.

In short, then, Habermas argues that in the name of creating freedom and autonomy, the dominance of technological rationality has done away with open domination only to replace it with more subtle and far-reaching forms of control. Modern ideology resides not so much in the domination of one class over another as in the domination of technocratic forms of reason over other forms of reason.

What other writers have seen as the end of ideology — the draining away of overall values and ideals in favour of pragmatic, technocratic government — Habermas regards as the very core of what modern ideology is.[8] This ideology means we have a deficient understanding of society, and the deficiencies have been particularly damaging to families.

The public/private realms

In *Public Man, Private Woman*, the feminist political philosopher Jean Bethke Elshtain has explored the status and fortunes of women throughout Western history according to varying relationships between the public and the private realms.[9] Her analysis suggests yet another reason for the strange treatment of the Coleman and Moynihan reports. In the case of the Coleman Report there seems to have been a blindness to the finding that real effects were being generated from the private world of family — the world, incidentally, in which women currently do have power. In the case of the Moynihan Report, the diversion of interest from the public realm of legislation, marches and civil action seems to have generated an intense rage. In both cases significant issues were raised and hastily reburied.

Elshtain's work on the public and private realms alerts us to a dynamic that may explain the failure to respond to the Coleman Report findings. If the separation between public and private realms is currently severe, virtually a chasm, the public would react as if the private does not exist. This is precisely the way the research and education community have reacted, as if they found it impossible to believe that 'real' effects and 'real' influences *could* be generated in the private world. Smith's doubts concerning the finding of the importance of parental influence was referred to in chapter 1 and illustrates this incomprehension. Smith was merely verbalising the commonsense knowledge of the day. No one contradicted him or thought he was in error.

The inability to see their own data and findings seems to be an example of what sociologists mean by 'ideology'. By ideology is meant a distortion of reality, but the concept of ideology is more complex than that. Holbach portrayed the mind as confused by a veil of opinions from which we can extricate ourselves only with the greatest difficulty. One of the problems of extricating oneself from this veil is that our very language and social institutions embody those distortions from which we seek to be delivered. 'Ideology is never merely or simply a distortion or falsehood. Expressions of ideology, like neurotic symptoms to the psychoanalyst, are clues to and features of a complex structure comprised of manifest and latent, apparent and more deeply rooted exigencies'.[10] The power of ideologies is related to the way they are used to justify action. A person who accepts an ideology does not think of it as arbitrary. 'They think of it as "self-evident", "what any rational man will hold", "realistic", "based on what human nature is", or — more recently — "what science tells us".'[11]

The reason to suspect that ideology is operating in the response to the findings of the Coleman Report is simply that the research and educational community seem to have failed totally to see their own very clear findings. If the Coleman Report findings were the opposite to what they in fact were, if it had been found that families had no effect on school learning and that school learning was entirely related to curriculum, number of books in schools, teacher training, class sizes, buildings and so on, the response of educators and researchers would make sense. But the findings were the reverse. School factors have little leverage to affect the learning of those students who are failing. Family factors do seem to have the leverage to affect the situation.

Elshtain's work opens the way to the interpretation that, in this case, the ideology to which the researchers and educational establishment seem to have succumbed (and it is one to whom members of the knowledge class are particularly vulnerable) is that the public world is the only 'real' world. This is but one aspect of what Habermas describes as the fundamental ideology of technically advanced societies: the domination of technocratic forms of reason over other forms of reason.[12]

Awareness of our tendency to seek solutions only in the public world raises the possibility that solutions may be sought that strengthen the private realm and that give a voice to the private realm and its values and ways of operating. This will be a totally different approach from seeking solutions that further denude the private realm, that strengthen the public realm further in relation to the private realm and that assume the current biases and trends must be continued whether they meet the needs of individuals and communities or not.

Elshtain's analysis opens the way to see family issues as in many ways similar to women's issues. Families and women are strongly identified with the private realm and both suffer from the denigration of the private realm by the public realm. Much of the women's movement's response has been to claim status and rights in the public realm. This is a vital task, and one that must not be abandoned. Not only must women achieve their rightful place in the public, they must change the public. But even when this is achieved, it is only half the task. We must reclaim some space and status for the private also. 'The redemption of everyday life' that Elshtain looks for, the 'recognition of its joys and vexations, its values and purposes, and its place in becoming human' is a task scarcely begun. The recognition of the value of the private realm will involve the recognition of families and the unique roles they perform.

Elshtain's analysis also opens for investigation the notion that the resistance to the findings of both the Coleman and Moynihan reports was rooted in an antagonism of public and private. The public was either blind to or antagonistic and hostile towards any recognition of the private. This links with the role of the New Class or Knowledge Class in the denigration of families and the withdrawal of support for families.

The influence of the New Class
Schumpeter, who first drew attention to this New Class, did so in terms of the bureaucracy within socialist societies who had come to be a new élite with considerable power. His analysis was later applied to the Knowledge Class within Western societies, the bureaucrats, intellectuals and those with influence in the media who were seen to have a power

comparable to the New Class. Their power stems from their influence and control of the powerful institutions that dominate public life. The Bergers have noted the 'imperialistic' drives of this class and their hostility to family issues.[13] It was members of this class, in particular, who were in a position to vilify Moynihan as a racist and to consign to oblivion his data and his attempt to raise the issue of the significance of family contexts to the war against poverty. It was members of the Knowledge Class who ignored the findings of the Coleman Report on the weakness of school factors and the strength of family factors in bringing about school achievement. In neither case were these findings in the interest of the Knowledge Class. To concentrate on schools, institutionalised child-care and social welfare programs is basically a work-creation policy for the New Class, the professionals who will draw salaries and administer the institutions and programs established. To fully respond to the findings of these two reports would be to admit the limits of the public realm, to reverse the process of withdrawing status, recognition and supports from families, and to put resources into a competing realm, the private, and into a different mode of operating, the norm-based, informal, intimate world of families and family networks.

Instead of following the norms of the 'objective' social scientist, to consider the data in a value-free way, the academic, research, social science and policy leaders succumbed to something they analyse in others but assume they themselves are free from: ideology. In this case the ideology of the New Class. They made the mistake of thinking that only the public realm counts; only the public realm is real; that there was something not quite right about findings that involved placing a value on families. It is another example of that invasion of the private realm by the 'rationality' of the public world to which Habermas has alerted us. The director of the Marriage Guidance Council of Western Australia reports a senior government bureaucrat saying to him, 'The problem with the Marriage Guidance Council is the word "marriage" in your title.' Such an attitude is common among the New Class professionals who dominate politics and the public service. But it is not shared by the bulk of the community.[14]

Sometimes discomfort with the word 'marriage' arises from the belief that marriage and family is an oppressive institution. It should not be forgotten, then, that the New Class have recommended, implemented and administered the policies which resulted in the erosion of family allowances that has resulted in families being so much worse off than they were over a decade ago. It is ironic that while tending to perceive *families* as the symbol of ultra-conservatism, the New Class have themselves administered this reversal from a more co-operative and sharing society to one which favours individualistic advancement. Thus the New Class themselves are strongly implicated in one of the most striking and reactionary trends in Australian life in recent years.

The family besieged

Invasion of the family by a market mentality or by bureaucratic attitudes is damaging to family integrity, as family operates on norms that are quite at variance with those that dominate the public sphere. For example, families operate on norms of loyalty and on the understanding that the relationships between people are unique. It is not possible to substitute another who can satisfactorily replace the particular role a loved human being plays in our lives. The public realm operates on principles of competition, self-advancement and that 'no one is irreplaceable'.

One of the key ways that the public world dominates the family is in the invasion of its 'market mentality' into family life. Nowhere is this seen more than in the tendency of the public realm to see the family and family relationships as commodities.

Families as commodities
In March 1987 the *Australian Financial Review*, in discussing whether family allowances should be abolished, asked the question, 'Should the social security and tax system reward adults simply because they have chosen to have children?'[15] In proceeding to answer this question ('No') the *Review* immediately pointed out that no one is forced to have child-

ren and that in many ways children are like commodities. Like durable goods, they are costly to acquire, last for a long time, give pleasure, but are expensive to maintain and repair, often disappoint and definitely have an imperfect second-hand market. The implication was clear, and in no way denied by the jocular tone: the choice to have a child is similar to the choice to indulge in an expensive commodity. If I choose to buy a Mercedes car or an expensive boat, should you have to help me pay the interest, upkeep and repair bills? It is rare to find a technocratic approach to family issues expressed so blatantly.

Co-operative responsibility for child-rearing

The value position behind the *Review*'s statement is totally the reverse of that adopted by the Australian community when the Lang Government pioneered child-endowment in 1927. The provision of child-endowment or family allowances is based on the acceptance of co-operative and community responsibility for child-rearing. It indicates that the community acknowledges that child-rearing has an importance to the whole society and that the parents cannot be expected to shoulder the burdens involved entirely alone.

The *Review*'s assumptions are the antithesis of co-operative, communal responsibility for child-rearing. The *Review* fails to acknowledge that families with dependent children make significant contributions to the common good. Because the contributions parents make in child-rearing are so vital, family groups cannot be stressed beyond their limits without negative results for the whole community. The failure of the *Review* to acknowledge parental contributions to the economy, and their recommendation that families with dependent members should 'compete', without compensation for their handicaps, against unencumbered individuals marks their stance as one of favouring competitive individualism over communal co-operation.

Costs of child-rearing

The Australian Institute of Family Studies has estimated the costs of child-rearing for Australian families in 1987 (see Table 3).[16] Different rates are given for low-income and

Table 3. Costs of children

	Age 2 $	5 $	8 $	11 $	Teenage $
Low-income Families					
Per week	21.92	28.12	34.48	36.59	54.48
Per year	1139.90	1462.27	1792.84	1902.80	2833.02
Middle-income Families					
Per week	32.98	37.01	47.76	60.29	90.64
Per year	1714.97	1924.65	2483.33	3134.90	4713.28

Sources
Lovering, K. (1984), *Cost of children in Australia*, Working Paper No. 8, Australian Institute of Family Studies, Melbourne; updated to 1987 Cost of Living (June 1987 CPI).

Notes
Included are food and clothing, fuel, household provisions, extra costs of schooling (but not fees), gifts, pocket money and entertainments. Not included are housing, transport, school fees or uniforms, child-care, medical or dental expenses. Holidays are a component of the middle-income figures only.
Low income = below average weekly wage; middle income = average weekly wage and above.

middle-income families, as the different groups spend quite different amounts on their children. In short, it costs middle-income families (families on the average weekly wage and above) over $90 per week to keep a teenager. This does not include costs of housing, transport, school fees or uniforms, medical or dental expenses. The costs for a two-year-old in a middle-income family amount to $32.98 per week, excluding the items referred to above and also excluding any cost for child-care. Low-income costs were calculated at $21.92 per week for a two-year-old and $54.48 for a teenager. Holidays were included in the middle-income figure, but not for the low-income one. While it is known that the cost of institutional care of children is much higher than care in the family home, few realise the magnitude of the discrepancy. In other words if a family fails to care for its children and the children end up in government institutional care, it then costs the taxpayer $50,000 per year (and sometimes much more) to pay others to do what parents do for nothing (in fact at a personal cost of between $2833 and $4713). ($90,000 per year is the cost per child for care and supervision in one Australian non-government agency caring for delinquent teenagers. Children or youngsters committed to full-time institutional care are usually only those who have become mentally or emotionally ill or delinquent, or whose behaviour cannot be managed in foster homes or family group homes.)

It can be seen, then, that as well as the actual money costs that parents pay to rear their children, they also contribute an enormous quantity of time, care, supervision, teaching, nurturing and love. To pay someone other than the child's parents to do this requires a daunting sum for an inferior service.

To deny parents some financial compensation is to be ignorant of current demographic trends and their inevitable effect on the future economy. A number of factors have reduced our birth-rate to a record low level. Young people are delaying marriage, delaying the birth of children and reducing the number of children they have.[17] A recent cartoon made the point quite graphically. A group of wrinkled and fragile old people crowd to peer through a hospital viewing window at a newborn baby. Wheezing and cackling with glee, they shout, 'We've come to see the new tax-payer!'

It has been calculated that whereas now there are six working adults to support each person on retirement benefits, in the not-too-distant future this will have fallen to three people working to one retired person. Only if it can be shown that the removal of family allowances does *not* affect the decision to bear children can it be considered a 'hard-nosed' economic policy. In fact, demographic research has shown that people's perception of the costs of children does impact on decisions to bear more children.[18] It is almost puerile to have to spell out that without children there can be no future, no growth, no market, no society and no economy.

The human ecology

It is now clear that unrestrained exploitation of the physical environment is not good business. Instead of being efficient and productive, it has been exposed as destroying the assets of our communal company, the planet. Instead of being realistic and pragmatic, it can be seen to have been based on the fantasies of growth without limits and of action free of consequences. But as the farmers who now are confronted with unsaleable livestock and farms with polluted soil are discovering, this *was* a fantasy. The reality is much grimmer and the consequences are real and not to be easily reversed, if at all. The destruction of the social ecology, which sustains our humanity, is just as short-sighted. Families are an irreplaceable component of that human ecology.

An attempt has been made to consider and to explain why families, despite their obvious contributions to society and despite evidence of their need for a more adequate infrastructure of support, have had such little claim on public resources or interest. The influence of the anti-psychiatrists, some forms of feminism, overly deterministic social theories, technocratic understandings of knowledge, the split between the public and private realms and the invasion of the competitive rationality of the public world into the norm-governed world of the family have all played a part in this situation. The belief that nothing is known of what creates competence in family systems and that no judgements can be made concerning the quality of family life (an example of the almost universally held belief that truth is relative[19]) also inhibits exploration and knowledge in this area.

It is quite possible to develop policies and programs to support families, as they are and in the conditions of the 1980s and 1990s. This does not mean imposing one traditional model of family on families or defining family in a way that excludes or stigmatises or demeans some families. The recent report on family policy for the government of Quebec is an example of an approach to family policy that declares the primacy of families among social institutions, accepts all family types and emphasises the right of parents to collective support.

Nor does developing family-support programs or family-education programs mean prying into family privacy. Families require privacy, time, space and control over their own processes and affairs. Yet not every aspect of family is private, and many decisions have public implications, such as decisions to have or not have children. Parental abdication of responsibility for children has public repercussions. Programs to enhance parenting skills, to facilitate young couples in choosing and establishing a marriage relationship, to enable parents to relate to adolescents in a way that increases the youngsters' self-esteem and confidence have all been developed, evaluated and found effective.[20] Other programs within schools and medical institutions involve better co-operation between institutions and families and result in greater empowering of families, enhanced development of family members and increased satisfaction within families.[21]

As so few of these programs are known to the public realm, some of them will be described in the next chapter.

Part 4

The Way Forward

11

Programs and Policies for Families

The need for multiple strands in family policy

Since Moynihan's controversial writing on black families in the USA, debate in many countries over support policies for families has tended to focus on the relationship between economic conditions and the problems families face. Moynihan emphasised the need to strengthen black families as a means of improving the economic condition of this group. More recent studies emphasised the reverse of this equation: poverty was seen as the major cause of stress, dysfunction and disruption in families; and improvement in family well-being was seen to be dependent on improvement in the economic and other environmental conditions of families. However, evidence of wide differences in competence between families of similar socio-economic resources indicates that the socio-economic factor is *not* the only relevant one. Some poor families create a life-enhancing environment for their members, and some affluent ones fail to do so. This fact, plus the considerable and mounting evidence of the impact of the family's own ways of relating to each other and to the outside world, leads to the conclusion that family policy must focus on economic opportunity *and* public support services *and* creative family *processes*. Consequently, a prime need in the family policy area is reform of the tax structure to reverse recent trends that favour individuals over family groups and penalise those who accept responsibility for dependents. The argument for policies promoting the economic and structural support of families has been well presented in other places. This last chapter will focus on the need for policies and programs that promote and support positive family processes.

The concept of preventive family policy has gained very little support in any country and has failed even to be seriously debated. It is rejected on the grounds that it implies that the problems families face are due to their own incompetence, because it invites further intrusion into and loss of autonomy of families, and because it assumes the imposition of middle-class values, or of one (traditional) model of family life on the variety of family forms in existence.

Despite the lack of support from governments or major institutions, many programs and approaches to the support and enrichment of family life have been developed and evaluated. The success of these programs calls into question the lack of serious debate on and funding for this area. The evaluation of the programs belies the widespread conviction that such programs necessarily involve invading family privacy, imposing values on families, stigmatising some family forms or manipulating and engineering family processes. Some of the programs will be described, as they indicate various ways in which the current needs of families may be met without the depressing side-effects that have been anticipated.

Two broad approaches to the enrichment and support of family groups have emerged. One concentrates on giving parents the opportunity to develop the skills, attitudes and resources that characterise effective parenting: this can be called the 'education for family life' approach. A different strategy is for institutions that impinge on family life to adapt their practices in ways that give recognition and status to families, which empower families, and which encourage the development of those traits known to be associated with effective family functioning. In practice, the two approaches are often combined, nevertheless some family education programs will be described first and some approaches in which institutions adopt practices that are more empowering for families will be described later.

Education for family life

Education for family life is one preventive measure that offers the possibility of families gaining access to skills, information and resources that will enable them to negotiate better with the institutions that frame their lives and to make up for deficits that may have occurred in their own experience of family life. But family education is not proposed only as a preventive or crisis-prevention measure. A relatively small number of families naturally exhibit patterns that result in a very high level of development in their children. There is no doubt that these patterns can be learnt by other families and that many parents are eager to learn and to practise such patterns, especially if the opportunity is presented at the right time. Every family as it develops through the stages of the family life-cycle can benefit from information, the learning of skills and the support of other families.

Programs developed

Programs have been developed for almost every stage of the family life-cycle, including pre-marriage and post-marriage, child-birth and infancy, childhood and adolescence. There are couple communication programs for couples at any and every stage of the family life-cycle, the best known being Marriage Enrichment and Marriage Encounter. Parent education and support groups such as PET (Parent Effectiveness Training), STEP (Systematic Training for Effective Parenting), the Playgroup and Playcentre movements are all well known. A few programs (such as Family Cluster and Understanding Us[1]) involve the whole family in appreciating their family's unique strengths, learning more satisfying ways to relate to each other and to other families, building stronger support networks and planning the future direction of their shared life. There are programs to assist families undergoing separation or bereavement and to help others negotiate the predictable difficulties of establishing a step-family.

A survey of published evaluations of almost sixty programs found almost all were measurably successful in achieving their aims. It is quite clear that it is possible to teach skills, change attitudes and alter couple and family interactions through relatively simple and short interventions and programs. For example, parent participation in parent education courses has resulted in parents being less autocratic and more democratic with their children, mother-child interactions being more positive, *children's* self-esteem increasing and families demonstrating more effective decision-making and reporting greater family happiness.

Research into couple communication courses found couples who had taken part demonstrating increased ability to negotiate conflict without it have a damaging effect on the relationship, increasing their expressions of appreciation and affection for each other and showing higher levels of empathy and warmth, which resulted in more closeness and sharing of intimate thoughts and feelings. One study found that couples who had attended a pre-marriage course with a follow-up segment six months after the wedding demonstrated that their major area of disagreement had a *positive* effect on their relationship, in marked contrast to the control group. Those who had taken part in this course also avoided the predictable slump in satisfaction and positive relating that affected almost all other couples in the early years of their marriage. A particularly significant change due to pre-marriage education programs is willingness to seek counselling or help should problems arise later in the marriage. Couples increased their range of communication styles and had more choices of how to relate. Changes were demonstrated at home as well as in laboratory tests.

In the past twenty years there has been an explosion of information about how people relate in groups, and much of this is relevant to how people relate in marriage and family. The process of learning the skills and attitudes associated

182

with satisfying family relationships has much in common with learning to relate in other situations. What does *not* work is *lectures* on how people ought to relate. A comparative study of different types of pre-marriage education found no effects at all from the traditional pre-marriage approach of a series of lectures from experts such as doctors, bankers and clergy. People learn to relate better by practising the skills of relating and by giving and receiving feedback on the new experience. In the family education field it is clear that participants benefit more when they learn to relate to their own family rather than learning the skills in an individualistic mode only (teenagers at school, mother at assertiveness course and father at management seminar).

For example, couples may be asked to write down and then tell each other what they like and admire in their partners. Later they may discuss with their partners, and possibly other couples, their reactions to this exercise. A teenager reflecting on her experience of a family education program declared this expression of admiration and liking to be 'magic'. 'You know how much you appreciate it yourself and how good it makes you feel and so you decide to do it for others.' Those who come from families where positive appreciation of others is not the usual practice find this a difficult and uncomfortable exercise. But usually their own appreciation of hearing unambiguous recognition and liking from others leads to the realisation that others benefit from *their* appreciation. This encourages them to practise expressing rather than suppressing liking and admiration.

One reason why it is important that family members learn together is that the new ways of relating are introduced into the family system during the learning process. This does not leave to an individual with a still precarious hold on a new skill the daunting task of trying out this skill on an incredulous family. (It is more difficult to alter long-established patterns of relating to one's life partner than it is to learn and implement a new way of returning a faulty purchase to a sales assistant whom one has never seen before and will never see again.) The initial discomfort of altering long-established patterns is faced with the support of the learning group and with the opportunity of seeing how other couples go about incorporating a new pattern into their particular style of relating.

Active game-like processes have been particularly effective with many groups. The use of drawing, clay modelling, music, ritual and symbol enable family members to share their hopes, dreams and expectations, even when they are scarcely known to themselves.

The major reason why people apply for divorce is that they are deeply lonely within their marriage. The failure or inability to communicate at an intimate and feeling level causes anguishing isolation and a sense of rejection leading to anger and depression. Yet we know a great number of ways to help couples prevent this erosion within their marriage.

Not all couples or families are good candidates for educative programs. Where there are long-standing, deep-seated problems in relating, it is unlikely that the couple or family will benefit from an educative approach. Seriously dysfunctional families are either chaotic or rigid and inflexible. In the latter case they cannot even imagine that things could be different from what they are. In other words, they have virtually lost their ability to benefit from a learning experience, though they can benefit from the more intensive experience of therapy if they are able to commit themselves to it.

The fact that not all families are able to benefit from these programs is no argument against them. On the contrary, it is an argument for the ready availability of family enrichment and education programs before a crisis develops and while things are going well. This is when families are most open to learning. And in any case, the majority of families are able to participate and benefit.

The common belief that these programs are aimed only at middle-class families and are acceptable only to them is erroneous. Some programs have been accepted by and are effective with a wide range of socio-economic groups. However, programs do need to be suited to the participants' needs, interests and general style, which often means they need to be adapted to differing ethnic or other cultural groups. There is a need for variety in programs and in sponsoring agencies so that these differences are catered for.

Often programs are led by non-professionals or by those with professional qualifications in teaching, social work, nursing, medicine and so on with a brief training in group leadership. In a number of evaluations, peer-led programs compared very favourably with those led by professionals. Volunteer, peer-leadership has obvious advantages in making programs more financially accessible. However, adequate training, supervision, support, evaluation and back-up are essential to make a volunteer program effective and to control the quality of the service.

The times when families are most open to learning coincide with key transition-points in the family life-cycle of birth, adolescence, marriage and death. Incidentally, these are the nodal points universally celebrated in primitive societies with the rites of passage. These powerful rituals provided essential learning to the participants for the next stage of the life-cycle, encouraged the changed attitudes and conception of self appropriate to the change of status, and attempted to thwart any temptation to regress to earlier roles or ways of being. The ritual made clear to the candidates, and to the community, the changed status and role of the candidate. It often provided a catalyst to those involved to mourn what had been lost in the transition to a new social role, thus making adaptation to the new role more likely. The universality of these rituals in human societies is evidence against the common belief that preparation, learning and ritual surrounding these key times of transition is somehow unnatural. What is unnatural is that the learning should be in a cognitive mode only, rather than incorporating experiential, interactional and creative modes.

Families and family members are open to learning at these key stages of the family life-cycle because they are suddenly confronted with a multitude of new situations and decisions. Usually they are totally involved emotionally with the new experience and have a great deal of energy to invest in mastering it. Two programs, each aimed at different stages of the family life-cycle, will be described to give some idea of the variety of approaches that have led to the learnings within families described at the start of this chapter.

Educating for parenthood

The work of Dr Burton White in establishing the impact of parenting style with toddlers on the development of later human competence was reported in chapter 1. Not surprisingly, considering that he found that the development of human competence was strongly related to parental style in these early years, White has continued his interest in teaching parents the effective parenting style he learnt from the highly competent families he studied.[2] In 1981 the Missouri State Department of Education hired White and his colleague, Dr Michael Meyerhoff, to design a parent-education program and help to set it up in four school districts, representing urban, suburban, small town and rural communities. One full-time and two part-time parent educators were employed to serve between sixty and a hundred families in each district. By January 1982 the program was under way and continued for three years at a cost of approximately $800 per family per year.

The program began in the final three months of the mother's pregnancy and continued until the child's first birthday. The parent educators arranged group get-togethers at which ten or twenty parents would meet at the project resource centre, which provided books, magazines, toys and other materials related to the early development of children. After the child was six months old there was an increasing emphasis on individual visits to the parent and child. The average contact was once a month for between an hour and an hour and a half.

In both individual and private sessions, staff gave parents information on the kinds of parenting practices likely to help or hinder their child's development. 'A Primer for Parents' (see pp. 188–9) is a summary of the approach recommended. White and Meyerhoff are not sympathetic to the intensive, highly structured approach of the superbaby programs. They recommend a comfortable approach that is enjoyable as well as effective and is based on what they observed happening in the homes where children were developing a high level of competence.

Linguistic competence in children developed where the

parents spoke to the child frequently almost from birth. These parents did not concentrate on flash cards and coaching. Instead, when the child approached them for comfort, assistance or to share excitement over some happening, they used simple language to talk about and to expand on what had happened. As the child's developing mobility made accidental falls, breakages and scaldings likely, they did not resort to restricting the child to a play-pen. Instead they made the living area of the house safe for (and from) the developing child. Thus a large and stimulating environment was provided for the baby: pots and pans, brooms and brushes, old magazines, whatever the parents were using and involved with was available for the baby to explore and manipulate. Expensive toys and games are not needed to develop children's intelligence: helping to bake biscuits, washing up, folding and sorting washing and tagging along at the supermarket are just as effective.

Social skills are just as important as intellectual ones. Many new parents operate under the illusion that children arrive in the world already civilised or pick up courteous behaviour automatically. Even when strong evidence to the contrary is presented, many parents have trouble putting a stop to unacceptable behaviour. However, the more effective parents studied by White, while lavishing love and attention on the newborn and responding almost unconditionally to every demand, began at about eight months of age to let the child know quite clearly that other people had to be considered. They did not hesitate to set realistic, but firm, boundaries to the child's behaviour before the first birthday.

White found that these effective parents were persistent in setting these limits. Almost any parent can be driven to make an objection, but the effective parents were swift and consistent in putting an end to undesirable behaviour. Nor were they punitive or aggressive. They used the most effective and least punitive methods, often removing the child from the scene and preventing a return.

Although the parent education program provided under White's supervision was entirely voluntary, the researchers report that first-time parents are always eager for guidance

187

A primer for parents

The following recommendations are based on the lessons White learned from the parents of linguistically, intellectually and socially competent pre-school children.

Things to do

Provide your children with maximum opportunity for exploration and investigation by making your home as safe and accessible as possible.

Remove fragile and dangerous items from low shelves and cabinets, and replace them with old magazines, pots and pans, plastic measuring cups and other suitable playthings.

Be available to act as your children's personal consultant during the majority of their waking hours. You don't have to hover, just be near by to provide attention and support as needed.

Respond to your children promptly and favourably as often as you can, providing appropriate enthusiasm and encouragement.

Set limits — do not give in to unreasonable requests or permit unacceptable behaviour to continue.

Talk to your children often. Make an effort to understand what they are trying to do and concentrate on what they see as important.

Use words they understand but also add new words and related ideas. For example, if your child gives you a red ball, say, 'This ball is red, just like my shirt. Your shirt is blue and it matches your pants.'

Provide new learning opportunities. Having children accompany you to the supermarket or allowing them to help you bake cookies will be more enriching than sitting them down and conducting a flashcard session.

Give your children a chance to direct some of your shared activities from time to time.

Try to help your children be as spontaneous emotionally as your own behaviour patterns will allow.

Encourage your children's pretend activities, especially those in which they act out adult roles.

---

that will help them in their new role as parents. An independent research team evaluated the effectiveness of White and Meyerhoff's parent education program. They found the social development of the project children to be outstanding,

Things to avoid
Don't confine your children regularly for long periods.

Don't allow them to concentrate their energies on you so much that independent exploration and investigation are excluded.

Don't ignore attention-getting devices to the point where children have to throw a tantrum to gain your interest.

Don't worry that your children won't love you if you say 'no' on occasion.

Don't try to win all the arguments, particularly during the second half of the second year when most children are passing through a normal period of negativism.

Don't try to prevent your children from cluttering the house — it's a sure sign of a healthy and curious baby.

Don't be overprotective.

Don't bore your child if you can avoid it.

Don't worry about when children learn to count or say the alphabet. Don't worry if they are slow to talk, as long as they seem to understand more and more language as time goes by.

Don't try to force toilet training. It will be easier by the time they are two.

Don't spoil your children, giving them the notion that the world was made just for them.

M. K. Meyerhoff and B. L. White, *Psychology Today*, September 1986, p. 44. Reprinted with permission of *Psychology Today*, Copyright 1986 (P. T. Partners, L. P.)

---

but there was no established test that enabled them to quantify this comparison with other groups. However, in the intellectual realm, on the Kaufman Assessment Battery for Children and the Zimmerman Preschool Language Scale, the project children scored significantly higher than would normally be expected. There is little doubt that these children's educational prospects have been significantly enhanced by this programme.

The researchers report that they had success with high-income and low-income families, with white and black families, with parents in their thirties and with teenage parents. In summarising the findings of the project they said:

We feel we have clearly demonstrated some basic principles that could revolutionize the traditional approach to education in this country and around the world. First you are likely to make the greatest difference in the academic prospects of young children if you reach them during the first three years, when the foundations for later development are laid.

Furthermore, the most inexpensive and efficient method is to work through the people who have the greatest influence on children's lives during this period — their parents. Finally, most parents, regardless of social status, educational level or cultural background, are eager to receive and can benefit from the information and support they need to be effective in their role as their children's first and most important teachers.

Calculations of the cost-benefit of programs to encourage a high level of early development among children in the USA were able to convince legislators that for every dollar spent in such programs, seven dollars would be saved in the future due to fewer children needing to repeat classes, less remedial teaching being required, less delinquency developing and so on.[3] The role of the family is as yet little recognised in formal schooling, yet there is no doubt that families play a vital part in developing the foundations on which schooling calls for its success.

A particularly vital stage of family life is the birth and early development of the child. The first child's arrival is particularly important, because parents form their patterns of parenting at this time. They are then particularly eager for information and resources. With later children they are not so easily influenced, tending to continue the patterns they have already established with the first child. Another equally vital stage in family life is the pre-marriage and early marriage period. This, too, is a time when patterns are forming and couples are interested to learn.

Pre-marriage education

FOCCUS (Facilitation Open Couple Communication, Understanding and Study) is another example of a project that has been designed to improve the quality of family life in a nonintrusive way. It was developed in 1985 by the Family Life Office in Omaha, Nebraska. This organisation investigated what was needed for pre-marriage education through surveys among a variety of professionals. Finally, three professionals in the field devised FOCCUS in response to those requirements. FOCCUS is not the first pre-marriage inventory compiled. It was preceded by the Pre-Marital Inventory (PMI) and PREPARE.

FOCCUS is a tool designed to aid couples in their preparation for marriage. It consists basically of a questionnaire, which identifies areas of concern that a couple may wish to discuss. Each individual completes the questionnaire alone, then the couple come together with a facilitator to discuss the results. To each questionnaire there is an answer that the writers consider indicates there is no need for concern regarding that issue. If one or both members have answers that differ from the desired one, that question is discussed. The questionnaire usually takes between forty-five and sixty minutes to complete.

The facilitator is expected to stress to the couple that FOCCUS is in no sense a test. It cannot be failed — or passed, for that matter. Nor is it intended to assess whether or not the couple is compatible enough to marry — the couple are the only judges of that. It is emphasised that the decision to marry cannot be based on FOCCUS alone. It also points out that the results of the questionnaire are by no means a fixed record of the status of the couple's relationship. It is applicable only at the time it is done and should therefore not be kept for future reference.

Lifestyle expectations

FOCCUS is organised into sections, the first being Lifestyle Expectations. This section is designed to highlight the areas of each other's lifestyles that are incompatible and those that are compatible. It gives the partners a better understanding of how they lead their lives as individuals and how that will or won't change once they are a couple. The emphasis is on their expectations of each other, which must be discussed in detail before they can know if they correspond. As research by the Australian Institute of Family Studies found that differences in expectations or changed expectations were a major cause of marriage breakdown, this focus on expectations is clearly relevant. It challenges the couple not only to clarify their expectations before they embark on marriage, but to intro-duce into their relationship a process of sharing, clarifying and negotiating expectations.

Friends and interests

The need for interdependence is established in this section. The questionnaire can indicate a tendency towards too much independence or dependence. Either extreme is considered to be a problem only if it worries one or both partners. The facilitator may, however, consider that the couple are un-aware of a potential problem area and suggest it be discussed. The couple decide whether to do so or not.

Personality match

This section focuses on the personality types of each individ-ual, and areas of possible misunderstanding are highlighted. The aim is to enable each individual to be more aware of her/his own temperament, behaviour patterns and preferences and also those of the partner. It should enable the partners to be more tolerant of their differences because they are better understood and appreciated. The study into their personalities is undertaken with the appreciation that all personality matches can constitute successful relationships, given enough tolerance and understanding.

Personal issues

There may be personal issues that worry one or both partners in relation to their partnership, a history of alcoholism in the family, for instance. This section facilitates discussion of any such issue that could be of concern.

Communication

Communication skills are directly addressed at this point. The essence of FOCCUS is to facilitate and encourage com-munication, and this section provides an opportunity for spe-cific communication skills to be learnt or improved. Skills that often require work are listening, sharing one's self-knowledge, resolving conflict, apologising and forgiving.

Key bonders

FOCCUS concentrates on what research has indicated are the 'key bonders'. They are primarily religion or values, children, sex and money. Common values or religious beliefs can work as a significant bonder, while differences in these areas can cause considerable conflict. It is an issue, along with sex and money, that is frequently not discussed easily or constructively after marriage. FOCCUS believes it should be discussed in the couple's preparation period.

Like religion, parenting can provide a positive bonding for the couple or conflict over differing parenting styles. Decisions will need to be made about the mode of parenting that will be adopted.

A couple's sexual relationship is one of the most important bonders in their marriage. However, there are often unrealistic expectations of each other's sexual roles, which can give rise to power games. FOCCUS helps to identify any aspect of the sexual relationship that should be discussed to prevent destructive patterns developing.

Money plays a prominent role in most marriage breakdowns. In examining how money will be dealt with, FOCCUS addresses the balance of power in the relationship.

The final issue raised in FOCCUS is whether or not the couple are ready to marry. Is it a totally free choice? What is their motivation? It may be that they are expecting a child. If so, how will they deal with that?

The constant emphasis in FOCCUS is that things will not magically change after the wedding. Problems won't resolve themselves. Individuals will not metamorphose. One's partner will not change more than 50 per cent of his/her qualities throughout the marriage. Reality must be accepted and built upon.

FOCCUS's main thrust is to identify *potential* problem areas and thereby prevent destructive patterns from emerging. It is a concrete and effective way of bringing to the surface issues that can lead to marriage breakdown. It is an active way of empowering couples to make autonomous, informed decisions.

In Nebraska, where the questionnaire was first developed, 14 per cent of those who discuss the questionnaire and attend an educative course either postpone or cancel their marriage (similar figures are reported for PREPARE and PMI). It has recently been introduced into Australia. Responses to it from priests and ministers who have facilitated it and from couples are remarkably positive. Pastors find it enables them to play a much more effective role in counselling the couple about to be married. Couples themselves appreciate the serious and sustained conversation about their relationship, initiated by FOCCUS and facilitated by an interested, concerned third party.

The relationship of institutions to families

A second approach to resourcing families is for institutions to alter their practice in order to recognise in concrete ways the power and influence of the family and its unique role. Some institutions have found that relatively minor changes in the way they perform their role can be empowering to families and can strengthen family ties and the shared responsibility of family members for each other. Klaus and Kennell's research into hospital practices with newborns is one example of this in the medical field, a family-centred approach to learning to read is an educational example and other examples relating to research and the church will also be described.

Health: mothers and infants
In chapter 1 the importance of enabling mothers to have uninterrupted time with their newborns was discussed. It was shown that the positive effects of early interaction between infant and mother persisted over five years, and was associated with enhanced development of the children, even to a raised IQ of seven points above what would normally be expected.

A number of directions are suggested by such studies. One is that the support of positive family functioning would be effective and cost-efficient. If we consider the amount of funds or resources that would be needed to achieve a seven point increase in IQ at later stages of life, or through schooling programs, the significance of early bonding between parent and child is apparent. For in spite of the millions of dollars spent on curriculum development, reducing class sizes, and providing buildings and facilities, only rarely can these result in a seven point increase in IQ scores maintained over a five-year period.

Secondly, the evidence discussed in this book shows conclusively that the private realm is more important than the public. To find that IQ at five years of age is related to the amount of time a mother spends *looking* at the infant at one month of age is astounding. The amount of time a mother spends gazing at an infant at one month is also related to the child's verbal ability at two years of age. Yet we persist in pouring millions of dollars into programs in the public realm (very few of which could claim such correlations) and ignore the private realm as if it was of no consequence and as if no significant effects were being generated there.

It should be noted that this powerful improvement is the result of a change in practice at a critical moment in the family life-cycle, and this alerts us to the vital nature of *the intersection of institutional and family worlds and of critical times in the family life-cycle.*

A 'reason' given for ignoring the positive possibilities of the family realm is that the family is private and cannot be invaded or manipulated by public institutions in the way schools and hospitals can. But enabling family interaction at the early stage of a child's life is simply to alter a practice at the *intersection* of family and institution. The effectiveness of the intervention is likely to be linked to its *occurrence at a vital moment in the family life-cycle.*

It should not pass without comment that in the case of mother-child bonding all the institution had to do was *to reduce its intrusiveness into an intimate family moment and return to the family some small measure of control over its own processes.* With hindsight it is amazing that the situation ever existed in which mothers *were not allowed* to be with their infants immediately following birth, yet this was universal in English-speaking countries. I am not denying or belittling the contributions of modern medicine to family well-being, but suggesting that bureaucratic procedures in hospitals are not always in the best interest of family members.

Research discussed earlier in this book suggests institutions do not always give primacy to practices that would be of optimum benefit to families. This raises the question of who needs to change. When family concerns are raised in the public realm, it is often in the context of family problems, or advocating the need for change within families. But it may be that institutions need to change in both their attitudes and practices towards families, and change in the direction of greater respect for family processes and realisation that problems may not always be caused by families. Institutions can make problems for families, and they should examine how their practices impact on families and search for practices that are supportive of the families' own creative process. It is always possible to discover new ways to build and enrich the partnership between institutions and families.

Education: the Belfield and Haringey Reading Scheme

This program was developed in Belfield, a depressed housing estate in London, where, at the time of the study, one-third of the parents were unemployed, and half the children belonged to a one-parent family. Two-thirds of the children qualified for free school meals. The project was intended to encourage the parents to listen to their children reading. The parents were to provide an 'audience' for the child, rather than to be teachers. All parents co-operated enthusiastically. Peter Wilby of the *Sunday Times* reported that 'in three years, not one parent has refused to help his or her child'.[4] Even if the parents themselves were illiterate, the outcome of the parents listening to the children reading was that the children's reading improved dramatically.

The same scheme was tried in Haringey, another working-class, multi-racial area of London. After two years, two-thirds of the children in a control group were *below* the national average for their age in reading (the expected achievement level for this socio-economic area), and over half the children who had taken part in the project were *above* the national average for their age. As Peter Wilby commented, 'for them, the scheme had effectively wiped out the educational disadvantage of being working-class'.[5] The project was compared with the alternatives of employing experienced teachers or remedial reading experts to hear children read. The parent-listening scheme was much more effective, as well as much more economical than either of these alternatives, indicating that the interest and time of the parents has a significance for the children that cannot be easily replicated. The professional qualifications of the remedial reading expert do not replace the interest and time of the parent in enabling the child to learn to read. Similar programs have been developed and tried in other places,[6] but few have attempted the evaluation reported for Belfield and Haringey.

The effectiveness of the Belfield and Haringey Reading Scheme indicates the importance of the institution *recognising* the family's role. The effectiveness of early education programs depends on family interaction (such as the amount of time parents spent with children or the parents' shared activity with the child). In fact, programs that introduced children's groups too early actually lowered children's achievement. It seemed that over-emphasis on groups gave parents the impression that their role was less than essential, and that the really effective agent was the professional expert in the group situation. As a consequence, parents reduced their own involvement in the education of their children. This resulted in falling measures of children's learning.[7]

In reviewing this research, Bronfenbrenner emphasises the need for 'ecological intervention', a strategy that can result in a major transformation of the environment for the child and for the family. Programs that were effective over time in raising the competence level of children had two factors in common: parental involvement with the child (they were family-centred rather than child-centred), and recognition by institutions of the primacy of the parental role.[8] This is precisely what is provided by the Belfield and Haringey Reading Scheme. Such programs increase shared family-time, encourage strengthened family responsibility and family ties, and recognise in a concrete way the family's role as the 'primary educator'.[9] Such programs enable parents to develop a relationship with the school and to participate meaningfully in the school's work, a factor known to improve a child's educational chances.[10]

In the Belfield and Haringey Reading Scheme, some of the parents learned to read, a bonus of the program. But the key factor is one that supports the conclusions of the Plowden Report, described in chapter 1. Children will succeed if they are convinced that school achievement is important to the parents.

In the Belfield and Haringey Reading Scheme all families were visited and all families took part, so there was no stigmatising of particular families. This also applies in the Australian version of the program at the Doveton Cluster of Schools in the Melbourne area. All communications with parents — meetings, home visits, lunches and supply of a video explaining the program — are planned to fit in with family time. The school is not prying into family privacy or being deflected from the task for which it has a mandate: to teach children to read. There is absolutely no suggestion that families are all the same or that only one model of family is acceptable. As all families are visited, and all take part, all models are accepted as valid. If parents cannot listen to children read, an older brother or sister, a grandparent or neighbour is encouraged to do so.

The family is the most effective and economical system for the rearing of children, and as Bronfenbrenner says, for 'making human beings human'. Yet Bronfenbrenner finds that the erosion of the 'ecology of family life' in the United States is undermining the contribution of families. 'A child requires public policies and practices that provide opportunity, status, example, encouragement, stability and, above all, time for parenthood, primarily by parents, but also by all adults in the society. And unless you have those external supports, the internal systems can't work. They fail.'[11]

There is a need for an enhanced status for parenting. Any significant change in the status of family and parenting will involve changes in other structures of society, especially changes in the world of work and the neighbourhood.[12] The Belfield and Haringey Reading Scheme increases family status because it involves a public institution recognising in a concrete way the role and influence of the family. This is to accord status to the family. It is an example of an educational program that takes the family factor seriously and harnesses the family factor to make the public institution's role more effective. Many other educational programs could be adapted to incorporate the family. For example, Coleman has drawn attention to lower drop-out rates in Catholic High Schools in the USA being related to the type of community around the school, especially the fact that the parents of students know each other. This fact opens the way for initiatives in other schools to create this type of community. Obviously, many more educational programs could be adapted to incorporate the family factor rather than to attempt to replace or ignore this vital factor. Next, we look at a research project that also adapts to the family factor.

Research: family issues

In chapter 10 it was alleged that certain views of society are inimical to positive perception of families. Researchers and social scientists have been charged with being major proponents and purveyors of these views and of being insufficiently aware of biases within their disciplines that are damaging to families.[13]

The possibility of such bias was brought home to me particularly strongly when I was asked to assist in gathering information from groups presumed to be opposed to the introduction of more liberal distribution of alcoholic liquor. I asked whether the parents of teenagers had been surveyed and was told they had not. When I asked why, as they were the group most likely to be concerned, I was informed that it was impossible to survey parents on such a question. 'You can't survey parents. Parents cannot understand these issues,' the researcher said. After some discussion, she began to plan a strategy to gather parental response to the proposed laws. The fact that parents are ordinary members of the community not incompetents, incapable of understanding the simplest issues is often forgotten. Carol McMillan's *Woman Reason and Nature* provides a fascinating insight into the genesis of this negative stereotype.

This tendency to see families as merely passive victims or recipients of initiatives emanating from the public realm is most evident in the lack of research into family perspectives. I can bring to mind only three small studies that explore family perceptions of family issues,[14] and this indicates that our researcher's assumption that 'You can't survey parents. Parents do not understand these issues' may be quite widespread.

Little is known of what family members see to be the sources of pressures on families. Nor is much known of any changes desired by families in government policies or in the interface between families and public institutions that could enhance the experience of family life. It seems to be more common for researchers to test their own perceptions and assumptions of what are the sources of pressure on families than it is to consult with families and gather their observations and reflections on family in society. There are few avenues whereby family perceptions may be expressed. The lack of open-ended research into what family members desire in the way of family policy blocks one important avenue through which a family voice could be heard. Bellah's *Habits of the Heart* provides a refreshing model for such research.

It was argued in chapter 6 that there is a need for further research into areas related to the positive possibilities of families. While a great deal is known of the factors associated with well-being in families, no study (with the possible exception of Elder's longitudinal studies of families during the Great Depression) has focused on how some families develop the characteristics that seem to account for the high level competence of their members.

A study by a group of Australian medical researchers indicates a different way in which researchers may modify their practice in order to take the family factor more into account. Dolby and colleagues used neurological and behavioural tests, not only to measure premature infant development, but, by demonstrating the tests to the parents, teaching the parents greater sensitivity to their infants' signals and increased knowledge of their babies' skills. These demonstrations led to smoother interactions between parents and children, to more self-confidence on the parents' part, and to improved scores for the infants on standard measures of development.[15] This small example illustrates how an approach that recognises the family factor and the right of the parents to the information generated by research into their infants can increase family self-esteem, skills, ties, responsibility and power.

The reader can best judge whether the example of this research project in sharing with the parents the knowledge generated through study of infants is the norm or whether it is a pattern that needs to be more commonly followed. In either case the example indicates that researchers, like other professionals employed by public institutions, can choose to operate in ways that enhance family power and autonomy or that undermine it. Researchers can take knowledge generated with the co-operation of families and direct it to the public realm of researchers, experts and professionals, thereby increasing the distance between families and professionals and experts, or they can share this knowledge with families.

Religion: the church and families

The churches play a very important role in relation to family issues. A consistent finding of research into well-functioning families is that church membership and the maintenance of the family's spiritual traditions and rituals are a source of strength for family life. One reason for this is that church membership often provides the basic network of support so essential to families. Especially for mobile families, the new parish often provides the pool from which friends, interest groups, baby-sitters, sympathetic professionals, advice on schools, housing, jobs and so on are gleaned.

Because members of religious groups have close links with their parish or synagogue at the key transition-points of the family life-cycle, especially birth, marriage and death, the churches have access to families in a quite unique way. The church is the only institution with the whole family as its client, which adds another dimension to its role as partner to families. In some countries the whole development of marriage guidance and marriage counselling was spearheaded by church bodies or individuals with strong church connections. Many of the programs to support and enrich family life were also developed within a church framework. Hence the church is a particularly important institution to observe in seeking clues for ways families could be supported and empowered.

201

However, while there is evidence that church-membership is often a strength in family life, surveys of church members indicate many needs in the family area. A church survey of families in the outer western region of Sydney in 1982–83 reported seven crucial reasons given by families for their sense of frustration and inadequacy.[16] They included consumerism and the pressures it brings to bear on family life, financial fears and worries that leave parents with a sense of inadequacy and pending failure as 'providers', and the absence of help in the form of education, instruction, advice, and/or counselling for families, especially in the early years of their development. In particular, the report stressed the sense of many families that they are very much alone in a crowded, urban society without extended family, local friends or even Christian community to rely on in times of celebration or in times of need.

An earlier survey of 825,000 members of the Catholic Church in the USA reported findings similar to the Sydney survey. The top eight needs identified by respondents included the need for support for family values and for family life education (parenting skills; pre-marital, marital and post-marital enrichment; sexuality education for parents and children, the ageing, handicapped and other areas). There were needs in relation to divorce, especially making the divorced welcome in the pews and ministering to their special needs, for increased communication skills, for teaching families how to communicate with each other, especially husband/wife, parent/teen and family/church. Families asked for help with pressures that militate against family life, including helping families deal with television, drugs, music, advertising, alcohol, mobility, affluence, unemployment and the changing attitudes of women.

The Sydney survey was a dialogue with families. The first responses of families were collated and summarised and fed back to the families. Later, the researchers returned to visit families again and to hear their response to the collated report of what they and other families had said. In this report the compilers speak of the 'living church . . . the families, the young marrieds, the lone parents, the youth, the handicapped, the unemployed, the burdened, the elderly' and conclude:

If the members of this living church were to form small integrated units of support and interest to address the issues that confront them in their daily living, then eventually there could come about a ground-level or grass-roots contribution to the challenging issues of our time.[17]

A number of different church-initiated programs will be described in order to see how another institution (other than education, medicine and research from which examples were given earlier) is responding to the needs of families.

Family Ministry

The Catholic diocese of Omaha in Nebraska, USA, is known for its particular model of Family Ministry. The Family Ministry program is based on certain assumptions. The first is that all families, no matter how hurting or fragmented, have tremendous strengths and the power to help and support other families. A second assumption is that individuals or families who have been through a certain experience have a quality of caring and support to offer others in a similar situation that is unique and healing.

From this principle follows the concept of like-to-like ministry: the real experts in the area of marriage and family are spouses and family members. There are times and situations that require specialised, professional services such as counselling, but the basic ministry to families lies in the day-to-day support that family members and families give each other. This principle is particularly evident in the area of family bereavement. The closeness and support that another who has experienced the death of a spouse, parent or child can offer a grieving family or family member cannot be replaced by the professional counsellor, though at times the professional counsellor may be needed to help untangle the web of pathological grief.

Family Ministry in Omaha is closely linked to the spiritual beliefs of the community and is seen to be a true form of Christian ministry or service. The director of the program, Sr Barbara Markey, stresses that when parents get up at night to give a child a drink of water, when they nurse a sick child, when they earn the family income and prepare the meals they are fulfilling the command to 'feed the hungry, give water to the thirsty, visit the sick'.

Other aspects of this program that have made it acceptable to parishes and families are that it is based on a commitment to networking and to non-competiveness. It is never the role of the Family Ministry team to duplicate what is already being done. Hence issues raised in various parishes can often be addressed by calling together those who are affected by the problem and calling on resources within the parish, within other parishes in the diocese or from outside agencies. The aim is always to empower people at the local level to establish their own response to the issue rather than attempt to do it for them, hence the emphasis on a facilitative empowering model rather than a focus on particular programs or strategies.

The Family Life Office is the headquarters of several programs of support for families, in particular a pre-marriage education program and the Rainbows program for children suffering the loss of a parent (discussed later). However, the core of the program is the leadership training for Family Ministry, run in conjunction with the nearby Jesuit University, Creighton College. The training, run on a number of weekends over two years, provides the participants — volunteers sponsored by parishes — with some basics of theology, liturgy, family dynamics plus skills to enable them to be the one in the parish who is in touch with families, who surfaces the family issues that need to be addressed and who calls in whatever help is needed to enable the parishioners to respond to their own issues. At this level too, the role is facilitative: it is not the family minister's role to attempt to be the one who does everything and who solves all the problems. The role is to call the relevant people together with whatever resources are needed and to start the process of responding to the issue.

The training, while basic, is backed up by ongoing support during and after the initial two years. The office supplies a telephone support line, the opportunity to freely consult with office staff and to be put in contact with other suitable resource people. There is also a staffed resource centre to provide books, tapes and programs related to family issues and family development. Regular information evenings, seminars and get-togethers provide the opportunity for Family Ministers from different parishes to swap notes.

At parish level this project has resulted in response to the financial crisis of farm families in rural areas, which include ways of alleviating the crushing poverty as well as responding to the spate of suicides that have ensued from the crisis. Families have reached out to each other to help overcome the stress, the grief and the sense of shame farm families feel when they fail to make a success of a farm that has been in the family for generations.

In parishes with many young families there are celebrations of the events of daily life: births, birthdays, wedding anniversaries, children starting school are all the centre of celebrations that bring people together and give status to the ordinary events of early family life, so much of which can be drudgery if performed in isolation and without reminder of the big picture.

In parishes with many elderly, the aged themselves have taken responsibility for caring for less mobile and active members. Some of the elderly said they are living more creatively than at any previous stage of life.

Omaha's model of Family Ministry has proven adaptable to a range of parishes and family situations from the outer suburban parish with young families and many children, to the older area with many elderly members, to rural areas suffering the devastating effects of rural depression. Evidence of its effectiveness in supporting families has created interest and inspired emulation in many other states and in other countries. It is just one example of the myriad of ways religious groups are seeking to respond to the new needs of today's families.

Small Christian communities
The sense of isolation reported in the Sydney Survey has been noted in many places and many congregations have responded by attempting to develop 'small Christian communities' within parishes. The Sydney parish of Terrey Hills has become well known for the way members have created small groups of families and individuals who meet regularly for prayer, Bible reading and reflection and mutual enjoyment

and support. Many of the activities that in other parishes revolve around the large congregation in Terrey Hills are done within smaller groupings within which members find the mutual sharing and support that the Sydney Survey found many families crave.

Other parishes have developed a variety of ways to strengthen and support the family's role and to strengthen the supportive networks between families. In North Ringwood the preparation for First Communion, First Reconciliation and Confirmation is done primarily within families. The families of the candidates meet in small groups for several weeks. The children learn the meaning of the Eucharist, Reconciliation and Confirmation within their own family and in discussion, games, sharing and prayer with other families. Their own reflection on the themes of gift, of promise, of thanksgiving, of forgiveness, of courage and trial are deepened from hearing from the adults and other children in the group what these realities have meant to them and why they struggle to make them more real in their lives.[18]

Even the geographic layout of this parish reflects the commitment to family support. A car park for parents dropping off children to school is located in a safe, off-street location, which encourages parents to get out of their cars and talk with others for a few minutes, establishing those informal networks that have been shown to be so effective in enabling children to learn and to stay on at school. Morning Mass is at nine o'clock, again to suit the mothers who often stay on afterwards for a cup of coffee and a chat to others. This means that on any morning a mother can call in and have the opportunity to share with others.

In explaining the establishment of this pattern, parishioners spoke of the village well. They had considered a modern community needed some equivalent of the village well where a woman could go at any time and find others with whom she could talk, celebrate life's daily joys, joke, and, when needed, comfort or be comforted, ask for help or offer help. Coleman's findings on the impact of the community that surrounds a high school on drop-out rates demonstrates the effectiveness of strategies such as these. Another small group that aims to both create a network of support for families and to offer the opportunity to learn skills of use in day-to-day life of the family is the Family Cluster.

Family Clusters

Many models of family support groups or Family Clusters have been developed. The following account describes the approach to Family Clusters developed by the US educator Dr Margaret Sawin. In Sawin's model a Family Cluster is a group of four or five families who contract to meet regularly with leaders over an extended period of time for shared learning related to their concerns, hopes, questions, joys, problems and dreams within the family.[19] A cluster provides mutual support, training in skills to facilitate family living and celebration of life and beliefs. Sawin developed the cluster model within the First Baptist Church of Rochester, New York. It has since been adopted by other denominations throughout the United States, in Canada and to a small extent in Australia. It has also inspired a number of adaptations and alternative ways of supporting and enriching family life and has been adapted to non-church contexts.

The length and timing of sessions is open to negotiation between leaders and participants. Sessions may be conducted at a family camp situation, over one or two weekends or by meeting one evening a week for an agreed period. Clusters often meet for two hours for eight to ten consecutive weeks. The schedule for a typical session begins with a 'straggle-in' time of fiteen minutes while families arrive, greet each other and begin to take part in activities, such as solving puzzles, writing on a graffiti sheet, making a model of their family in clay or with Leggo or drawing something they like to do with their family. After a brief sandwich meal, about twenty minutes are devoted to games and singing and a further ten to airing the concerns of the group. The structured learning activity follows and lasts about an hour. The final ten minutes are given to evaluation and closure.

Family clusters differ from education programs such as PET in that all family members can attend (even babies can be accommodated in its flexible approach) and the emphasis is on enjoyment, fun and on families supporting each other and learning from each other. Family Clusters focus on family strength rather than family pathology and provide a setting where family strengths can be recognised and affirmed. Families see the different ways other families approach family issues and have the opportunity of adopting any patterns that seem to them to be valuable.

The all-age nature of the learning group is another strength. The children are sometimes the first to respond to a new situation, and readily lead the older members into a situation where games, music, play-acting, drawing and making things provide opportunities for members to communicate their perspectives in new modes, and at the same time to learn new ways of relating within the family.

Family Clusters may focus on any area of interest to the families. A church group may focus on preparation for a sacrament such as the Eucharist or Confirmation, on a season such as Easter or Christmas, or on a theme such as forgiveness. Both church and other groups may choose topics such as values, family stories, the environment, choosing a lifestyle, consumerism, peace, our community or whatever concerns the particular families involved.

However, most families, no matter how healthy, can benefit from learning skills of communication and conflict-resolution and from opportunities to increase individual and family self-esteem. So these tend to be a large part of the agenda of a first series of meetings.

In interviews with sixteen families who had taken part in three different clusters, each led by a different leadership team, all members said they would attend another series of sessions and would recommend other families to do so, though one family made the condition that certain emphases be included. Most members could relate learnings related to self, family and others. Many members could report evidence of improved communication within the family and other settings. Members valued the experience of community, increased understanding of self, family and others, improved ability to communicate and the intergenerational and non-competitive nature of the groups. They liked the shared experience of going somewhere together as a family and actively participating in stimulating, challenging tasks. There was resentment of a few attempts by leaders to use 'schooling' type methods to restore order, and two families expressed disappointment that they were not challenged more by the learning processes. Leaders found the leadership role demanding, but satisfying, some (who were experienced educators) rating it as some of the best educational work in which they had ever been involved. The following comments taken from interviews give some idea of the members' response to this experience.

Fathers said:
'We joined to get to know other families. We were amazed that we got to know each other better.'

'My children saw me not just as a parent but as a person.'

'I felt loved.'

'I liked acting like a big kid.'

'I loved getting to know the little kids and having them get to know me.'

'Family cluster is a party. It's not a training. It would be a pity if it became a training.'

Mothers said:
'It's a non-competitive group. School and most situations are very competitive.'

'It was a renewal for us as a family. A time to be together that we wouldn't have had otherwise.'

'The best part was the shared experience. We all went somewhere and did something together.'

'I felt that our family was O.K.'

'I was very impressed with the teenagers.'

'There was a heightened sense of community, of identity with other families. I see it in the faces of the children when they meet one of their favourite adults in the street. There's a special bond, an increased care and concern for one another.'

Teenagers said:
'I found out how I affect other people, how other people feel when I do certain things. I've become more tolerant.' (sixteen-year-old boy)

'I found out that lots of the things I do without thinking about them are very hurtful to other people, so I try not to do them. I realised parents are people, not jailers.' (fifteen-year-old girl)

'The adults didn't treat us as mini-adults.' (fourteen-year-old girl)

'You weren't forced to [say things], but you were expected to, and you wanted to and you found you could.' (thirteen-year-old boy)

Younger children said:

'Before it was hard to talk to adults. We didn't know what to say. Now we know what to say.' (eleven-year-old girl)

'It makes a family a closer family and brings you closer to other people.' (eleven-year-old girl)

'It would be good if there was another cluster. We had so much fun. It would be good if other people could join in.' (eight-year-old boy)

'I learnt that other people liked me. People don't look as if they like you.' (eight-year-old girl)

'I liked the games. You play games with other kids. You don't usually play games with Mum and Dad.' (nine-year-old girl)

'Everyone was not just a child or a parent or a member of a family, but was a person in their own right and got a chance to speak.' (eleven-year-old boy)

A case-study evaluation of six families who had taken part in a series of twelve cluster sessions found that, following the cluster experience, every family had taken steps to create more shared family time.[20] It was also evident that the members felt a much deeper sense of belonging to the parish in which this cluster was held. They felt much closer to the other families and to individuals within the other families. It was particularly stressed that adults had got to know teenagers and younger children, and this was corroborated by the children's reports. These cross-generation friendships were appreciated on both sides. This finding was of interest because this parish was one known for its sense of community, and the families who took part were all well established in the area with many friends. This case study indicates that even in very good parishes there exists the possibility of developing ways by which even stronger networks of support could be built. As one adult said in the evaluation: 'Before we began, we said we knew those other families. We didn't really know them. Now we know them.'

Friendship and support for grieving children

In 1983 Mrs Suzy Yehl, the divorced mother of three boys, realised that her children were suffering as much grief over her divorce as she was. Finding little support for them, Suzy soon saw the need for a program that would help the children of divorce as adult programs had helped her. She began to develop such a program and so the Rainbows program to provide peer-support for children grieving the death of a parent or sibling, or the divorce of parents, was born.

Each week for twelve weeks the children who take part meet in small groups of three to five children with a caring adult to talk about how they feel in their new family situation. Through talking and listening to others, the children are able to express some of the hurts, fears, doubts and angers that are part of a human response to the loss of a loved person. They discover that they are not the only ones to experience these feelings and that in fact they are normal to feel the way they do. One seven-year-old boy, after several weeks in the program, said to his teacher, 'I think all the other children in my group are lying.' Further discussion revealed that he had been so convinced that he was the only person who felt as he did that his first response to hearing other children speak of similar situations and how they were reacting was to conclude that they must be making it all up.

The Rainbows program can be introduced to a youth group, parish or school, any place where children attend regularly. Some counselling agencies have introduced it. Schools are in a good location, because school can be the still point in a turning world to a child going through the trauma of separation and divorce or the sickness and death of a parent.

Suzy says that we know children do not come to school and leave their feelings outside the classroom door. 'The school setting can provide the guidance of nurturing and caring adults, peer support and a secure place for sharing so that healing and acceptance can take place.' Thousands of children in the USA have taken part in the program, which has recently been introduced to Australia. An evaluation at one of the first Australian schools to introduce Rainbows found teachers, leaders and children strongly positive about the program. Teachers had commented that some children who were once withdrawn and disruptive were becoming more settled and more involved in classroom activity. Parents had commented to the parish priest on incidents where they had been able to have an honest, open conversation with a previously 'unreachable' child. The parish priest commented, 'We have learned so much. The children have trusted us with their stories and shown us that young hearts can bear so much. We hope we've eased the pain and shown them a Rainbow or two. Next year we hope to do it a bit better.'

The examples given above are a small sampling of a multitude of programs and approaches to supporting families, especially to support families to establish the kinds of relationships within the family and between the family and the outside world that is associated with well-being. These programs demonstrate that it is possible to support families of the late twentieth century in ways that respect the dignity of families and institutions. This work must continue because we can have no human society without strong families and today's families face many new challenges.

Family policy

There has been a demand for family policy in many countries for many years. It was one of the hoped-for outcomes of the White House conferences on family in the USA. In Australia the 1985 report of the Senate Standing Committee on Social Welfare recommended, unsuccessfully, the establishment of an Australian Children and Families Commission. The roles of this proposed Commission were to include 'promoting the stability of the family' and 'examining the means of maintaining the family entity as the fundamental group unit in society'.

Such proposals have failed to materialise for a number of reasons. Steiner's objections were summarised in chapters 4 and 6 and are based on these notions: family is the last bastion of privacy which must not be invaded by the public realm; no notion of strength in families exists; the differences between family types are so great that no family policy can be developed without imposing one model of family on the diversity of family forms. All these objections have been challenged throughout this book: family needs privacy but not every aspect of family life is private; the public realm is already invading families and one reason for public policy is to protect families from that invasion; we know a great deal of the factors that are associated with strength in family systems, and public policy should be fostering those strengths and limiting the factors that weaken family well-being; sometimes the differences in family types have been exaggerated so as to obscure the common ground that exists between families of different types and the common needs all families have for an environment supportive of marriage and family life.

Steiner's major and underlying objection is that under the Carter administration family was unveiled as a major policy area but without a theory to explain and guide public intervention. All that has gone before is intended as a contribution towards the development of that missing theory. The critical elements of this proposed theory are: evidence of the impact of families on individual and communal competence and well-being; evidence of a progressive fragmentation of families so that the process of making human beings human is breaking down; evidence that we do know the factors that are essential to family competence and health and that the essential factors reside in the family's internal dynamics and processes and its relation to the outside world; and evidence that there is an antipathy or tension between the public and private realms that in recent times has undermined and invaded family autonomy and strength and is destroying the supportive environment that families need.

Another aspect of the difficulties Steiner has identified in government adopting a family policy is that it is so difficult to discern and agree on what family policy is and should be. Moynihan comments:

A fair point. Yet experience suggests that policy will emerge, given a conducive institutional setting; perhaps more accurately, policy will be discerned and in some rough way assessed. Does the United States have a trade policy? It has many. Let the secretary of agriculture propose to subsidize farm exports, and the U.S. trade representative soon enough will make a judgement of the policy implications. A civil rights policy? A fiscal policy? An environmental policy? Institutions attend to such matters. Usually several; commonly with conflicting views. But the subject is not simply overlooked; it is somebody's business . . .

In the area of family, no such ministry or department exists, hence the interests of families are lost between a multitude of different departments: the economy, health, education, social welfare and so on. This is true of virtually every Western country. The director of the Marriage Guidance Council of Western Australia wrote recently:

> Australia persists in having 'Ministers for Family Breakdown' rather than 'Ministers for Supporting the Family' at both Commonwealth and State levels . . . The simple and extraordinary fact is that there is no Commonwealth Government Department and no Minister charged with responsibility for developing and implementing policy to support families and prevent family breakdown. The Commonwealth Attorney-General's Department, which funds marriage counselling organisations, has no policies and denies it has a policy role. Other Departments and Ministers are almost entirely concerned with remedial programmes to help families seriously at risk or already experiencing breakdown . . .
> What is needed as a minimum structure is a Minister responsible for family policy, backed by a specialist policy unit . . . Without a Minister being responsible for implementation, no family policy statement is going to be taken seriously; and without appropriate, specialist public services, no family policy is going to be implemented.[19]

A group of family agencies in the USA has proposed six principles which could be used to guide policy-making and program development in the family area.

Institutions and families

In 1986 in the USA, the House Select Committee on Children, Youth and Families began the work of identifying different kinds of criteria to be used in assessing the effectiveness of social programs. An initial framework was developed and the Minority Deputy Staff Director asked Steven Preister of the American Association for Marriage and Family Therapy to set up a task force to examine and develop one fundamental type of criteria, namely, family criteria.

The Family Criteria Task Force, an *ad hoc* group consisting of members with senior responsibility in a number of family-related organisations (the American Association of Marriage and Family Therapists, the Family Impact Seminar, the American Home Economics Association, Family Service America and the National Council on Family Relations), met from April 1987 to February 1988. It has proposed six principles to guide policymaking and program evaluation from a family perspective.[22] The Task Force believes that one of the major goals of adopting a family perspective in policymaking and human services should be to strengthen the partnership between families and social institutions. It is intended that if the proposed criteria gain public acceptance they be used to assess the effects of proposed and existing policies and programs on family life and well-being.

The authors of the report draw attention to the fact that the call for a systematic analysis of how laws and regulations affect families was one of the top six recommendations of the 1980 White House Conference on Families, gaining the support of almost 90 per cent of the over 2000 delegates.

Noting that one of the difficulties with family policy discussions has been the intensely bitter emotional and value disputes that have been aroused, the report writers defend their strongly value-laden criteria. Asserting that values issues are invariably present in policymaking, they deny the possibility of value-free policy, but assert that the value content can be rigorously and calmly examined. They note the tendency for liberals to fear that the main goal conservatives have in the family policy field is to put mothers back in the home, re-establish patriarchy and diminish the role of government. Similarly, conservatives believe that liberals care more about alleviating the consequences of divorce than strengthening marriage, value teenagers' rights more than parental authority and see little danger in government intrusion into the home.

At the same time the Task Force considers that value conflicts over family issues have been greatly exaggerated, obscuring the fact that a broad middle ground exists on many family-policy goals. They perceive a growing consensus that absent parents (usually fathers) should be required to pay child support; that welfare mothers should be expected and helped to become self-supporting; that employers should adapt work schedules and demands to take account of family responsibilities; and that governments should assist poor families with child-care. The Family Criteria Task Force therefore proposes the six principles with some degree of hope and confidence that they will attract a wide spectrum of support from the American public. The Principles of a Family Perspective that they propose are as follows:

1. *Policies and programs should encourage and reinforce family, parental and marital commitment and stability, especially when children are involved.*

   An assumption of this Report is that the well-being of society is promoted by the well-being of families. Hence, it is in society's best interest to ensure that public policies and programs support family stability.

2. *The first presumption of policies and programs should be to support and supplement family functioning, rather than substituting for family functioning.*

   A primary objective of family policies and programs should be the strengthening of families' own abilities to manage and fulfil their own functions, including care of their own members. Services that substitute for families should be provided only in those situations where it is clear that the family will not be able to function sufficiently even with support, or when the burden on the family is excessive.

3. *Policies and programs must recognise the strength and persistence of family ties, even when they are problematic.*

   Policies or programs that attempt to assist or change one person in a family must take into account the influence of the family on that person, and how the desired change or service may affect the family system as a whole. For example, current alcoholism research identifies the dynamic of a co-dependent partner of an alcoholic and the lifelong effects of alcoholism on offspring of alcoholics, particularly adult children of alcoholics.

Further, changes in family relationships (for example, through divorce or adoption) are not simply events; they are processes which family members must deal with over time.

4. *Policies and programs must treat families as partners when providing services to individuals if families are to fulfil the various tasks society expects of them.*

Families need to be provided with information and resources that will empower them and to the extent possible, be given rights to make or share in decisions. Families' rights especially need protection in the education and health care of children and when children are removed from their parents.

Further, policies and programs need to acknowledge that there is a continuum of family involvement. Some families can and will be more involved in this partnership than others, but all families should be given the opportunity for some level of involvement.

5. *Policies and programs must recognise the diversity of family life.*

Families come in many forms and configurations. Programs and policies must take into account their different effects on different types of families, since an objective of a policy or a program may be beneficial for one type of family but may harm another. The diversities that need to be taken into account include different types of family structure; different stages of the family life-cycle; different ethnic, cultural, racial and religious backgrounds; socio-economic differences; and differing community contexts.

6. *Families in greatest economic and social need, and those determined to be most vulnerable to breakdown, should have first priority in government policies and programs.*

Targeting the vulnerable has long been a tradition in our government's responsibility to promote the general welfare. A corollary of this principle is that policies and programs should seek to prevent serious crises rather than targeting all resources on remedial services.

Advocacy for families

The *Strategy for Strengthening Families Report* proposes another function for institutions that have responsibility for family issues or whose functions impinge on the well-being of families: the role of advocacy for families and family issues. By challenging the perception of family issues as too conflict-ridden for consensus to be a possibility, and by attempting to explicate a common ground, the Family Criteria Task Force are playing a positive role in establishing agreed criteria, which would be used to judge whether or not programs and policies are supportive of families.

Conclusion

The failure to provide an adequate infrastructure of support for families is a serious social issue and one that is a challenge to every level and group in society. The scandal of homeless children and child poverty, of rising levels of addiction and child suicide, of increasing poverty among women, of children whose childhood is marred by parental conflict or neglect or of the loss of their family and childhood home can be addressed only through a new focus on families. We must create the conditions that enable increasing numbers of families to find the satisfaction, the love, the intimacy and the personal fulfilment and growth that, with all our current cynicism, we wish to every couple on their marriage — and which every couple desires for themselves.

It is a challenge at the personal level to value our families and the intimacy and support they can provide above the status and material rewards that can be gained from the public world. It is a challenge to all to work out the optimum balance between adapting to changing social conditions and defending and preserving the traditions, values, rituals and ways of life that are essential to our humanness.

It is easy to become gloomy and despairing when acknowledging the full picture of what is happening to families. But there is room too for hope. In some ways to study what is happening with families is like studying what is happening to our physical environment under the impact of industrialisation and advanced technology. The devastation is so great that it can tempt one to denial, apathy or flight. But we will not find the resources to counter these threats from an abstract and academic analysis alone. It is only when we care passionately in an immediate and concrete way that we can be moved to put aside our concerns with our own personal survival and with enhancing our individual interests. People care passionately about their own family. So it may be that family is the one issue that can generate a response that will halt the destruction of the physical and human environment that is essential to human life and — in fact — to life at all.

Notes

Introduction, pages vi–xiv
1   T. McCarthy, 'Translator's introduction' to J. Habermas, *The Theory of Communicative Action*, vol. 1, Beacon, Boston, 1983, p. v.
2   Habermas, *Communicative Action*, vol. 1, p. xii.
3   B. Berger and P. Berger, *The War Over the Family: Capturing the Middle Ground*, Penguin, Harmondsworth, 1984; F. Mount, *The Subversive Family*, Allen & Unwin, London, 1983.
4   C. Gaspari, 'The family's future prospects', in *Lumen Vitae*, 1981, pp. 39–47.
5   C. Lasch, *Haven in a Heartless World: The Family Besieged*, Basic Books, New York, 1977.

Chapter 1, pages 1–20
1   J. B. Elshtain, *Public Man, Private Woman*, Princeton University Press, Princeton NJ, 1981, p. 327. Elshtain quotes S. Hampshire, 'Joyce and Vico: the middle way', *New York Review of Books*, 18 October 1973, p. 8.
2   J. Itard, *The Wild Boy of Aveyron*, Prentice Hall: Englewood Cliffs, NJ, 1962, p. 4.
3   M. Pines, 'The civilizing of Genie?', *Psychology Today*, 15, 9 (1981) pp. 28–34.
4   Elshtain, *Public Man, Private Woman*, pp. 294–6; B. Bettelheim,

The Children of the Dream, Collier-Macmillan, London, 1969.
5   Elshtain, *Public Man, Private Woman*.
6   R. M. Kantor, *Commitment and Community: Communes and Utopias in Sociological Perspective*, Harvard University Press, Cambridge, Mass., 1972.
7   D. Cooper, *The Death of the Family*, Random House, New York, 1971.
8   K. Keniston, 'The sources of student discontent', *Journal of Social Issues*, 23, 3 (1967) pp. 108–37; W. A. Watts and D. Wittaker, 'Profile of a non-conformist youth culture', *Sociology of Education*, 41, 1 (1968) pp. 178–200; J. Habermas, *Toward a Rational Society: Student Protest, Science and Politics*, translated by Jeremy Shapiro, Beacon Press, Boston, 1971.
9   J. L. Freedman, *Happy People: What Happiness is, Who Has It and Why*, Harcourt Brace Jovanovitch, New York, 1978; J. L. Freedman, 'Love and Marriage = Happiness (Still)', *Public Opinion*, Nov./Dec. 1978.
10 L. Radic, 'Family life is more satisfying than work, play, religion, and possessions, Survey finds', *Age* (Melbourne) 13 March 1986, p. 4.
11 Freedman, *Happy People* and 'Love and Marriage'.
12 P. and B. Berger, *War Over the Family: Capturing the Middle Ground*, Penguin, Harmondsworth, 1984, p. 178, based on Freedman, 'Love and Marriage'.
13 M. H. Klaus and J. H. Kennell, *Maternal-Infant Bonding*, Mosby, St Louis, 1976.
14 M. H. Klaus *et al.*, 'Human maternal behaviour at the first contact with her young', *Pediatrics* 46 (1970) pp. 187–92.
15 M. H. Klaus *et al.*, 'Maternal attachment: importance of the first post-partum day', *New England Journal of Medicine*, 286 (1972) pp. 460–3.
16 J. H. Kennell *et al.*, 'Maternal behaviour one year after early and extended post-partum contact', *Developmental Medicine and Child Neurology* 16 (1974) pp. 172–9.
17 N. Ringler *et al.*, 'Mother-to-child speech at two years — effects of early post-natal contact', *Journal of Pediatrics*, 86 (1975) pp. 141–4.
18 D. Hales *et al.*, 'How early is early contact?' Defining the limits of the sensitive period.' Paper prepared for presentation at the meeting of the Society for Research in Child Development, New Orleans, 1976. Cited in U. Bronfenbrenner, *The Ecology of Human Development*, Harvard University Press, Cambridge, Mass. 1979
19 Hales *et al.*, 'How early', p. 1.
20 N. Ringler, 'Mother's speech to her two-year-old child: its effect on speech and language comprehension at five years', cited in U. Bronfenbrenner, *The Ecology of Human Development*.
21 J. H. Kennell *et al.*, 'Evidence for a sensitive period in the human

mother', in *CIBA Foundation Symposium 33* (new series), Elsevier, Amsterdam.

22   A. S. Honig, 'Parents of preschool children', in R. R. Abidan (ed.), *Parent Education and Intervention Handbook*, Charles C. Thomas, Springfield, Ill., 1980, pp. 386–91; M. Eastman, 'Family Education: Implications for the Development of Family Education from a Study of the Family Cluster Model', Ph.D. thesis, Monash University, Melbourne, 1987.

23   B. L. White *et al.*, *The Origins of Human Competence*, Lexington Books, Lexington, 1979.

24   U. Bronfenbrenner, 'Is early intervention effective?' in H. J. Leichter (ed.), *The Family as Educator*, Teachers' College Press, Columbia University, New York, 1974.

25   M. K. Meyerhoff and B. L. White, 'Making the grade as parents', *Psychology Today*, September 1986, p. 42.

26   B. L. White, 'The family: the major influence on the development of competence', in N. Stinnett *et al.* (eds), *Building Family Strengths*, The University of Nebraska Press, Lincoln, Nebr., 1979.

27   R. H. Bradley and B. M. Caldwell, 'The relation of infants' home environments to mental test performance at fifty-four months: A follow-up study', *Child Development*, 47 (1976) pp. 1172–4.

28   J. S. Coleman *et al.*, *Equality of Educational Opportunity*, US Department of Health, Education and Welfare, Washington, 1966, p. 22.

29   M. S. Smith, 'Equality of Educational Opportunity: the basic findings reconsidered', in *On Equality of Educational Opportunity: Papers Deriving from the Harvard University Faculty Seminar on the Coleman Report*. Frederick Mosteller and Daniel P. Moynihan (eds), Vintage Books: New York.

30   J. S. Coleman, (1972), 'The evaluation of Equality of Educational Opportunity', in ibid.

31   D. J. Armor, 'School and family effects on black and white achievement: a reexamination of the USOE data', in ibid. p. 224.

32   Ibid. p. 225

33   C. Jencks, *et al.*, *Inequality — A Reassessment of the Effect of Family and School in America*, Penguin, Harmondsworth, 1972.

34   Plowden Report, *Children and their Primary Schools: A Report of the Central Advisory Council for Education (England)*, HMSO, London, 1967.

35   R. C. Whitfield, *Education for Family Life*, Hodder & Stoughton, London, 1980.

36   United Kingdom Department of Education and Science, *A Language for Life* (The Bullock Report), HMSO, London, 1975.

37   Smith, 'Equality', p. 261.

38   M. Eastman, 'Family Education: Implications for the Development of Family Education from a Study of the Family Cluster Model', Ph.D. thesis, Faculty of Education, Monash University, Melbourne, 1987.

221

39 L. C. Comber and J. P. Keeves, *Science Education in Nineteen Countries*, IEA,. Almqvist and Wiksell, Stockholm; John Wiley, New York and Chichester, 1973.
40 R. C. Whitfield, *Education for Family Life*.
41 H. H. Penny, 'The training of Aborigines for teaching in the Aboriginal schools of the Northern Territory'. Report to the Education Research Development Committee, Woden, undated (C. 1980). A summary appears in Education Research Abstracts, 1, 1 (1981) pp. 9–11.
42 K. Marjoribanks, *Ethnic Families and Children's Achievements*, Allen & Unwin, Sydney, 1979.
43 R. W. Connell, *et al.*, *Making the Difference: Schools, Families and Social Division*, Allen & Unwin, Sydney, 1982.
44 P. Amato, *Children in Australian Families: the Growth of Competence*, Australian Institute of Family Studies, Melbourne, and Prentice Hall, Sydney, 1987, p. 238.
45 The Institute for the Development of Educational Activities and The National Association of Elementary School Principals, *The Most Significant Minority: One-Parent Children in the Schools*, 1980, pp. 8, 9, 11, 12, 13, 16.

Chapter 2, pages 21–37

1 W. B. Westley and N. B. Epstein, *The Silent Majority*, Jossey-Bass, San Francisco 1969.
2 R. Blum *et al.*, *Horatio Alger's Children*, Jossey-Bass, San Francisco, 1970, p. 253.
3 Ibid. p. 31.
4 S. B. Coleman *et al.*, 'Life cycle and loss — the spiritual vacuum of heroin addiction', *Family Process*, 25 (1986) pp. 5–23.
5 J. M. Eisenstadt, 'Parental loss and genius', *American Psychology*, 33 (1978), pp. 211–33.
6 M. D. Stanton, *et al.*, 'A conceptual model', Chapter 1 of *The Family Therapy of Drug Abuse and Addiction*, The Guildford Press, New York, 1982. Stanton and Todd cite five literature reviews of family dynamics associated with drug addiction, p. 8; Blum, *et al.*, *Horatio Alger's Children*. See review of literature of separation, family disorganisation, unstable marital relationships and homelessness and drug addiction, p. 24.
7 Eisenstadt, 'Parental loss and genius' pp. 220–1; M. Wolfenstein, 'Loss, rage and repetition'. *Psychoanalytic Study of the Child*, 24 (1969) 432–460.
8 Ibid. p. 458.
9 D. Cooper, *The Death of the Family*, Random House, New York; R. D. Laing, and A. Esterson, *Sanity, Madness and the Family*, Tavistock, London, (1964); R. D. Laing, *The Politics of the Family*, Random House, New York, 1971.
10 T. A. Lidz *et al.*, 'The intrafamilial environment of the schizophrenic patient: Marital schism and marital skew'. *American Journal of*

Psychiatry, 114 (1957) pp. 241–8.
11   L. C. Wynne *et al.*, 'Pseudo-mutuality in the family relations of schizophrenics', *Psychiatry*, 21 (1958) pp. 205–20.
12   R. V. Blakar, *Studies of Familial Communication and Psychopathology*, Universitetsforlaget, Oslo, 1980, pp. 101–2.
13   Gregory Bateson, *et al.*, 'Toward a theory of schizophrenia'. *Behavioural Science* 5 (1956) pp. 251–64.
14   Blakar, *Studies in Familial Communication*.
15   B. R. Rund, 'Communication deviances in parents of schizophrenics', *Family Process*, 25 (March 1986) p. 144. The foregoing implies that schizophrenia is often an 'intergenerational disease'. The parents' communication patterns were learnt in their family of origin.
16   S. Strauss and W. T. Carpenter, *Schizophrenia*, Plenum Medical Book Company, New York and London, 1981, p. 84–6.
17   John Bowlby, *Attachment and Loss*, vol. 2. *Separation: Anxiety and Anger*, Penguin Education, Harmondsworth, 1978, p. 362. First published by The Hogarth Press and the Institute of Psychoanalysis, 1973.
18   Obviously either parent can impose this destructive pattern. I use 'she' because, to date, that is the pattern most often reported in the literature. The most common destructive pattern of fathers is withdrawal and passivity.
19   G. H. Elder, Jr. *Children of the Great Depression: Social Change in Life Experience*, University of Chicago Press, Chicago, 1974, p. 250.
20   G. H. Elder and R. C. Rockwell, 'Economic depression and post-war opportunity: a study of life patterns in hell'. In *Research in Community and Mental Health*, ed. R. A. Simmons, JAI Press, Greenwich, Conn., 1978.
21   A personal communication from G. H. Elder cited in U. Bronfenbrenner, *The Ecology of Human Development: Experiments by Nature and Design*, Harvard University Press, Cambridge, Mass., 1979, p. 275.
22   Elder and Rockwell, 'Economic depression', p. 274.
23   G. H. Elder, 'Historical change in life pattern and personality'. In *Lifespan Development & Behaviour*, vol. 2. P. Baltes and O. Brim (ed.), Academic Press, New York, 1979. Cited in Bronfenbrenner, *The Ecology of Human Development*, p. 280.
24   Bronfenbrenner, *The Ecology of Human Development*. See Bronfenbrenner's analysis of Elder's research in relation to the question of parental and peer influence, p. 280–3.
25   B. Cass, *Income Support for Families with Children*, Social Security Review, Issues Paper No. 1: Commonwealth of Australia, 1986.
26   Brian Howe, 'Scheme aims to cope with the legacy of the sexual revolution', *Age*, 21 April 1988, p. 13.
27   J. M. Lewis *et al.*, *No Single Thread: Psychological Health in Family Systems*, Brunner/Mazel, New York, 1976; L. Pratt, *Family Struc-*

ture and *Effective Health Behaviour: The Energised Family*, Houghton-Mifflin, Boston, 1976; T. Baranowski *et al.*, 'Family self-help: promoting changes in health behaviour', *Journal of Communication*, Summer 1982, 161–72.

28   J. Lynch, *The Broken Heart: The Medical Consequences of Loneliness*, Basic Books, New York, 1977; L. F. Berkman and S. L. Symes, 'Social networks, host resistance and mortality: a nine-year follow-up of Almeda County residents', *American Journal of Epidemiology*, 109 (1984) pp. 186–204; T. Holmes and R. Rahe, 'The social readjustment rating scale', *Journal of Psychomatic Research*, 11 (1967) pp. 213–18; B. L. Bloom, S. J. Asher and S. W. White, 'Marital disruption as a stressor: a review and analysis', *Psychological Bulletin*, 85 (1973) pp. 867–894.

29   C. Wallis, 'Stress: can we cope?', *Time*, 6 June 1983, 64–70.

30   C. B. Thomas and K. R. Duszynski, 'Closeness to parents and the family constellation . . .', *Johns Hopkins Medical Journal*, 134 (1974) pp. 251–70

31   H. I. McCubbin *et al.* (eds), *Family Stress, Coping and Social Support*, Thomas, Springfield, Ill., 1982.

32   S. Minuchin, B. Rosman and L. Baker, *Psychosomatic Families*, Harvard University Press, Boston, 1978.

33   S. Minuchin, *Families and Family Therapy*, Tavistock, London, 1974.

Chapter 3, pages 39–48

1   J. Bowlby *Separation: Anxiety and Anger*, vol. 2 of *Attachment and Loss*, Penguin Education, Harmondsworth, 1978, pp. 300–24.

2   Ibid. 315–18.

3   Ibid. 269–71.

4   Ibid. p. 367.

5   R. Blum, *et al.*, *Horatio Alger's Children*, Jossey-Bass, San Francisco, 1972, ch. 12 and 13.

6   Ibid. p. 231.

7   Ibid. p. 276.

8   D. Edgar, Introduction to J. McCaughey, *A Bit of a Struggle: Coping with Family Life in Australia*, McPhee Gribble Penguin, Ringwood, Australia, 1987.

9   McCaughey, *A Bit of A Struggle*, p. 53.

10   Ibid. p. 54.

11   Ibid. p. 200.

12   Ibid. p. 202.

13   P. McDonald, *Settling Up: Property and Income Distribution on Divorce in Australia*, Prentice Hall, Melbourne, 1986.

14   L. Bumpass, 'Children and marital disruption', *American Journal of Sociology*, 85, 1 (1979) pp. 49–65.

15   O. D. Duncan, D. L. Featherman, and B. Duncan, *Socioeconomic Background and Achievement*, Seminar, New York, 1972.

16   R. M. Hauser and D. L. Featherman, 'Equality of schooling: trends

and prospects', *Sociology of Education*, 49, April 1976, 99–120.
17   D. C. McLelland, *The Achieving Society*, Van Nostrand, Princeton, N.J., 1961; C. Gasparis, 'The family's future prospects', *Lumen Vitae*, (1981) pp. 39–47.
18   V. M. Dickinson, 'The Relation of Principled Moral Thinking to Commonly Measured Sample Characteristics and to Family Correlates in Samples of Australian Senior High School Adolescents and Family Triads', PhD Thesis, Macquarie University, Sydney, 1979.
19   A. Greeley, *The Young Catholic Family*, Thomas More Press, Chicago, 1980.
20   Ibid.
21   J. Habermas, *Toward a Rational Society: Student Protest, Science and Politics*, translated by Jeremy J. Shapiro, Beacon Press, Boston, 1971.
22   K. Keniston, 'The source of student discontent', *Journal of Social Issues*, 23, 3 (1967) pp. 108–37.

Chapter 4, pages 51–62

1   S. Minuchin, *et al.*, *Families of the Slums: An Exploration of their Structure and Treatment*, Basic Books, New York, 1967; J. M. Lewis, *et al.*, *No Single Thread: Psychological Health in Family Systems*, Brunner/Mazel, New York, 1976.
2   J. V. Carew, I. Chan and C. Halfar, *Observing Intelligence in Young Children*, Prentice Hall, Englewood Cliffs, NJ, 1976; D. Baumrind, 'Parental disciplinary patterns and social competence in children', *Youth and Society*, 9, 3 (1978) pp. 239–75. B. L. White *et al.*, *The Origins of Human Competence: The Final Report of the Harvard Preschool Project*, Lexington Books, Lexington, 1979; V. M. Dickinson, 'The Relation of Principled Moral Thinking to Commonly Measured Sample Characteristics and to Family Correlates in Samples of Australian Senior High School Adolescents and Family Triads', PhD thesis, Macquarie University, Sydney, 1973. D. C. Bell and L. G. Bell, 'Family process and child development in unlabelled (normal) families', *Australian Journal of Family Therapy*, 3, 4 (1982) pp. 205–10.
3   R. M. Blakar, *Studies of Familial Communication and Psychopathology: A Social-Developmental Approach to Deviant Behaviour*, Universitetsforlaget, Oslo, and Columbia University Press, New York, 1980; R. M. Blakar, 'Schizophrenia and familial communication: a brief note to follow-up studies and replications', *Family Process*, 20, 1 (1981) pp. 109–12; T. Gottman, *Marital Interaction*, Academic Press, New York, 1979; D. L. Krueger and P. Smith, 'Decision-making patterns of couples: a sequential analysis', *Journal of Communication*, Summer 1982, pp. 121–34.
4   P. Steinglass, 'A life history model of the alcoholic family', *Family Process*, 19, 3 (1980) pp. 211–66; F. Steir, M. D. Stanton, and T. C. Todd, 'Patterns of Turn-Taking and alliance formation in fami-

ly communication', *Journal of Communication*, 32, 3 (1982) pp. 148–60.

5   Robert B. Hill, *The Strengths of Black Families*, Emerson Hall, New York, 1971; J. M. Lewis, and J. G. Looney, *The Long Struggle: Well-Functioning Working-Class Black Families*, Brunner/Mazel, New York, 1983; R. Clark, *Family Life and School Achievement: Why Poor Black Children Succeed or Fail*, University of Chicago Press, Chicago, 1983.

6   V. Satir, *Conjoint Family Therapy*, Science and Behaviour Books, Palo Alto, Calif., 1964; V. Satir, *Peoplemaking*, Science and Behaviour Books, Palo Alto, Calif., 1972; S. Minuchin, *Families and Family Therapy*, Tavistock, London, 1974; S. Minuchin, B. Rosman and L. Baker, *Psychomatic Families*, Harvard University Press, Boston, 1978.

7   J. McCaughey, S. Shaver and H. Ferber, *Who Cares?* Macmillan, Melbourne, 1977; P. Boss, H. McCubbin and G. Listerman, 'The corporate executive wife's coping patterns in response to routine husband-father absence', *Family Process*, 18 (March 1979) pp. 79–86; H. I. McCubbin *et al.*, 'Developing family invulnerability to stress: coping strategies wives employ in managing separation', in Jan Thost (ed.), *The Family and Change*, International Library Publishing, Sweden, 1980; H. I. McCubbin *et al.*, *Family Stress, Coping and Social Support*, Thomas, Springfield, Ill., 1982.

8   N. Stinnett and K. H. Sauer, 'Relationship characteristics of strong families', *Family Perspective*, 11, 4 (1977) pp. 3–11; D. H. Olson, *Families: What Makes them Work*, Sage Publications, Beverley Hills, 1983; G. Ochiltree and P. Amato, 'The child's use of family resources'. *Key Papers: The XXth International CFR Seminar on Social Change and Family Policies*, Institute of Family Studies, Melbourne, 1984, pp. 247–322.

9   D. Curran, *Traits of a Healthy Family*, Winston, Minneapolis, 1983.

10 G. Steiner, 'Family policy as latter day children's policy', in International CFR Seminar *Social Change and Family Policies*, Australian Institute of Family Studies, Melbourne, 1984, p. 217.

11 Ibid. p. 219.

12 Baumrind, 'Parental disciplinary patterns'. In the 'harmonious' family, the boys are aimless, passive and lacking in achievement orientation while the girls display superior competence. Blakar, *Studies and Familial Communication* and 'Schizophrenia and familial communication'. There are differences between urban and rural families and between Icelandic and Norwegian families, but these do not blur the differences in communication patterns between schizophrenic, anorexic, borderline psychotic, heart disease and normal control families.

13 W. A. Westley and N. B. Epstein, *The Silent Majority*, Jossey-Bass, San Francisco, 1969.

14 Lewis *et al.*, *No Single Thread*, p. 48.

15 Ibid. p. 48.

16 T. Lidz, *et al.*, 'The intrafamilial environment of the schizophrenic patient: marital schism and marital skew', *American Journal of Psychiatry*, 114, 241–248.

17 W. R. Beavers, 'Healthy, mid-range and severely dysfunctional families', in *Normal Family Processes*, ed. F. Walsh, Guildford, New York, 1982.

18 The researchers found some evidence that there are less destructive outcomes if it is the father that is dominant rather than if the mother is dominant, though they do not attempt generalisations on that issue.

19 D. Cooper, *The Death of The Family*, Pantheon, New York, 1971.

Chapter 5, pages 63–88

1 S. Minuchin, *et al.*, *Families of the Slums: an Exploration of their Structure and Treatment*, Basic Books, New York, 1967; F. Walsh, *Normal Family Processes*, Guildford New York, 1982. R. Blum, *et al.*, *Horatio Alger's Children*, Jossey-Bass, San Francisco, 1972; N. B. Epstein, *et al.*, 'McMaster model of family functioning: a view of the normal family', in Walsh, *Normal Family Processes*; J. Riskin, 'Research on non-labelled families: a longitudinal study', in Walsh, *Normal Family Processes*.

2 Minuchin, *et al.*, *Families of the Slums*.

3 S. Minuchin, *Families and Family Therapy*, Tavistock, London, 1974, p. 200.

4 Minuchin, *Families of the Slums*.

5 N. B. Epstein, *et al.*, 'McMaster model of family functioning: a view of the normal family', in F. Walsh (ed.) *Normal Family Processes*, Guildford, New York, N.Y., 1982.

6 R. M. Blakar, *Studies of Familial Communication and Psychopathology: A Social-Developmental Approach to Deviant Behaviour*, Universitetsforlaget, Oslo, and Columbia University Press, New York, 1980, and 'Schizophrenia and familial communication: a brief note to follow-up studies and replications', *Family Process*, 20, 1 (1981) pp. 109–12.

7 J. M. Lewis *et al.*, *No Single Thread: Psychological Health in Family Systems*, Brunner/Mazel, New York, 1976; D. Curran, *Traits of a Healthy Family*, Winston, Minneapolis, 1983.

8 Lewis *et al.*, *No single Thread*; C. Hansen, 'Living in with normal families', *Family Process*, 20 (1981) pp. 53–75 (data gathered in 1966–67 and published posthumously). D. C. Bell and L. G. Bell, 'Family process and child development in unlabelled (normal) families', *Australian Journal of Family Therapy*, 3, 4 (1982) pp. 205–10

9 V. M. Dickinson, 'The Relation of Principled Moral Thinking to Commonly Measured Sample Characteristics and to Family Correlates in Samples of Australian Senior High School Adolescents and Family Triads', PhD. thesis, Macquarie University, Sydney, 1979.

10   V. Satir, *Conjoint Family Therapy*, Science and Behaviour Books, Palo Alto, 1964; V. Satir, *Peoplemaking*, Science and Behaviour Books, Palo Alto, 1974; Lewis *et al.*, *No Single Thread*; Hansen, 'Living in with normal families'.

11   Bell and Bell, 'Family process and child development'.

12   Blum *et al.*, *Horatio Alger's Children*, p. 264.

13   Ibid.

14   Ibid.

15   Lewis *et al.*, *No Single Thread*, p. 59.

16   Blum *et al.*, *Horatio Alger's Children*, p. 279.

17   Minuchin *et al.*, *Families of the Slums*; Minuchin, *Families and Family Therapy*; Lewis *et al. No Single Thread*; J. M. Gottman, 'Emotional responsiveness in marital conversations', *Journal of Communication*, Summer 1982, 108–12; A. Brandt, 'Avoiding couple karate', *Psychology Today*, October 1982, 38–43; Curran, *Traits of a Healthy Family*.

18   Gottman, 'Emotional responsiveness'; Brandt, 'Avoiding couple Karate; Curran, *Traits of a Healthy Family*.

19   B. Jackson, *Fatherhood*, Allen & Unwin, London, 1984.

20   P. McDonald, 'Marriage and the Family: the Australian perspective', in *MAGT*, Newsletter of the Melbourne Association of Graduates in Theology, October 1987. p. 7.

21   Lewis *et al*, *No Single Thread*.

22   F. Steier, M. D. Stanton and T. C. Todd, 'Patterns of turn-taking and alliance formation in family communication', *Journal of Communication*, 32, 3 (1982) pp. 148–60.

23   P. Watzlawick, J. H. Beavin and D. Jackson, *Pragmatics of Human Communication*, Norton, New York, 1967.

24   Blakar, *Studies of Familial Communication*.

25   S. Miller, E. W. Nunnally and D. B. Wackman, 'Minnesota Couples Communication Program: Premarital and marital groups', in D. Olson (ed.), *Treating Relationships*, Graphic, Lake Mills, 1976.

26   L. C. Wynne, I. Ryckoff, J. Day and S. Hirsch, 'Pseudo-mutuality in the family relations of schizophrenics', *Psychiatry*, 21 (1958) 205–20.

27   Brandt, 'Avoiding couple karate'. See also Gottman, 'Emotional Responsiveness'.

28   Watzlawick *et al.*, *Pragmatics of Human Communication*, p. 52.

29   J. Habermas, *The Theory of Communicative Action*, 2 vols. Beacon, Boston, 1983.

30   Watzlawick *et al.*, *Pragmatics of Human Communication*.

31   R. D. Laing and A. Esterson, *Sanity, Madness and the Family*, Tavistock, London, 1964; R. D. Laing, *The Politics of the Family*, Random House, New York, 1971; Minuchin *et al.*, *Families of the Slums*; Lewis *et al.*, *No Single Thread*; Blakar, *Studies of Familial Communication*.

32   Bell and Bell, 'Family process and child development'.

33   Gottman, 'Emotional responsiveness'.

34 D. L. Krueger and P. Smith, 'Decision-making patterns of couples: a sequential analysis', *Journal of Communication*, Summer 1982, pp. 121–34.
35 Brandt, 'Avoiding couple karate'.
36 Krueger and P. Smith, 'Decision-making patterns'.
37 A. P. Bochner, D. L. Krueger and T. L. Chmielewski, 'Interpersonal perceptions and marital adjustment', *Journal of Communication*, Summer 1982, p. 135.
38 Lewis *et al.*, *No Single Thread*; D. Olson *et al.*, *Families: What Makes Them Work*, Sage Publications, Beverley Hills, 1983.
39 Blum *et al.*, *Horatio Alger's Children*, p. 268.
40 G. Gallup, *Gallup Youth Survey*, Associated Press, 1979. Reported in D. Curran, *Traits of a Healthy Family*.
41 D. Baumrind, 'Parental disciplinary patterns and social competence in children', *Youth and Society*, 9, 3 (1978) pp. 239–75.
42 Gallup, *Gallup Youth Survey*; T. Ronka, 'Developing new methods in family education'. Finnish report to the OECD/CERI Project, *The Educational Role of the Family*. Organisation for Economic Co-operation and Development, Centre for Educational Research and Innovation, 1983.
43 G. Ochiltree and P. Amato, 'The child's use of family resources'. *Key Papers: The XXth International CFR Seminar on Social Change and Family Policies*, Institute of Family Studies: Melbourne, 1984, pp. 247–322.
44 Ronka, 'Developing new methods'.
45 Minuchin, *Families of the Slums*.
46 Lewis *et al.*, *No Single Thread*.
47 Ibid; Hansen, 'Living in with normal families'; Epstein *et al.*, 'McMaster model'.
48 B. Dordevic, 'The modern family in Yugoslavia and its capabilities in exercising educational competencies', in *The Educational Role of the Family*, Yugoslavian national contribution to the joint CERI/ Japanese Seminar on the Educational Role of the Family, OECD/ CERI/IE/83.03.
49 Lewis *et al.*, *No Single Thread*.
50 Epstein *et al.*, 'McMaster model'.
51 Ibid.; Hansen, 'Living in with normal families'; Baumrind, 'Parental disciplinary patterns'; R. Clark, *Family Life and School Achievement: Why Poor Black Children Succeed or Fail*, University of Chicago Press, Chicago, 1983.
52 D. Baumrind, 'Socialization and instrumental competence in young children', in W. W. Hartup (ed.), *The Young Child: Reviews of Research*, vol. 2, National Association for the Education of Young Children, Washington, DC, 1972; Lewis *et al.*, *No Single Thread*; Hansen, 'Living in with normal families'; Clark, *Family Life and School Achievement*; J. M. Lewis and J. G. Looney, *The Long Struggle: Well-functioning Working-Class Black Families*, Brunner/Mazel, New York, 1983.

53 J. V. Carew, I. Chan and C. Halfar, *Observing Intelligence in Young Children*, Prentice Hall, Englewood Cliffs, NJ, 1976; B. L. White *et al.*, *The Origins of Human Competence: The Final Report of the Harvard Preschool Project*, Lexington Books, Lexington, 1979; Baumrind, 'Parental disciplinary patterns'.

54 Olson *et al.*, *Families*; Blum *et al.*, *Horatio Alger's Children*

55 D. Edgar, 'Emerging changes in family life and their effects on the "health" of society', *Transactions of the Menzies Foundation*, 9 (1985) pp. 35–9.

56 Lewis and Looney, *The Long Struggle*; Clark, *Family Life and School Achievement*.

57 Baumrind, 'Socialization'.

58 Blum *et al.*, *Horatio Alger's Children*, p. 52.

59 Ibid. p. 53.

60 Ibid. pp. 271–4.

61 Ibid. p. 281.

62 J. G. Stachowiak, 'Functional and dysfunctional families', in V. Satir *et al.* (eds), *Helping Families to Change*, Jason Aronson, New York, 1975.

63 J. S. Coleman, 'Families and schools', *Educational Researcher*, 16, 6 (1987) p. 35.

64 Ronka, 'Developing new methods'.

65 M. Eastman, *Education for Family Life*, Australian Institute of Family Studies, Melbourne, 1983.

66 J. McCaughey *et al.*, *Who Cares?*, Macmillan, Melbourne, 1977; J. McCaughey, *A Bit of a Struggle: Coping with Family Life in Australia*, McPhee Gribble/Penguin, Melbourne, 1987.

67 Committee for the Family, 1983.

68 M. Cochran, 'Social ties and parent-child outcomes: The networks of single and married mothers', in M. Cochran *et al.*, *The Ecology of Urban Life: A Summary Report to the National Institute of Education*, The Comparative Ecology of Human Development Project, Cornell University Press, Ithaca, NY, 1982.

69 Cochran, 'Social ties'.

70 M. Cochran *et al.*, *Contexts for Childrearing: The Ecology of Family Life in Syracuse, New York*. Final report of the National Institute of Education, Cornell University Press, Ithaca, NY, 1981, Cochran, *The Ecology of Urban Life*.

71 Curran, *Traits of a Healthy Family*.

72 Ibid. p. 139.

73 K. Okonogi, 'Contemporary family and education', *Monbujiho*, June 1983, pp. 41–6. Quoted in OECD/CERI 1983.

74 J. Bowlby, *Attachment and Loss* vol. 2, *Separation*, Penguin Education, Harmondsworth, 1978, pp. 368–410.

75 I. C. Wynne *et al.*, in Walsh, *Normal Family Processes*, p. 152.

76 Lewis *et al.*, *No Single Thread*, pp. 102, 122.

77 W. A. Westley and N. B. Epstein, *The Silent Majority*, Jossey-Bass, San Francisco, 1970; Hansen, 'Living in with normal families';

Epstein *et al.*, 'McMaster Model'.

78　Lewis *et al.*, *No Single Thread*; N. Stinnett and K. H. Sauer, 'Relationship characteristics of strong families', *Family Perspective* 11, 4 (1977) pp. 3–11; Olson *et al.*, *Families*; Lewis and Looney, *The Long Struggle*.

79　Lewis *et al.*, *No Single Thread*, p. 194.

80　Ibid. pp. 67–70, 103, 207, 225.

81　S. B. Coleman *et al.*, 'Life cycle and loss — the spiritual vacuum of heroin addiction', *Family Process*, 25 (1986) pp. 5–23.

82　G. Caplan, 'The family as a support system', in G. Caplan and M. Killilea (eds), *Support Systems and Mutual Help*, Grune and Stratton, New York, 1976.

83　J. Lynch, *The Broken Heart: The Medical Consequences of Loneliness*, Basic Books, New York, NY, 1977.

84　R. N. Bellah *et al.*, *Habits of the Heart: Individualism and Commitment in American Life*, Harper and Row, New York, NY.

85　Ibid.

86　B. Berger and P. Berger, *War Over the Family: Capturing the Middle Ground*, Penguin, Harmondsworth, 1984, p. 228.

87　Ibid. p. 229.

88　Lewis *et al.*, *No Single Thread*; Lewis and Looney, *The Long Struggle*; Clark, *Family Life and School Achievement*; J. Riskin, 'Research on non-labelled families: a longitudinal study', in Walsh (ed.), *Normal Family Processes*, pp. 67–93.

Chapter 6, pages 89–96

1　G. Steiner, 'Family policy as latter day children's policy', International CFR Seminar *Social Change and Family Policies*, Australian Institute of Family Studies, Melbourne, 1984.

2　Steiner 'Family Policy', p. 219.

3　A. Bloom, *The Closing of the American Mind*, Simon & Schuster, New York, 1987, p. 25.

4　Ibid. p. 26.

5　Ibid. p. 30.

6　Ibid. p. 40.

7　R. Clark, *Family Life and School Achievement: Why Poor Black Children Succeed and Fail*, University of Chicago Press, Chicago, 1983.

8　T. Ronka, 'Developing new methods in family education'. Finnish report on the OECD/CERI Project: The Educational Role of the Family, 1983.

9　Ibid. p. 23.

10　J. Stachowiak, 'Functional and dysfunctional families', in V. Satir (ed.) *Helping Families to Change*, Jason Aronson, New York, 1975.

11　J. E. Dizard, 'The Price of Success', in L. K. Howe (ed.), *The Future of the Family*, Simon & Schuster, New York, 1972.

12   C. Lasch, *Haven in a Heartless World: The Family Besieged*, Basic Books, New York, 1977; U. Bronfenbrenner, 'Reality and research in the ecology of human development', *Proceedings of the American Philosophical Society*, 119 (1975) pp. 439–69; U. Bronfenbrenner, *The Ecology of Human Development: Experiments by Nature and Design*, Harvard University Press, Cambridge, Mass., 1979; S. B. Kammerman, *Parenting in an Unresponsive Society*, The Free Press, New York, 1981.

13   F. Mount, *The Subversive Family*, Allen & Unwin, London, 1983.

14   Lasch, *Haven*; Mount, *Subversive Family*; B. Berger and P. Berger, *The War over the Family*, Penguin, Harmondsworth, 1984.

15   E. Friedman, *Generation to Generation*, Guildford Press, New York, 1984.

16   See, for example Piaget's work on the development of intelligence, and Habermas's on species-wide stages in the development of communicative competence.

17   The word Negro is used here as that is the word Rainwater uses in his study. Rainwater explains his choice of language. At the time the study was undertaken, the world Black was used only by radical activists attempting to change black-consciousness and was not a word accepted by the Negro communities themselves. Rainwater used the word most acceptable to the community he studied. Since then the language use has changed.

18   L. Rainwater, *Behind Ghetto Walls: Black Families in a Federal Slum*, Allen Lane, The Penguin Press, London, 1970.

19   V. Turner, *Rites of Passage*, 1957.

20   E. Friedman, *Generation to Generation*, Guildford Press, New York, 1984.

Chapter 7, pages 99–126

1   E. Bott, *Family and Social Network: Roles, Norms and External Relationships in Ordinary Suburban Families*, 2nd ed. (first edition published 1957), Tavistock, London, 1971.

2   J. L. Freedman, *Happy People: What Happiness Is, Who Has It, and Why*, Harcourt Brace Jovanovitch, New York, 1978; J. L. Freedman, 'Love and Marriage = Happiness (Still)', *Public Opinion*, November/December 1978.

3   D. Edgar, 'Emerging changes in family life and their effects on the health of society', *Transactions of the Menzies Foundation*, vol. 9 (1985) pp. 35–9.

4   N. Zill, 'Divorce, marital happiness and the mental health of children'. Findings from the FCD National Survey of Children prepared for the National Institute of Mental Health workshop on Divorce and Children, Bethesda, Md., 1978. Available from the Foundation for Child Development, 345 East 46th Street New York, N.Y.

5   M. J. Bane, *Here to Stay: American Families in the Twentieth Century*, Basic Books, New York, 1976; K. Everley, 'New Directions in

divorce research', *Journal of Clinical Child Psychology*, 6, 2 (1977) pp. 7–10; G. W. Smiley *et al.*, 'Some social, economic and relationship effects for families and young children following marital separation'. Paper presented to the Australian Family Research Bureau, Canberra, 1983.

6 D. Marsden, *Mother Alone: Poverty and the Fatherless Family*, Allen Lane, The Penguin Press, London, 1969; J. S. Wallerstein and J. B. Kelly, *Surviving the Break-up: How Children and Parents Cope with Divorce*, Grant McIntyre, London, 1980; D. Edgar, 'Emerging changes'.

7 P. McDonald, *The Economic Consequences of Marriage Breakdown in Australia*, Australian Institute of Family Studies, Melbourne, 1985; P. McDonald, *Settling-up: Property and Income Division on Divorce in Australia*, Prentice Hall, Melbourne, 1986.

8 L. Bumpass, and R. R. Rindfuss, 'Children's experience of marital disruption', *American Journal of Sociology*, 85, 1 (1979) p. 51; S. Hoffman 'Marital instability and the economic status of women', *Demography*, 14, 1 (1977) pp. 67–77.

9 L. Weitzman, *The Divorce Revolution*, 1986, p. xii; L. J. Weitzman, *The Divorce Revolution: The Unexpected Social and Economic Consequences for Women and Children in America*, The Free Press, New York, N.Y., 1986 p. xii.

10 Ibid.

11 B. Cass, *Income Support*.

12 Ibid.

13 Ibid.

14 S. Preister, 'Contemporary American families: facts and fables', a paper presented at the 82nd annual convention of the National Catholic Education Association, St. Louis, Ms.

15 Weitzman, *Divorce Revolution*, 352, quoting a conversation with Dr Arthur Norton, March 1984.

16 S. Griffen, 'Facing the real issue in marriage breakdown', *Age* (Melbourne), 8 March 1984, p. 13; D. Lardner, 'Sharp rise in the cost of divorce', Media Release, National Marriage Guidance Council of Australia, 13 August, 1985.

17 J. Burgoyne, R. Ormrod and M. Richards, *Divorce Matters*, Penguin, Harmondsworth p. 190.

18 Weitzman, *The Divorce Revolution*, p. 321.

19 Ibid., p. 354.

20 G. Elder, 'Historical change in life pattern and personality', in P. Baltes and O. Brim (eds), *Lifespan Development and Behaviour*, vol. 2, Academic Press, New York, 1979.

21 A. Mitchell, *Children in the Middle: Living Through Divorce*, Tavistock, London, 1985; O. D. Duncan, D. L. Featherman and B. Duncan, *Socioeconomic Background and Achievement*, Seminar, New York, 1972; M. E. J. Wadsworth and M. McLean, *Parents' Divorce and Children's Life Chances*, cited as being 'in press' in Burgoyne *et al.*, p. 204 note 6.

22   L. Bumpass, and J. Sweet (1972), 'Differentials in marital instability', *American Sociological Review*, 37, 6 (1972) pp. 754–66.
23   R. M. Hauser, and D. L. Featherman, 'Equality of schooling: trends and prospects', *Sociology of Education*, 49 (April 1976) pp. 99–120.
24   D. Edgar, 'Director's Report', *Institute of Family Studies Newsletter*, 10 (August 1984) p. 3.
25   Portfolio Program Estimates 1985–86, Budget Paper No. 6, Attorney-General's Portfolio; Griffen 'Facing the real issue'; Social Security Budget Information 1986–86.
26   A. Burns, 'Divorce and the children', *Australian Journal of Sex Marriage and the Family*, 2 (1981) pp. 17–26.
27   Wallerstein and Kelly, *Surviving the Break-up*.
28   B. R. Bloom *et al.*, 'Marital disruption as a stressful life event', in George Levinger and Oliver C. Moles (eds), *Divorce and Separation: Context, Cases and Consequences*, Basic Books, New York, 1979.
29   M. Eastman, 'Family Education: Implications for the Development of Family Education from a Study of the Family Cluster Model', PhD thesis, Monash University, Melbourne, 1987.
30   Headlam, 'Marital separation', p. 22.
31   A. Parks, 'Children and youth of divorce in Parents Without Partners Inc.', *Journal of Clinical Child Psychology*, 6 (1977), pp. 44–8; Hetherington, Cox and Cox, 'Play and social interaction'; Wallerstein and Kelly, *Surviving the Break-up*.
32   Parks, 'Children and youth'.
33   J. Lynch, *The Broken Heart: The Medical Consequences of Loneliness*, Basic Books, New York, 1977.
34   J. M. Eisenstadt, 'Parental loss and genius', *American Psychologist*, 33 (March 1978), pp. 211–23; Wallerstein and Kelly, *Surviving the Break-up*. The authors note that for some children the stress of divorce acts as a spur to achievement.
35   Wallerstein and Kelly, *Surviving the Break-up*; A. Mitchell, *Children in the Middle: Living Through Divorce*, Tavistock, London, 1985.
36   Wallerstein and Kelly, *Surviving the Break-up*.
37   J. F. McDermott *et al.*, 'Child custody decision-making: the search for improvement', *Journal of the American Academy of Child Psychiatry*, 17 (1978) 104–16.
38   Wallerstein and Kelly, *Surviving the Break-up*; Burns, 'Divorce and the children'; Connell, 'Where's my daddy gone?'; Wallerstein, 'Children of divorce'.
39   G. Brown, T. Harris and R. Copeland, 'Depression and loss', *British Journal of Psychiatry*, 130 (1977) pp. 1–18.
40   A. Roy, 'Vulnerability factors and depression in women', *British Journal of Psychiatry*, 133 (1978) pp., 106–10.
41   A. Roy, 'Role of past loss in depression', *Archives of General Psychiatry*, 38 (March 1981) pp. 301–2.
42   Ladbrook, 'Health and survival'; Zill, 'Divorce, marital happiness';

234

Roy, 'Role of past loss'; Wallerstein, 'Children of divorce', p. 240.
43 Burgoyne, Ormrod and Richards, *Divorce Matters*, p. 134.
44 R. Dunlop and A. Burns, *Don't Feel the World Is Caving In*, Australian Institute of Family Studies, Melbourne, 1988.
45 Wallerstein, 'Children of divorce', pp. 222–3.
46 Ibid, p. 239.
47 Ibid, p. 240.
48 Ibid.
49 Ibid. p. 241.
50 S. Hirst and G. Smiley, 'Access — What is really happening?' Paper presented to the family law practitioners conference, Brisbane, 1979. S. Hirst and G. Smiley, 'The access dilemma — a study of access problems following marriage breakdowns', Family Court of Australia, Principal Registry Library, 1980.
51 Burns, 'Divorce and the children', p. 22.
52 F. F. Furstenberg *et al.*, 'The life course of children of divorce: marital disruption and parental contact', *American Sociological Review*, 48 (October 1983) pp. 663–4.
53 G. Ochiltree and P. Amato, 'The child's use of family resources', *Key Papers: The XXth International CFR Seminar on Social Change and Family Policies*. Seminar sponsored by the Committee for Family Research of the International Sociological Association and the Institute of Family Studies. Australian Institute of Family Studies: Melbourne, 1984, pp. 247–322; Mitchell, *Children in the Middle*.
54 Weitzman, *Divorce Revolution*.
55 M. Eastman, *Family Education*. p. 41.
56 T. Holmes and R. Rahe, 'The social readjustment rating scale', *Journal of Psychosomatic Research* 2 (1967) pp. 213–18.
57 J. Chapman, 'Leaders in today's schools'. An address given to the State Conference of the South Australian Primary Principals' Association, 2 July 1984.
58 J. Dominion, *Marital Pathology*, Dartman, Longman & Todd and British Medical Association, London, 1980.
59 Weitzman, *The Divorce Revolution*, p. xi.
60 Ibid. p. 376.
61 Ibid. p. 374.
62 J. Crawley, 'Helping families stay together'. Paper presented at the Australian Institute of Public Policy Seminar, 'Family chaos and social welfare', Perth, 18 October 1988.

Chapter 8, pages 127–140
1 R. C. Whitfield, *Education for Family Life*, Hodder and Stoughton, London, 1980.
2 M. M. Smith, 'Basic findings reconsidered', in Mosteller and Moynihan (eds), *On Equality of Educational Opportunity*, Vintage, New York, 1972, p. 312.
3 Ibid. p. 315.

4   J. S. Coleman, 'The Evaluation of *Equality of Educational Opportunity*', in Mosteller and Moynihan, op. cit. p. 165.
5   Mosteller and Moynihan, op. cit.
6   J. B. Elshtain, *Public Man, Private Woman: Women in Social and Political Thought*, Martin Robertson, Oxford, 1981.
7   J. S. Coleman, 'Families and schools', *Educational Researcher*, August-September 1987, p. 36.
8   C. Beed, 'An Exploratory Study of Mothers' Ideals for their Children's Social Programs.' M. Ed. thesis, Monash University, Melbourne, 1986; Committee for the Family, 'The Christian family in the Outer Western region of Sydney', Catholic Diocese of Sydney, Outer Western Region, Blacktown, 1983.
9   Coleman, 'Families and schools', p. 36.
10 Coleman, 'Families and schools', p. 37.
11 R. Blum *et al.*, *Horatio Alger's Children*, Jossey-Bass, San Francisco, p. 280.

Chapter 9, pages 141–157

1   D. P. Moynihan, *Family and Nation*, Harcourt, Brace, Jovanovich, San Diego, 1986, pp. 22–36, 40.
2   Ibid. p. 23.
3   Kenneth Clark, *The Dark Ghetto*, quoted in Moynihan, *Family and Nation*, p. 24.
4   Moynihan, *Family and Nation*, p. 27.
5   Ibid. p. 31.
6   Ibid. p. 30.
7   D. P. Moynihan, 'The deepening schism', *The Public Interest*, cited *Family and Nation*. p. 46.
8   U. Bronfenbrenner, 'Reality and research in the ecology of human development', *Proceedings of the American Philosophical Society*, 119 (1975) pp. 439–69.
9   Moynihan, *Family and Nation*, p. 53.
10 E. H. Norton, 'Restoring the traditional black family', *New York Times Magazine*, 2 June 1985, p. 93.
11 Moynihan, *Family and Nation*, pp. 134–5.
12 Ibid. pp. 99–100.
13 Ibid. pp. 142–3.
14 G. C. Loury, 'Moral leadership in the black community', in *Black Leadership: Two Lectures in the W. Arthur Lewis Lecture Series*, Princeton Urban and Regional Research Center, Princeton, NJ, 1984.
15 W. J. Wilson and R. Aponte, 'Urban poverty', *Annual Review of Sociology*, 2 (in press).
16 M. L. King, Westchester Address, reported by Moynihan, *Family and Nation*, p. 37.
17 B. L. Hooks, cited in Moynihan, *Family and Nation* p. 55.
18 Glen Loury, cited in Moynihan, *Family and Nation*, p. 42.
19 E. H. Norton, 'Restoring'.

20 William Raspberry, cited in Moynihan, *Family and Nation*, p. 145.
21 Cited in Moynihan, *Family and Nation* p. 167.
22 Ibid. p. 174.
23 M. J. Bane, cited in Moynihan, *Family and Nation*, p. 143.
24 R. A. Dentler, cited in Moynihan, *Family and Nation*, pp. 88–9.
25 B. Cass, *Income Support for Families with Children*, Social Security Review, Issues Paper No. 1, Commonwealth of Australia, 1986.
26 Moynihan, *Family and Nation*, p. 159.
27 Australian Catholic Social Welfare Commission *A Fair Go for Families*, available for ACSW, Canberra.
28 D. Ironmonger, 'Australian households: a $90 billion industry'. Paper delivered to the 1989 Summer School at the University of Melbourne: 'Changes in the household: implications and future strategies'. Available from Dr Ironmonger at the Household Research Unit, Centre for Applied Research on the Future, University of Melbourne, Parkville, Vic. 3052, Australia.
29 H. Henderson, *The Politics of the Solar Age*, Anchor/Doubleday, 1981.
30 M. Waring, *Counting for Nothing: What Men Value and What Women are Worth*, Allen and Unwin/Port Nicholson Press, New Zealand, 1988.

Chapter 10, pages 159–176

1   C. Lasch, *Haven in a Heartless World*, Basic Books, New York, 1976.
2   D. Cooper, *The Death of the Family*, Random House, New York, 1971.
3   J. B. Elshtain, 'Preface: political theory rediscovers the family', in J. B. Elshtain (ed.), *The Family in Political Thought*, University of Amherst Press, Amherst, 1982.
4   C. McMillan, *Women, Reason and Nature*, Basil Blackwell, Oxford, 1982.
5   Elshtain, *The Family*.
6   R. Bernstein, *The Restructuring of Social and Political Theory*, University of Pennsylvania Press, Penn. 1978, p. xxii.
7   J. Habermas, *Theory and Practice*, Translated by John Viertel, Beacon, Boston, 1974, pp. 41–81.
8   A. Giddens, 'Can Jurgen Habermas be a Marx for our time?' *Australian Society*, 4, 5, 1985. pp. 17–19.
9   Elshtain, *Public Man, Private Woman*.
10 J. B. Elshtain, *Public Man, Private Woman*, Princeton University Press, Princeton, NJ, 1981, p. 335.
11 R. J. Bernstein, *The Restructuring of Social and Political Reality*, University of Pennsylvania Press, Philadelphia, p. 108.
12 J. Habermas, *The Theory of Communicative Action*, 2 vols, Beacon, Boston, 1983.
13 B. Berger and P. Berger, *War Over the Family: Capturing the Middle Ground*, Penguin, Harmondsworth, 1984.

14   J. Crawley, 'Helping families stay together'. Paper presented at the Australian Institute of Public Policy Seminar, 'Family chaos and social welfare', Perth, 18 October 1988.

15   'The case against family allowances', *Australian Financial Review*, Wednesday, 4 March 1987, p. 12.

16   Australian Institute of Family Studies, 'AIFS Research: Report on the progress of major Institute Studies', *Family Matters*, 19 (1987) p. 9.

17   Frank Maas, 'Financing the family', *Family Matters*, 19 (1987) pp. 10–11.

18   Ibid.

19   A. Bloom, *The Closing of the American Mind*, Simon & Schuster, New York, 1987, ch. 1, especially pp. 25–7.

20   M. Eastman, *Education for Family Life: A Survey of Available Programs and Their Evaluation*, Australian Institute of Family Studies, Melbourne, 1983.

21   M. Eastman, 'Supporting creative family processes as an object of family policy', MMFW Conference, Melbourne, 1986.

Chapter 11, pages 179 – 219

1   P. Carnes, *Understanding Us*, Interpersonal Communications Programs, Minneapolis, Mn, 1981.

2   M. K. Meyerhoff and B. L. White, 'Making the grade as parents', *Psychology Today*, September 1986, pp. 38–45.

3   J. R. B. Clement, *Changed Lives: The Effects of the Perry Pre-School Program on Youths Through Aged 19*, Monograph 8, High Scope, Ypsilanti, Michigan, 1984; Consortium for Longitudinal Studies, *As the Twig is Bent . . . Lasting Effects of Pre-School Programs*, Lawrence Erlbaum Associates, Hillsdale, New Jersey, 1983.

4   P. Wilby, 'The Belfield experiment', *Sunday Times*, 29 March 1981, pp. 33–5.

5   Ibid. p. 33.

6   M. Wright, 'Learning to share: the school, home and reading enjoyment program', *Primary Education*, May/June 1985, pp. 20–2.

7   U. Bronfenbrenner, 'Is early intervention effective?', in H. J. Leichter (ed.), *The Family as Educator*, Teachers College Press, Columbia University, New York, 1974.

8   Ibid.

9   For other studies indicating the essential role of the family in the growth and development of competence, see E.S. Schaefer, 'Parents as educators: evidence from cross-sectional, longitudinal and intervention research', *Young Children*, 27 (1972) pp. 227–39; J. Kagan, 'The psychological requirements for human development', in *Raising Children in Modern America: Problems and Prospective Solutions*, Little, Brown, Boston, 1976; B. Berger and P. Berger, *The War Over the Family: Capturing the Middle*

Ground, Penguin, Harmondsworth, 1984. A review of studies on this topic is included.

10   R. Clark, *Family Life and School Achievement: Why Poor Black Children Succeed or Fail*, University of Chicago Press, Chicago, 1983.

11   U. Bronfenbrenner, in *Innovator*, September 1984.

12   U. Bronfenbrenner, 'Reality and research in the ecology of human development', *Proceedings of the American Philosophical Society*, 119 (1975) pp. 439–69; U. Bronfenbrenner, (1980), 'On making human beings human', *Character*, 2 (1980) p. 2; U. Bronfenbrenner, 'Children and families: the silent revolution', *Australian Journal of Sex, Marriage and the Family*, 3, 3 (1982) pp. 111–23; M. Cochran, *et al*. 'Contexts for childrearing: the ecology of family life in Syracuse, New York', Final report to the National Institute of Education, Cornell University, 1981. S. B. Kammerman, *Parenting in an Unresponsive Society*, The Free Press, New York, 1981; D. Edgar, 'Emerging changes in family life and their effects on the 'health' of society', *Transactions of the Menzies Foundation* 9 (1985) pp. 35–9.

13   C. Lasch, *Haven in a Heartless World: The Family Besieged*, Basic Books, New York, 1977; J. B. Elshtain (ed.), *The Family in Political Thought*, University of Massachussetts Press, Amherst, 1982; J. B. Elshtain, 'Political theory rediscovers the family', Preface to *The Family in Political Thought*; J. B. Elshtain, 'Towards a theory of the family and politics', Introduction to *The Family in Political Thought*.

14   M. Eastman, *Family Education*. Committee for the Family, 'The Christian family in the Outer Western Region of Sydney', Catholic Diocese of Sydney, Outer Western Region, Blacktown, 1983; C. Beed, 'An Exploratory Study of Mothers' Ideals for their Children's Social Programs', M.Ed thesis, Monash University, Melbourne, 1986; A. J. Wearing *et. al.*, 'Consumer research for the public sector: human services in Victoria', *Urban Policy and Research: A Guide to Urban Affairs*, 1 (1983) p. 3.

15   Dolby, English and Warren.

16   Committee for the Family, 'The Christian family.'

17   Ibid.

18   C. Noar, Sacramental Preparation Programs, Collins Dove, Melbourne, 1988.

19   M. M. Sawin, *Family Enrichment with Family Clusters*, Judson Press, Valley Forge, 1979.

20   M. Eastman, Family Education.

21   J. Crawley, 'Helping families stay together', Perth, Oct. 1988.

22   T. Ooms and S. Preister (eds.), *A Strategy for Strengthening Families: Using Family Criteria in Policymaking and Program Evaluation*. The Family Impact Seminar and AAMFT Research and Education Foundation, Washington, 1988.